The Voyage of Storm Petrel
Book One

The Voyage of Storm Petrel

Book One
Britain to Senegal
Alone in a Boat

Clarissa Vincent

Published by: girl in a gale books.
Copyright © 2010 Clarissa Vincent
All rights reserved. No part of this book may be reproduced in whole or in part (other than for purposes of review), nor may any part of this book be stored in an information retrieval system without written permission from the publisher.
A catalogue record for this book is available from the British library.
Typesetting and design by Clarissa Vincent
Illustrations Copyright © 2010 Becky Gilbey

The Voyage of Storm Petrel
Book One

Britain to Senegal alone in a boat

Acknowledgements

The inspiration to set sail on a long voyage was Anne and Neville on a newly built Wharram Tiki catamaran called Peace Four, in Bristol Marina. They left for Spain within days of the start of the voyage of Storm Petrel and nurtured me, like a mother gull, all the way to Portugal. To Kresza who loved bashing around the North Sea, France and Belgium in bobble hats and duffel coats with me and my dream of one day sailing to Spain. Often alone I'd imagine conversations with Kresza and laugh at the rawness and vulnerability of being far from land in a small boat. Thanks to Becky Gilbey for her gorgeously sensual illustrations throughout the book. To my Mum and Dad for their unfailing support and worry while I was out on the wide grey sea of life. Thanks to Felix Grant for constantly encouraging me to do whatever I wanted to do.

Forward

Lone voyagers are brimming with contradictions. They can afford few self-doubts if they are to survive the trials of solitude, the relentless demands of single-handed sailing and the potentially overwhelming power of wind and sea. Yet what is such an adventure if not a journey of self-discovery which will test one's confidence and self-awareness to the limit? It is likely to be a life-changing experience. And so it was for Clarissa Vincent. As the familiar English coastline disappeared over the horizon and Storm Petrel settled into the steady rhythm of the sea, canvas taut, heeling jauntily to the breeze, Clarissa too was beginning to spread her own wings, free at last to embrace a new identity and live on her own terms. A passage that was originally intended to stop at Spain slipped almost seamlessly into a voyage to West Africa, eventually negotiating treacherous mud banks and shallows as Storm Petrel worked her way hundreds of miles up the River Gambia. And with her went music. Friends will tell you that if you follow the sinuous sounds of a saxophone on a sunny afternoon, or subtle guitar chords quietly floating on a warm evening's air, you will likely find Clarissa. For making music is as essential a part of her everyday life as breathing. Hand her an instrument and the melodies will flow, as they often did during undemanding spells at sea, while the nautical miles slid relentlessly under Storm Petrel's keel. Clarissa's voyaging may be over - at least for the present - but her musical journey knows no bounds, and, thanks to the internet, reaches out to audiences worldwide. Meanwhile I hope you enjoy reading the Voyage of Storm Petrel as much as I have.
Andrew Blackford

Chapters

An Almost Unmanageable Mess of Safety	1
Nazare and Peniche	56
Ergfada	115
On Not Being an Omen	190
The Light, The Silence	250

Chapter 1

An Almost Unmanageable Mess of Safety

When I look in your face I can't help believing all you say: but that's just what might happen with a witch too. How are we to know you're a friend?" "You can't know," said the girl. "You can only believe - or not."
(CS Lewis, *The Chronicles of Narnia*, The Voyage of the Dawn Treader, P. 518).

How to begin? A bar, a café, my usual place to reflect on so many new experiences. A paradigm shift I suppose; a total life change. I had sailed to Spain as I had wanted, no intended, for at least a decade. It took seven days and I was there now for the winter. There was no way I could face going all that way back, ships everywhere, as busy as Harwich harbour, one of the busiest ports in the world, even right in the middle of the Bay of Biscay, hundreds of miles from land, giant ships just hanging around. I suppose they were waiting for slots and orders, but there they were, lying there, not going anywhere.

There was a thunder storm, or five thunder storms surrounding me and shooting lightning between them, accompanied by dark booming. And then the wind came. I had languished in gentle winds with just enough force to keep SP (Storm Petrel) moving solidly south. One of my fears was strong winds. Suddenly I was in a force 6 with waves rising steeply in the darkness. It felt like a Thelwell cartoon, as I huddled at the helm with my hat pulled around my ears, with oil-skins, safety harness and life jacket combining into an almost unmanageable mess of safety. Waves arrived at the stern like white cartoon ghosts, 'whooooaaaarrrr', to either collapse into hissing spume, or clambered on to the deck and ran around looking for ways in to the boat. Hardly any made it into the cockpit, that is what boats are designed to do, keep the water out and the people in.

I had left unintentionally really, from Milford Haven in Wales. For weeks the weather had been settled and the boat was as ready as it would ever be, with extra food, water, spares, documents, and diesel (extra fuel was given kindly by my Welsh friend Ty). I could sail around Land's End into the English Channel and then make off towards France. At least I'd be away from the Bristol Channel. But a much more audacious plan was unfolding.

The bar was full of mature men playing cards and smoking cigars or white cigarettes. A few women were amongst them. I think most of them would have seen the war of 60 years ago, but they all seemed to have legs and to be wearing good glasses. A man stood in the middle with a stick, he wore a flat cap and smoked a pipe, he was older, with whiter hair and tired eyes. His look seemed to say, 'The place is full of youngsters, how the times are changing'. One man looked to be straight out of the film 'Amelie', a cigarette held near his face and one eye cocked over towards the bar to watch the barmaid who was his ex. Each customer she served gave him more to be jealous about. His white t-shirt and jeans looked relaxed enough but his sideways looking expression said, 'I've a broken heart, it was 10 years ago, we were in love'.

The floor was covered with diagonal brown and cream tiles. There was an ornate, heavily gloss painted post in the middle of the room. A waiter with a white shirt, black trousers and a little curly patch at the top of his forehead served tiny cups of coffee. I ordered a café con leche (coffee with milk) and got a weenie little cup which was actually delicious, so I had a second. When I was in Spain twenty years ago I would drink café con leche because it came in a long glass with a long spoon and lasted well, serving to quench thirst as well as stimulate it. These tiny cups increased thirst, but at least the rich coffee cured my aching back. I was suffering a little from the seven days and nights slouching in the cockpit all the way from Milford Haven.

These men were definitely not war veterans, they were more friendly and lively - they were younger. My own world view had to be updated - old men in bars do not necessarily remember the war. 20 years ago the old men in bars probably were involved in the European war. I had noticed this form of change in a different way in the UK. There used to be many old men in charity shops, where I found most of my clothing. They often could be heard breathing heavily near the bras and nighties, or scuffling in the changing rooms. It was part of the charity shop social service to offer these people a somewhere to be in their latter years without being hassled. The old ladies who ran charity shops were wise enough to keep an eye on the old men, but compassionate enough to sell them the bits of strappy lingerie, held in shaking fingers, without criticism. Nowadays charity shops have been rationalised to tight profit margins and the old men have disappeared.

Charity shops are now run by youngsters with MAs in business studies. In fact the prices have almost converged between new clothes and second-hand, although charity shops offer more choice and once in a while a real gem is discovered. The sailing jacket which wrapped me against the Biscay thunder was breathable fabric made by Helly Hansen and cost £8. Not at all bad. But I miss the old grotty shops with their tired old clothing and tired old men. The times are changing.

Hopelessly and in terrible Spanish, I asked the yacht club barman what the weather would be like in the winter. He offered me the local paper with little boxes for each day of the week, each containing symbols, such as smiling suns or a rain cloud with a drooping wet expression to show what type of weather to expect. Somehow I moved the conversation over to the seasonal climate of Atlantic Spain. I knew the word for snow and ascertained it does not snow in La Coruna, but by October it would no longer be hot. I suffered this as a form of disappointment because it meant I would have to sail several hundred miles further south to keep in warm weather over the inevitable winter. In just four weeks October would stamp a colder pattern into the days. There was no rest for the lotus eater, who must fly south, pursued by an intolerance of winter. My intention was to spend a winter in a warm climate. I was not off around the world, or across the Atlantic, I just wanted to be in gentle sunshine and evade the British winter.

Rising at seven am after going to bed at nine pm I took stock. Without the engine working I could not charge the batteries, apart from a trickle charge from the two solar panels. I rationed electricity into essentials such as charging my mobile phone, charging AA batteries for my Psion hand-held computer and digital camera. These were important at anchor, the core of my activity; communication; writing; recording images. Under sail the essentials were different; navigation lights; vhf radio; compass light; and 12 volt power lead for the gps (global positioning system).

    I removed the foresail to repair a strip of tabling along the aft edge (the leach) which had nearly come right off. Tabling adds strength at the edge and I was lucky the sail did not rip in half. The trouble was not stitching coming undone through chafe, the usual cause of sail damage, but deterioration of the cloth by ultraviolet. This would have been avoided by having an ultraviolet protection strip (a sacrificial strip) sewn onto the part of the sail which is exposed when the rest was rolled away on the fore-stay I had enquired at Bristol Sails earlier in the year but the price, over a hundred pounds, deterred me from having it done. There were so many considerations and expenses in the time leading up to departure. One could spend twenty or thirty thousand pounds fitting out a small boat for a big voyage. I spent about two thousand pounds, however this figure could not describe the amount of thought and planning which went into making it actually happen. It had actually happened. I was now unsure about how things would work out in the next few months. Several people said they would like to come and visit which would be pleasant. If I took out the wood burning stove there would be a decently long guest berth, but I could not think of a way to keep possession of the stove, off the boat. As far as I could tell I would not need a solid-fuel stove in Spain. Surely it would be defeating the object if I had to start ordering a delivery of coal, I might as well be back in the UK. A diesel stove seemed a good idea. Small, light, bulkhead mounted, run off the main fuel tank, but expensive. They would be a lot less work to run than the solid fuel stove. In cold weather a diesel stove could be left ticking over to warm and dry out the boat. If one of these was mounted on the bulkhead where the wood stove was the space freed up would enable the port berth to be nearly full length again.

Heading Southwards at Last

I woke up, wanting to sail away from Milford Haven to wherever I could. The Cleddau had been a very pleasant stay, particularly with Ty and his family and friends to meet up with. The estuary itself was a large attractive area of sheltered waters. I filled up to maximum amount of diesel and drinking water, as well as doing another session in Tescos of Pembroke Dock. With all the preparations of the last three months I felt rather disappointed after Peace Four departed for Bayona from Dale. I thought Dale would become the limit of my voyage. A few chilly nights and misty mornings coupled with the talk of locals, 'Soon the nights'l be drawing in', had me even more depressed and thinking I'd be stuck in the Bristol Channel for another winter. For the past year and a half I had aimed at heading further (plus ultra - more further) under sail, but really I had wanted to do a long southerly headed voyage since buying my first sailing boat in 1990.

I left Dale half expecting a 37 mile passage to Lundy, or maybe a daring 70 mile hike to Padstow. Any other southerly ports were unsuitable due to strong tides. However, as I sailed out of the Cleddau I almost thoughtlessly headed away from the coast and towards the distant Scilly Isles, 125 miles south-south-west. I admit I had carefully studied the possible route to Spain and entered a number of way-points into the gps which would serve as a basic approach to the journey. This involved getting westing from the UK to prevent a westerly gale blowing me into the Bay of Biscay too far. Also I had to get past the Scilly Isles and the associated TSS (Traffic Separation Schemes). My choice was to go way to the west of the Scilly Isles and their shipping lanes. This gave me the bonus of getting off the continental shelf for a large part of the voyage. The continental shelf has a fearsome reputation in heavy weather for causing very large and steep breaking seas. As it was the waves were pretty huge in the region of the shelf.

The point is I had made quite detailed and comprehensive passage plans prior to making such a casual decision to head to Spain that day. Far out of sight of land dolphins swam and dived around the boat. Flocks of gannets and shear-waters were all around. A gannet sitting on the sea looked as big as a swan. A line of eighteen gannets flew along the horizon, followed by a line of four. The mainsail flapped redundantly this side and that. The foresail was rolled away because there was very little wind. The sea softly swayed the boat and a south west swell came from the Atlantic Ocean.

If I hadn't set off towards Spain that day I would never again feel confident enough. As many of the requirements as could be were in place. Weeks of light north west winds resulted from the Azores high stabilizing and long range weather forecasts gave light to moderate north west winds right down to Spain. I could not resist having a go. The gps indicated 100 miles to the Scilly Isles, which I hoped to pass to the west. From there I would head almost due south towards La Coruna in North West Spain The radio played beautiful music perfectly accompanying my position; a magical full moon night in the open sea with a song called *'Foretold in a Language of Dreams'*, by Zitherbell.

I had noticed the diesel engine gives lots of heat if it is run for more than an hour. At night it was really cosy to sit on the companionway steps with the main hatch drawn back to close the gap around my shoulders. I would rest my head and arms under the spray hood and the main part of my body and legs were warmed and sheltered by the engine and cabin. To know how to arrange a boat for voyaging without using it over a long period would be impossible.

During the voyage, wracked with tiredness and beset by rhythmic rolling I could only think of selling the boat if I ever managed to get to land again. The last few hundred miles seemed interminable and each day I was convinced I was closing the coast. At 200 miles to go I felt myself to be quite close to land. Then at 100 miles I became anxious about being able to get around the chunk of land north of La Coruna. The wind was quite strong and I could only comfortably run downwind, otherwise the large breaking crests hit so hard I was concerned about SP being damaged or at least having the cockpit repeatedly swamped with wave tops. Finally reaching land a part of me felt I had already attained my goal and could happily sell the boat, return to the UK and put it all safely down to experience.

I repaired a split in the mainsail and also noticed the main halyard was chafing through. Either one of these could cause major difficulties offshore. I had no spare mainsail and a broken halyard would be almost impossible to repair at sea, without a bosun's chair with which to climb the mast, but even those require another person to assist. The other option was to fit mast steps and I had studied long and hard the various designs on boats in marinas. I had drawn plans for my own but had not the resources to go ahead with the project. To buy them ready fabricated was about fifteen pounds per step and I would need at least ten, so it was another idea on hold.

Keith, a friend who sailed across Biscay with Anne and Nev and another friend, aboard Peace Four, a few days ahead of me, owned a catamaran. He had an interesting device: A form of ladder set into the sail slide groove and hoisted up the mast on the main halyard or any spare halyard if the main one has parted. The ladder was made of stiff webbing. One of these would cost half the amount of new mast steps. These and other realizations had me thinking it was sheer luck which carried me to La Coruna. Plus I was not in possession of resources, either mechanical or financial, to match a cruising boat's needs. This depressive part of me was happy to quit while ahead and see the voyage so far as an audacious and risky success and as pure luck. The words to a Genesis song floated in my mind, 'Gambling only pays when you're winning'.

Mishaps at sea are not at all adventuresome and I felt lucky to have had no mishaps on the passage to Spain. Everything on the boat had a crust of salt on and this made me realize what a hostile environment it was, out there. With the diesel engine broken down and the tiller feeling sloppy, I wondered if I was looking reality in the eye. I did not have the sort of money a marine diesel mechanic would ask. I knew the tabling on the jib was about as much as I could run to for repair bills. The rest I had to make do myself and this is where things looked a little brighter. Systems I had installed aboard which worked well and had not failed gave me great satisfaction and confidence. The two solar panels were a boon, each day the sun trickled power into the ailing batteries. The two LED cabin lights were excellent investments. They had been expensive, £48 for the pair and they give very low light output, but the advantage they had was a very low power drain (just 0.5 amps each). In fact the solar panels would support the LED lights entirely. I looked forward to getting navigation lights based on LED technology, but it was emergent technology and so not widely available at reasonable cost.

I liked La Coruna, the anchorage was free and the city big enough to hide in. In a small towns locals quickly notice a stranger and I would feel vulnerable, being alone, but in the city, no one knows your name. I was an urban soul in Bristol where I learned to hide myself among the masses by being like them; shopping - wanting - inattentive but wary of others and above all pleasant. I found difficulty writing about the voyage, not out of trauma or even shock, but because I needed to build a wider perspective in order to take it in. Words to express how the Bay of Biscay felt to be in were yet to appear. Other sailors cross often and for those 'The Bay' is a relatively short hop. There were, however , none of the type of boats cramming the north coast of France, over from England for their summer holidays, none of them dared to strike out this far. I liked that. Most of the visiting boats in La Coruna were German, French, Dutch or Scandinavian. Most seemed bound further south and would be making Atlantic crossings in the next few months. SP was of the smallest of the visiting boats. The largest was a German yacht of around twenty five meters in length which arrived one evening and anchored nearby.

I went to unravel the idiosyncrasies of the Spanish mobile phone market in the Post Office. I could buy a Spanish SIM card for my UK Orange phone because I'd had the foresight to 'unlock' it. This had cost a tenner from a semi-legal but extremely efficient young man in Bristol market. The job took him about five seconds. An unlocked phone can be used with a number of different SIM cards. I would then be able to use a local Spanish internet service provider. The costs of the Spanish SIM card seemed particularly favourable after midnight, just 0.6 Euros per minute, less than 1/2p per minute, but surely too good to be true. If so, I would happily wait until after midnight to do email and internet work. The other big advantage was I would no longer have to pay to receive calls from outside Spain, it was costing me 30p per minute to listen to people saying, 'No! I don't believe you're in Spain! You're having me on, aren't you?' The attention was nice for a while, but I began getting the less frequent friends, those who only called once every couple of months, who were really just expressing guilt for not getting in touch. A new Spanish mobile number would be a breath of fresh air and I could only give it out to the people I wanted to.

I did several small repairs to the sails and running rigging. A sail slide I thought was broken simply needed sewing back onto its tape. A chafe hole where the main rubbed against the spreader in downwind legs needed a herring bone stitch. A serving was wrapped around the main halyard, the rope which raises the mainsail. Also I served the eye where the shackle joins the main halyard, to serve is to tightly wrap a rope with protective thread to prevent chafe. The foresail needed further repair but it tore because of ultraviolet degradation and simple stitching was not sufficient. I needed to have a purpose made ultraviolet protection strip put onto the leach, the trailing edge, of the sail. This would likely cost around £100. I had a spare but scruffy foresail which was slightly smaller, but could be used instead. However the damaged sail was a lovely big one and in good condition apart from the tabling hanging off. The sails had worked hard over 500 miles of fresh to strong winds. Anne and Nev aboard Peace Four had spent the last two weeks repairing gear from their Biscay crossing. It is traditionally a stretch of ocean which extracts a price from those who cross it.

What was I doing, wandering in Spain, for that was mostly what I did. I strolled around different parts of the city, always looking for something or other. On some level I felt like a modern Laurie Lee who wrote, *'As I Walked Out'* about walking through Spain. I also remembered Herman Hesse's *'Wandering'*, a book of short stories about different journeys, all travelling to travel rather than to reach a destination. I saw reaching Spain as the beginning of my travels, even though I had wanted to do that journey for a long period of my life. It was always only a qualifier, an entrée to a richer and hopefully less salty journeying where the land, its people and cultures would be as much a part of the experience as the sailing. The boat was an effective way to carry my possessions and somewhere to rest. Travelling with a rucksack is so exhausting because there is nowhere to feel at home. I did not wish to fall asleep in a car park, as I did once on reaching Alicante when I went there twenty years before. The boat demanded responsibility which was a good thing. The boat kept me focussed, with certain procedures which could not be negotiated or neglected.

I spent the day pricing a few gallons of engine oil and it seemed it would cost twenty six Euros This meant I had to postpone buying oil until my replacement debit card arrived at the Lista de Correos, at the local post office. Otherwise I would have nothing left to finance the wandering and that would put me in a bad mood. The strolling functioned as exercise too, after seven days on the boat, mostly slumped in the cockpit or in my bunk, I was weak. When I stepped ashore it was with a heady, dizzy feeling, of the ground being too unmoving. All the tiny pushes and shoves aboard the boat are suddenly gone and my legs felt like jelly. My head seemed to carry on swaying as if it had set up an automatic feedback to the constant movement aboard. When this stopped the mind swam on in its own after image of swaying and lurching.

I walked a different way into the city, around the sea front, the 'Balcony of The Atlantic' as La Coruna markets itself. It was a greyer, cooler morning. I had taken advantage of the temperature to get the outboard engine going again. I stripped the carburettor, blowing through the main jet and cleaning the petrol/air mix adjuster and I cleaned the spark plug after looking at it to see if it showed any sign of irregular combustion. It looked slightly reddish, so I was none the wiser but there was fuel and oil getting to the plug which showed greasy wet. While pottering with the engine a large Scandinavian gaff rigged ketch left the anchorage, into the fog outside the harbour. La Coruna is a stopover for many cruising boats, but hardly any seemed to linger. This fact made me feel as if I too should be heading south, but I had decided to wait for my debit card and my forwarded mail. Then I would be able to buy engine oil and navigation charts. I would perhaps get a Spanish SIM card for my mobile phone, although that depended on whether it would work to my advantage in Portugal too. I seemed to have decided Portugal was the best place to winter, for its warmer climate. So having got the outboard running, to my great satisfaction because I did it all myself, I walked into the city via a convoluted and more functional part of La Coruna. There were shops and cars and people as usual but the cool grey day made everything relaxed. It was like a typical September day in northern Europe. I felt a lot more at ease, even at home, in the grey air and vaguely chilly streets. Out at sea deep in the fog, a ship blew its foghorn at intervals and I wondered how the gaff rigged Scandinavians were finding the day.

I went again to my café, allowing a long forgotten coffee habit to re-groove. I wrote at a marble table and two students alighted on tables next to me, drawn to my self absorbed aura, which was a non-threatening stance. This was what I noticed first about this particular café; students with books, photocopies, pens and serious faces sat in the window seats. Not many, just three or four individuals at a time but it told me I could sit in this café and feel unhassled. Earlier in a supermarket called Gadis a middle aged man with black curly hair emerging from the back of a grey cap, asked for money. I passed by. On the way out I passed him by again wondering whether he was authentic as a beggar. To my relief another person gave him some coins, but I was struck by the humility in his voice as he thanked the giver. It sounded quiet, gentle and sincerely grateful. I left the supermarket entrance feeling as if I would have preferred to have given something.

The Gadis visit was a frustrating one because I really did not need to go into a supermarket. I had a desire for something to eat such as peanuts or a banana, but realized as I wandered the aisles, I was using the shop as a place to hide. From what? From myself? I had been stressed about being away from the UK with very limited resources while all my friends were reduced to SMS text messages on my mobile. Walking the streets was a way to relax after intense activity, just browsing in shops was a chance to let all the thoughts of the day filter through to their proper places. But I was filling in time, looking for peanuts without salt, trying to find something not there to be found. When I left the Gadis shop, I was approached by several street vendors who appeared to be the equivalent of UK Big Issue sellers. They had a low level of threat but nonetheless made me feel uncomfortable after I refused to buy a sad looking paper all in Spanish, called La Calle - The Street or similar.

I did give one Euro to a statue cowboy street artist. He had silver painted chaps up to the thigh, a toy gun in a holster and a leather cowboy hat on. His skin was street-performer-silver. As I dropped the coin, of course he moved to kiss my hand and then flipped his action into an offer of a red boiled sweet. I laughed and complemented his act. I felt restored and the usual hot sun was now out again. I headed for my favourite café and the marble table.

I planned to aim towards Cascais in Portugal. It was recommended as a place where cruisers gather for the winter, with a decent sized city and a year round tourist trade. I hoped to stretch my budget even further by playing the saxophone. The previous night I'd retrieved it from where it had been roped into storage in the bows, to play some songs. It sounded good and was another way to escape the ongoing striving to survive that life can become. Music was one of the saving graces of my life. I had a guitar aboard too and I frequently picked it up like a smoker picks up a cigarette. Also I had my new fretless electric bass guitar stowed up forward. I brought it along partly because it was a recent acquisition and so I just wanted it with me. I would love to get involved with more than just sailing ideas over the coming year. If I settled for a while in a tourist area who knows I could end up playing in a band, I was that optimistic.

The internet café was very cheap. Two hours sorting through 144 emails cost just three Euros The equipment was very old though and there were just three working PCs, with dismantled units lying around the place. I would not risk doing any secure transactions, such as internet banking. The possibility of keystrokes being recorded or networked PCs being monitored for passwords etc. was too risky. There was a chocolate bar I saw in Gadis, called 'On Line'. That made me chuckle. Somehow, I cannot imagine Spanish households having PCs set up as in the UK. Obviously many do, but Spain is still very much locked into creaky traditional social worlds. The culture was very advanced when allowed to be so but the majority of people seemed inclined to log on to a mainly

Spanish way of living. There was a difference between the UK and Spain which was hard to pinpoint. It was to do with the way each country consumes goods. There were none of the big digital electrical stores like Dixon's. Instead I saw the odd specialist retailer selling printers. There was not the rash purchases of family PCs with sound systems, printers, scanners, and a digital camera thrown-in in Spain. I had seen the fervour to get computers in the UK. People going out to spend a thousand pounds on a box of components as if it would be the answer to all life's problems. That may or may not be the case but in this part of Spain, Galicia, there was not the disposable income, or it did not show at least.

There were many quite expensive looking women's clothes and shoe shops in La Coruna. They never became crowded in the way British ones get with everyone queuing to spend. The Coruna shops seemed to have one customer in at a time. There were not the great W H Smith's magazine racks with dozens of people browsing, not just browsing, but reading a magazine cover to cover and afterwards either buying an unread, competing magazine, or nothing at all. In Coruna magazines were in abundance but trapped behind glass like flies on a hot day, fading and untouchable. It was not a hands-on culture. When I wanted to choose a navigation chart, all I could do was point to one in a catalogue. The assistant would then run around to another shop to collect my choice. I just wanted to look at lots, compare them and know it was what I could use. I would have preferred to have been directed to the shop where the assistant was running to, so I could get my hands and eyes into the stock charts. I could gain all sorts of impressions of the area by looking at different scales of charts with smaller or wider areas. To travel into an area one needs to have an internal picture in the mind's eye onto which all incoming information is mapped, however impressionistic, and browsing charts is part of this.

In the years leading up to the Biscay crossing I had often heard about the rough seas at the point where the continental shelf rises up out of the Atlantic Ocean depths. The chart indicates a change from around 100m to 4,000m over a distance of just 30 miles. In heavy weather this area is known to be extremely dangerous for big seas. The large Atlantic swells are modulated by the shallowing so that they shorten and become higher. My experience was not of heavy weather but of fresh winds of force 5-6. The waves were very large with breaking crests. They could be seen rising up six or seven metres above the rest of the seas and tumbling forward in sparkling foam. This occurred over many many miles. Once in a while a huge container ship appeared dead ahead. I had then to alter my course away from the danger. The chance the ship could see me would be tiny. My radar reflector was a proper modern one but they do very little in the movement and scale of the ocean. Seeing the massive size of those ULBCs (ultra large bulk carriers) I worried again about my habit of heaving-to for fifteen minutes of sleep whenever I needed it. The tiny flickering paraffin hurricane lamp flame would be negligible I suppose. The only thing in my favour was the sheer amount of room out there. The actual chance of being hit was reduced by that alone.

The problem though was the high number of ships. On a line from north west France to north west Spain, the main shipping lane, there are dozens and dozens of ships at any one time. To make a landfall from the UK to Spain it was necessary to cross the lanes at some point. I crossed the main shipping lanes about in the middle of the Bay of Biscay, but I then had to contend with shipping heading further east to ports such as Bordeaux and Brest. A device some cruisers were using, called a 'SeaMe', was a transponder which upon receiving the radar sweep of another vessel, emits a strong signal in reply. The result is a signal which appears on the ships radar as large as that of another ship. Another device was a CARD (collision avoidance radar detector). This senses the radar of a ship as it sweeps the boat and gives an audible warning to the sailor as well as indicating the approximate direction from which the radar was sensed. Both safety devices cost several hundred pounds. There was a simple answer to the question 'What price safety?' It was 'Too much'.

Real safety comes from looking after oneself so natural alertness and decision making is not impaired. I seemed to manage with fifteen minute sleeps. Some nights I got dozens of fifteen minute sleeps in a row which would add up to several hours. Other nights I had to keep sailing, out of busy areas, or, because the wind was too strong for the steering sail to work effectively. I did end up extremely tired and found it difficult to be together enough to know what was happening at the point of closing within 12 miles of La Coruna. For a while I was unable to sort out the pilotage to find the right bit of coast to head for. The gps was telling me to go one way, whereas I was determined to head another. In the morning things became easier as I fixed my position relative to the Ria de La Coruna. But the wind fell away entirely leaving me drifting engine-less a thousand meters off the entrance. It was early afternoon when I finally dropped anchor behind the protective harbour mole, in La Coruna port.

Walking the streets was a way to relax after intense activity, just browsing in shops was a chance to let all the thoughts of the day filter through to their proper places. But I was filling in time, looking for peanuts without salt, trying to find something 'unfindable'.

The Milky Coffee of Human Kindness

After heavy rain and a long walk in search of navigation charts I eventually made my way back to my café. The usual waiter was back, the previous day must have been his day off, he spotted me draping my wet fleece over a chair while peering out of the window at a particularly tall woman with bright red hair, who happened to be passing. Then the waiter strolled over to the table I was at and handed me a café con leche, my usual coffee with milk. "Buenos, y gracias" (good and thank you) I remarked and the waiter chuckled. This small enfolding of myself into the local milieu made me feel warm and relaxed. I realized it was human contact I missed most. I hoped to make some friends on the way south.

For now I would generate my own communication by just being myself, where I happened to be at the time, so La Coruna was the best place for me at that moment. If I was in the Algarve surrounded by wintering yachts with enthusiastic voyagers aboard I might feel a sense of loss of the intensity of my present experience. The trouble with mass migrations would be everyone would be offering the latest information and tips to make life easier. There would be no room to discover anything new for myself. Also the local Spanish people would then stereotype me as a tourist, as a yachty, which would put a barrier up against getting to know people on their own terms. I once enjoyed cruising in the Bristol Channel for similar reasons; off the beaten track one can be truly individual.

I saw a wonderful chandlers, for fishing boats, it was full of wire cables, wooden blocks with bright sheaves and hooks built into them. There were gritty, solid and basic materials such as nylon bar for making bow rollers and bushes on anchor winches, there were shackles, eye bolts, ropes, warps and no electronic gadgetry anywhere to be seen. I also found another chandlers where I was shown the specific Spanish navigation charts I would need. They cost about the same as British Admiralty ones in the UK, around fifteen pounds each. It was a difficult process deciding which charts to carry and more to the point which to pay out for. The one I chose missed out the first 25 miles from Coruna, starting at the Islas Sisargas. Looking at the bit I would not be getting, for any navigational hazards, I came to the conclusion it would be safe to head around the Islas Sisargas with a 5 mile offing, before sailing into the area covered by the new chart. The danger would be strong winds or gear failure putting me close to the coast before I had sailed into the chart. Then I would have to rely on the gps giving me course and distance to specific points, such as the Islas Sisargas, which I had listed in the Nautical Almanac. I had aboard a brand new Macmillan and Silk Cut Nautical Almanac which was valuable for the information it held, such as harbour plans, covering right down to Gibraltar, nearly 600 miles south. As an absolute minimum one can use a large scale passage planning chart combined with the Almanac's harbour plans and get by, but it is then wise to stay well offshore.

The rain stopped, the sky brightened a little. I looked at more engine oil prices. The Spanish brand, Repsol, was half the price of Castrol. I had a strongly conditioned message ringing in my ears, 'always buy the best quality oil'. But would I be simply paying for the Castrol name? And was it not cultural superiority to think 'Spanish oil' was not good? Something inside me knew the Repsol would be fine, even as a counterpoint argued for the homely name of Castrol. The trouble was it would all end up swilling around in the bilges soon anyhow. And this was how my brain cogitated and my days went by. I bought a fresh baguette and some Camembert with a bottle of water for lunch. The baguette was lovely but the cheese turned out to be the plasticky stuff in individual tin foil wrappers. A few initial moments of satisfaction of my hunger pangs but then the processed cheese became tedious. I had a raging appetite for some real Camembert, but at least I'd eaten something. That night I ate what was left from the previous day, a particularly enjoyable fresh vegetables and pasta mix. I used and liked very much some big Spanish tomatoes which have pink meaty insides, loads of juice and cook well.

At the post office (Lista de Poste) my forwarded mail had still not arrived. I supposed it would take three days, rather than two to arrive. I looked around the café and through the windows at shoppers and workers outside. Several people in the café looked back at me and I felt it was time to wander out, how much time does one coffee buy at a table? I'd been there about half an hour. I saw some blue sky and decided to go again to the internet café as until I got my replacement debit card through the post there was nothing I could really do, apart from wait cheaply. Later back aboard I hanked on the spare foresail. When at anchor it is best to keep a sailing capability in case the anchor drags or the boat needs to be moved at short notice. One problem I had was the batteries were so low it would be touch and go whether the engine will turn over enough to start. Once it started, however, they would quickly recharge. I relied very much on electrics; apart from navigation lights and radio, I needed to charge the mobile phone and AA batteries for the

Psion hand-held computer and the digital camera. Also I would feel happier when the engine would be able to keep the batteries high enough to run the laptop computer. Then I could shift digital photographs of the Biscay crossing from the camera to the laptop. There were super images of dolphins playing around the bows of Storm Petrel of Narnia. I remembered the man in Wales who said, "Narnia? When did you last go there?" Well, mate, I've had dolphins playing around my boat so stick that up yer jumper.

Thursday 5th September. I notched the tree of life with a date, well actually a fig. Three fresh green figs from a tiny fruit shop on the way to town gave me immense satisfaction. A deep ruby plum the size of an orange had me exclaiming with joy at fresh fruit. The apple in my bag from the Gadis cheap supermarket was utterly outshone by these fruits. The sun shone warmly and I carried my saxophone hopefully to find a spot to do some busking. I came across a trio made up of two accordionists and a double bass player. They wore black shoes, trousers and waistcoats with white shirts. Their greased back hair and polished shoes gave the impression of a dance band of the 1940s. The song they played as I strolled up was slow and delicate, with a chromatic descending bass line. It was a JS Bach fugue or similar. I watched passers by, children being given coins to put in the box and small dogs letting go last night's meal. The former gave a smile to the players, whereas the latter failed even to mildly amuse or distract them. Dog pooh was mostly picked up efficiently by the owner using plastic bags but I had seen owners of large dogs who seemed oblivious of the outpourings. The music framed the street for me, the houses, shops, windows, dresses, shoes, cigarettes, and sunshine coming out of a blue sky with big white cumulus floating in it. Through the music, which had become more Neapolitan in style, I saw Spain being Spain.

Buzzing away from SP in my Avon Redcrest dinghy, I felt a strong attachment to the little sailing boat. By now I had chucked out the rancid water I'd bunkered in as Biscay emergency supplies. I had also eaten my way through some of the mound of tinned food bought in preparation for the long voyage and so SP sat a lot better on her water-line. During the daytime at anchor I flattened down the spray hood to allow maximum sunlight onto the two solar panels which were mounted on the sliding hatch. This was not ideal for exposure to the sun but the only really convenient place on the boat. All the other positions seemed to create an obstruction to sail or boat handling. If I had enough money to buy bigger panels I think they could be mounted against the dodgers; two rectangular canvas spray barriers either side of the cockpit. One panel would always be out of the sun while the other would be in it, but a panel the size of one dodger would be quite powerful. These big solar panels would cost over three hundred pounds each. My present system of two 5 watt panels cost around £75 (and this was already reduced by half in a chandlery sale). They managed to supply cabin lighting as well as just about charge the mobile phone. I did not know how I would cope without the minimal power I got at present. That engine really needed fixing.

I phoned Annemarie back in Bristol Marina one night. She had forwarded the mail which hopefully included my debit card replacement. I was unaware of the time it took to get mail in Spain from the UK, I guessed about three days. Annemarie was very helpful in forwarding my UK mail to wherever I asked, she was also a bright cheerful homely voice on the phone. She was overworking as usual, trying to establish herself as an independent woman with freedom of choice and professional standing in a competitive world. I thought about how Annemarie creates a certain amount of her own stress by trying to attain too much. When a boat is driven faster than its hull speed, all that happens is a standing wave builds up in front which the boat then has to climb over; life is like that too. As I watched and listened to the busking trio I realized how much freedom is in just stopping and staring for a while. My past travelling experiences in Spain with a guitar were garlanded with this 'joy of the moment' and it can only really be had in very unique circumstances and it is necessary to shed off responsibilities to the point where one is as vulnerable to bad fortune as a sparrow. There was a concurrent thought in my mind as I wrote - all of what I had just said was rubbish and the truth was I had massive responsibilities to my self and my boat, each day was a struggle to keep the voyage going, a balancing of limited resources to that end. So, there was the laid back me, wanting the world to sit down and solve it's problems like that. And there was the adult me who had a lovely sailing boat in Spain and this me gripped life as tenaciously as a gecko on a hot monastery wall.

I was looking forward to seeing lizards, I would know I was far enough south when I saw geckos. I would call it the 'gecko index'. Felix informed me they can be found in any harbour throughout the Mediterranean, but on the Atlantic coast I reckoned I must travel a lot further southwards to gain a temperate enough climate for perennial geckos. And that is what I wanted to do. After being exposed to the sublime music of the busking band I was disinclined to blow my saxophone. I was never a very good musician, although I did have moments of remarkable flair. I felt it would be better to wait for the moment when my playing was needed rather than compete with really excellent players. I went again to the cheap internet café. I wanted to look at the website of a single-hander I met in Milford Haven. Karen was half way around her 'Round Britain Challenge'. She was sailing a little plywood Caprice (18 feet, like Shane Acton's 'Shrimpy'). We got on because we were both single-handers? Our excited chat was interrupted by an anti-terrorist police inspection of our documents. Karen joked that she could have sailed into Dale from almost anywhere in the world, such as Israel. This comment showed her young age and it did not make the macho policeman laugh one bit. Despite up to date ships radio license and RYA Yacht master qualifications he eyed me suspiciously. It was a little too much for him to come across two single-handers on one pontoon, who were both female. He cleared us both from his concern and swept away in an orange and black rubber rib thing. Next morning Karen had headed away towards Lundy Island and I made my way up river in search of water, food and charts for my Biscay voyage. I found Karen's website and read her log. She made it to Lundy, then Padstow and on around Land's End to Penzance. She was doing a great thing and I was moved to leave a long message on her guest book, expressing my appreciation of her indomitable spirit. I also took great pleasure in telling her of my own success in reaching Spain.

I enjoyed the camaraderie which existed between single-handers We are a special breed of sailor, moved by solitude and wilderness as much as the attention seeking aspect of arriving in port alone; fluffy lost chicks needing protection. We do not seek attention but neither do we often get much. I think well crewed boats fail to understand the single-hander and vaguely mistrust their ability to do alone, what takes five strong men on many boats. Pascal said, *'Man's unhappiness comes from not being able to sit down in a room by himself'*. The single-hander does just that - spends a lot of time sitting down alone and ready for the right solution to present itself. Single handed sailing is a philosophy in action.

The small fruit shop on the way to the town centre sold me the most delicious peaches, nectarines and plums. I was forced to sit in the big square as I bit into the large peach. The flesh was a mixture of dry firmness and sweet juice, none of which dripped out as I ate. The stone came away from the middle in its ripeness and I marvelled at the way we have the wool pulled over our eyes by supermarkets with their bad quality produce compared to the fruit I had found. I had my daily apple in my bag, brought from Gadis, the supermarket. I had decided to include fruit in my daily diet to keep my health good. The Gadis apples were cheap and local and I chose them for those qualities, but they tasted bland and sharp. When I had finished the peach of all peaches I started on a nectarine, golden red like a plum but not as dark coloured. It was completely gorgeous. Next was a soft, dark purple, almost black, plum. It had such a red insides I worried passers by would think I was eating a freshly carved out heart. This fruit revelation had bought Spain right into my mouth and I walked away from the town square with more Spanish in my gait, I felt in my intestines to be part of the place. The fruit was building itself into my bodily molecules and transforming me away from the English state to a semi-Spanish version of Clarissa.

The accordions and double bass trio were playing the same Bach fugue I heard as I came across them yesterday. A group of Arab speaking men talked in a bar nearby. They were guttural and had big open handed gestures; I liked them without knowing who they were. A poster shop sold large scenes of the New York skyline with the twin towers intact. Two small decorative dogs on leads confronted each other with ugly, dripping snarls saying, 'I am the pavement dog here, and I shall annihilate you'. A group of bronzed travellers, young, with braided hair, hand rolled cigarettes, juggling sticks, playing African drums, sat around like a micro-tribe. I did not give them money because I had already dropped nearly a Euro into the collecting box of another pair of street musicians. A young girl and boy in their late teens played tenor sax and electric guitar. Reading from music supported on a metal stand they did sophisticated versions of *Desafinado* and *Summertime*. I asked if they knew *'A Taste of Honey'* but they did not have the music, although they enthused about the tune.

They were Argentinian students. I am strongly wrenched by street music. Maybe my past as a busker travelling Europe and then stagnating for years in the UK without getting away had left me a little sad. For years I played every day with my eyes closed and my ears tuned; I sincerely wanted to dedicate myself to being a really good musician. What I lacked was a formal approach. I sometimes looked at various colleges or private tutors, but it never really happened. Now I see this young pair playing better than I probably ever did and a part of me feels sad I never learnt to play properly. The reason for my resistance was fear of becoming a slave to what I loved. However, to have been able to keep music as a spontaneous affair was a form of success even more difficult to attain than a formal education, or at least as difficult. It was the Zen of musicianship, learning to play by not learning to play. As I encountered various buskers I felt a powerful connection with a long term relationship in my life. Music takes one away to its own place, what the Hare Krishna's called the 'music planet'. The power of music is to transport the listener to a different dimension. When I passed a good street musician I was transformed along with the day itself, into a more trusting, more innocent, less pained and less worrisome individual. When I used to play regularly on the street occasionally people would say, 'Thank you,' in such a sincere way it was clear they had felt some profound relief.

Again I checked the Lista de Poste and again nothing had come. With sad eyes the woman who looked for my letter declared, 'Esta nada,' (there is nothing). To have no mail was to be left feeling dejected but I forced out an optimistic, cheery, "Gracias" (thank you) otherwise I wanted to break down in front of her on the counter, beating my empty paws, sobbing, 'Nobody loves me, boo hoo'. The first possible day for my expected mail was disappointing. I would have to wait 'til the following day and each day after that I would be even more certain of something coming. I could not leave Coruna until I had money to buy engine oil and charts. The emerging problem with the engine was insufficient battery power to turn it over to start it. A jump lead start from another boat would then let the engine fully recharge the batteries itself. Providing it ran for a reasonable amount of time without losing all its oil into the bilge.

One day came beautifully warm. I passed through a most wonderful square, a recent discovery, consisting of eight huge plain trees encircling a fountain and stone benches. There was a magical, peaceful atmosphere under the high leafy canopy. I looked up at the bits of blue sky showing through and there were glistening flying beings and gossamer threads way up in the top leaves, a world apart and unique to this grove. I originally had set the brass ships clock to Greenwich mean time, but it was so far away from Spanish local time I moved it forward two hours to that. GMT was useful for navigational purposes such as interpreting tide tables and getting shipping forecasts on the radio. GMT is known as UT or UCT, Universal Time or Universal Clock Time. UT is used in the nautical almanac to avoid confusion as different countries apply various daylight saving times as well as being in different time zones. Spain keeps time zone +1. Therefore local time in Coruna is two hours ahead of UT or Greenwich Mean Time. It was confusing. I eventually kept the ships clock on UT so it could act as a control amongst all the change around me. I always woke up at at 8.30am and continued to do so although now this meant rising at 9.30am Spanish time which was a little late by my preference. Annie of Peace Four always said, rise early and go to sleep with the sunset, then you will be able to sail in the more placid morning time. The west coast of Spain and Portugal often has a north wind which strengthens in the afternoon to around force 6.

At a headland this is a lot of wind because it is speeded up by being squeezed around the point. I was working a passage plan up in the back of my mind. It would be fairly straightforward, just a matter of choosing the next ria to head into. The rias are glacial estuaries. Oddly, they are often deeper than the sea outside due to the scooping effect of the glacier which gouged out such deep furrows into the landscape. After the ice age when the sea levels rose, the rias filled with sea-water. As my Spanish friend Paco would say, 'Amayyssing!' Paco lived in Cambridgeshire in the UK and made the most beautiful mosaics. He was a good example of natural creativity, I mean untutored. He started decorating his back garden with broken tiles stuck in cement. He became deeply involved in design and techniques to create a large complex mosaic, a wandering river of colour extending to a vertical section on the side of the house., truly *amayyssing* to see. Paco and his partner Luisa lived in southern Spain for years. Luisa was an artist too, an international caricaturist and she worked for good money and large companies. They moved to Peterborough where a significant number of my friends had settled. It is strange how we all need to gather into kinship groups. In the end life is about being with loved ones and I felt a little lonely in La Coruna. I hoped to meet others such as me at some point.

It was such early days, it was hard to tell how my travels would pan out. Another boat sailed in from the UK last night. The sailor passed close by and called to me, "Where are all the boats?" I knew exactly what he meant. I too expected a celebratory mood in La Coruna; single-handers exchanging charts and notes and parties aboard bigger boats after escaping the UK wintertime. I was being idealistic and perhaps it was a little late in the season. South bound yachts were likely to be already south and those returning to teaching jobs or whatever they do in the UK, already safely tucked into gale proof marinas in England. So, I sought community online. The internet café provided a welcome link to my peer group and a respite from the constant culture gap that was being English in Spain.

Exhausted, in two ways, I sat again in the same café, busy with Corunians. The clatter of dominoes on marble tables splattered away my stress and made me smile at the energy of play. Two strands to my stress,

1. Constant rocking and rolling of the boat out at anchor. I was losing sleep as I fought the tendency to be tipped onto the cabin sole. Even the lee cloth was no good because the movement was a rocking and pitching and lee cloths are designed to support the body on one tack.

2. Money. I received the forwarded mail at the post office but to my disappointment there was no debit card.

I cashed a tenner someone had sent as postage for some halyards he wanted sending from his boat in Bristol Marina. The tenner ended up with me in Spain and came in handy until I could get some proper money through. I very much needed to get moving again and could not wait another eight days for forwarded mail to arrive. Working on this problem I checked my purse and realized I had a second debit card for an almost redundant account. I checked with a local bank and was pleased to find if I had money in the account I would be able to draw on it in Spain. Then an offer of help arrived out of the blue. A friend phoned up having read of my engine oil problems and offered to pay for oil using a credit card, providing I carried on wandering Spain and writing my dispatches.

In the early hours of one morning I was spending a sleepless night rocking and rolling around with the paraffin lamp and Radio Treize (Spanish Radio Three); looking out at the wobbling harbour I was alerted by a particular yacht. It looked too close to the rocks. I kept an eye for a few hours until I saw figures with torches on deck. The yacht now looked too close for comfort to the slabs of sandstone which form the base of the Digue de Abrigo Barrie de la Maza. I got dressed and stuffed a couple of Maglight torches into my fleece pockets. Then I put oars and spare petrol into the waltzing Avon dinghy. The engine started after a lot of fiddling with controls in the dark. I made it to the possibly endangered yacht as the whole crew made it on deck and were hauling the anchor up and motoring away from the swell and swish of the harbour mole. They paused as I loomed into the scene with a torch on the yellow spray hood of my dinghy to make me visible. "Are you OK?" I called, silence and stares. "Are you OK? I saw your boat close to the, er," I gestured at the heaving sandstone blocks 15 metres away. "It's OK, I'm just taking my anchor," the Scandinavian or German person gestured towards the fairway.

I understood they were in control and said, "OK no problem" and turned away into the choppy blackness to find my little boat. I knew they'd recognized my concern and the value of my offer to help. In the light of morning they were nowhere to be seen. I laughed to myself how it would have been pleasant to find an envelope with some cash in it as a gesture of thanks for my heroic intentions. Thanks came from another direction entirely, in the shape of a little UK yacht popopopopoping past, having just arrived from the UK. A Folkboat derivative, as is SP, but not the same mark. This was one of my favourite small, long keel, yachts, a Contessa 26. She was named 'True Blue', a lovely name to reflect the salty deep sea nature of the class. It looked so sweet with its low slung cabin and long curved tiller, like a little crescent moon, a new one, kissing the horizon. It was a new moon too and with bigger tides and it was probably the increased tidal range which had lifted the yacht's anchor out of a secure footing.

The next day I felt like rowing to the nearest cruising yacht to ask if I could spend half an hour with them. I needed human contact, being at anchor for so long was isolating. But, company came to me, in the shape of three customs officials in a rigid inflatable boat launched from a large customs cutter. They hailed me and boarded as I was attempting to send an email. They were very polite and did not ask to poke around or go into the cabin. I gave them all mine and the boats details and they left pleasantly. I wanted to gush how nice it was to have three reasonable people aboard. I let them go without the linguistic complication of expressing the loneliness of a long distance solo sailor. What did concern me was a friend who often visited Ireland had given me several blocks of compressed peat. These make excellent fuel for the wood stove with the aroma of a Spanish smoked ham, which in my opinion is one of the finest aromas known to mankind. I suddenly realized the mistaken discovery of these peat blocks could be mistaken for bars of hashish. Then the boat would be ripped apart and I would have to put it back together again. I wondered about burning the peat, but the weather was not cool enough to have a fire and they were much too precious to discard.

This fruit revelation had bought Spain right into my mouth and I walked away from the town square with more Spanish in my gait, I felt in my intestines to be part of the place.

A 'Tool Box' Day
I lay in the following morning until awoken by my mobile ring tone. It was my friend again offering to pay for engine oil on a credit card. I declined assistance in the hope things would work out but the phone call had made me feel as if I had options. I gained the feeling of possessing the psychological tools for the tasks in hand. The day became like a toolbox full of 'wrenches' - to open stiff nuts, 'grips' - to take a strong hold of reality, a 'cold chisel' - to break apart stuck situations. There were 'operating manuals' and 'a plane' too, for some plain speaking. The day kinked into disappointment as my debit card failed to appear yet again. Then an old woman ripped me off by selling me a duff tomato, a rotting peach and a sharp nectarine. I should have known she was not bright when she put all three items in one plastic carrier bag and hung the lot on a pair of scales. During this sham she eyed up my shoes and clothing and said, "Tres" I stiffened. "Tres! No!" I replied, not believing the price could be so high. I was being asked to pay 3 Euros, the equivalent of over £2. "Dos?" I offered 2 Euros in the hope of not being cursed. She muttered about not having any money and I got away with being half ripped off for my disappointing fruit. The reason she had no money was she had spent her whole life grabbing other peoples, I mused to myself angrily.

The tool box day rattled along as I pondered 'faith'. In my thoughts I saw faith as merely a survival stance one must adopt in order to get over temporary setbacks. One knows what's needed will come, given time, such as the summer warmth after winter, or a more cheerful mood after disappointment. And that is natural faith, not the life embroiling Christian belief version, just the reality of time passing. Where one cannot yet know for sure whether an outcome will be favourable there is cognitive dissonance. Faith is the process of going through this dissonance. However, faith does have an undeniably spiritual resonance, it is a function of perspective and vision. One holds faith by focusing on discreet possibilities. To gain perspective it is necessary to draw back from a situation. If nothing can be done, withdrawal is the only choice. Faith is partly knowing one can allow distance to grow and enable one to draw closer to an answer in the long run. My 'toolbox' lay metaphorically open as I awoke to that helpful phone call and as the day blustered around me I began picking up those 'tools'. Metaphorically I 'hammered' at the bank doors when I was trying to find a way to get some cash. With a 'cold chisel' I levered customer services into giving me full attention and a definitive explanation of my options.

I then decisively punched my phone into action, calling my parents to ask them to transfer some money into the account I could access out in the wilds of Galicia. It may as well have been Narnia for all the communication difficulties, particularly where money moved. It was necessary to have an account in Spain to transfer money there, but how could a poor adventurer like me get into the system to start with? The decisive use of my 60p per minute mobile phone had a positively helpful response from my dad. He quickly agreed to 'dovetail' with my imminent need for money.

The waiter in the usual café was not the kindly one with the frontal curls; instead he looked as though he would have preferred a career in the aristocracy, in some position near to the 'thumb screw' department. He was small beady eyed, greased back hair and weasel voiced. I tipped too much, giving a whole Euro for a coffee which had cost 70 Cents. It doesn't sound too much but inflating the price of everything to a round pound or a whole Euro can only spoil things. That is what my still open 'tool box' told me as I sat squirming in my hard wooden chair now in need of a loo, but I lost my cognitive grip in the dank corridor for the toilets where five thin brown doors had labels as follows: 'Personal' - a second 'Personal' - 'Señoras' - 'Urinario' - 'Caballeros'. The two 'Personal' doors were either locked or were being held shut by stooping figures in the gloom. 'Señoras' sounded to me like 'Men'; as in 'The Senior'. I continued holding in my stressed coffee driven pee and considered 'Urinario' as much too like 'urinal' to be any use. The 'Caballeros' sounded like little tin soldiers, with thumb screws in their trouser pockets, so I peered into 'Señoras' and was pleasantly surprised to see a loo with a sink and nice clean paper. It was even pink coloured inside. And the light worked. After the 'test of the five doors' I sat in relief thinking about the little Contessa 26 that had arrived out at the anchorage. It had a UK ensign and a single-hander aboard. It was just like me and SP. I wanted to go and see it.

Back at the Real Club Nautico, where I parked my inflatable dinghy while ashore, I made noises with my 'tool box' again. Rattling my 'set of files' I found out the price of a nights berth. 'Grinding my chisels sharp' I got a price for getting my batteries charged. Finally I 'swept the shavings' of a busy day away by finding out the price for having the boat towed into the marina berth from the anchorage and then 'bolted on' the accessories of water and electricity. To my disappointment I was told nothing could be done because it was too windy to tow the boat in. I 'planed off' the rough face of my annoyance in my reactions by saying, "OK. Mañana". Mañana is stereotypically Spanish, meaning 'tomorrow'. But it was the only answer and therefore the fact that I said it for them gave them a chuckle because they were relieved of saying it themselves and playing out a stereotype. Spontaneous use of a Spanish word had occurred earlier when I was in the bank. Impatient at being made to wait while I sought every possible option on my little £10 note, I think the person serving me was slightly disdainful of the small amount I was manoeuvring. Before letting it slip from my control I insisted on getting a conversion price including commission. Then there was a small confusion as I decided whether or not I wanted to go ahead at the rate quoted, until out of the blue I said, "Venga!" The assistant laughed at the clarity of my expression. Venga means 'Go! Do it! Come on!' The tension of my problems melted in a bright flare of direct communication.

My metaphorical tool box lay open still and I made use of the bright tools in a new phase of a new moon. I had not yet spotted the thin crescent in the sky but I had noted its occurrence in my diary. When I got back aboard SP I decided to try the engine. I expected the batteries to be well down and unable to turn over the flywheel. I also expected the low oil pressure light to be winking at me but since arrival in La Coruna the sun had been totting up energy units via the solar panels. Furthermore, it was an uncommonly energized day with my metaphorical toolbox haunting me since I awoke. To my surprise the engine turned and bumped into life. The 'low oil pressure' light remained off. The engine popopopopoped itself around for half an hour without anything untoward happening. The batteries were fully charged again and my confidence was fully restored. I skipped around the decks singing, "I'm on my way!"

I tidied away the metaphorical toolbox day and sat around chuckling to myself about the engine and grinning at the sky over my guitar, or watching the big fishing boats drag clouds of white gulls across the harbour. Terns went, 'kirrick kirrick' overhead, temporary migrants like me, on the way to the warmth of Portugal for the winter. A bigger ship slid growling into the estuary, fussed around by two toy plastic tugs, with noises erupting from steel sides while it turned. I played my relief at being happy again out on the guitar. My audience was the odd gull flying over and the stick persons walking along the Digue de Abrigo Barrie de la Maza, who could only see me strumming, not hear over the distance, but at least I felt somebody out there knew I existed. Boats of all sorts caused washes far out in the harbour and I watched these waves of energy approaching as I soloed along with 'Radio Tres' (Spanish National Radio) and the boat leapt and rocked at their passing. Finally the sun left a little sailing boat moon full and by out in the deep blue alone. Annie of Peace Four SMS texted to say they had a spare chart of Portugal. Exactly the one I needed. Was it the new moon, or patience, maybe faith, or was it the set of psychological tools which kept life turning? All of it. All of it. As much the 'kirrick kirrick' of the terns as anything.

The difficulties continued with money access. I decided to go ahead with a Moneygram, suggested by a good friend worried by my cashless state but, even this failed. The English speaking telephone voice explained the system was down and to try later or tomorrow. Maybe it being September the eleventh meant the world banking system was going to be in disarray. I put it down to not enough people sitting down and being still. I was guilty too as I strutted around the city trying to make it work for me. If I just sat down and kept still I would have realized I, in some ways, had the world in my pocket. I'd sailed my yacht to Spain. I was planning to stay over the winter. I even seemed to be countering the slight back pain I felt, by maintaining correct posture at all times. I had friends emailing, SMS texting and phoning with offers of help with my money situation. I had a chart of Portugal waiting for me in Las Camarinas as well as two special friends aboard a beautiful Wharram catamaran there. The only thing now stopping me sailing around to Las Camarinas was the weather forecast. A southerly force 7 was not at all good. The barometer had been falling for three days. However, it had started to slowly rise.

After changing the ten pound note into Euros I bought oil for the engine. With the engine looked after the best I could do, I would sail to Las Camarinas as and when the wind had some north in it and moderated. I had asked for my debit card to be sent to Las Camarinas instead. I really needed friends by now. I had been a long period without them. A phone call the previous night from a friend in the UK went on for twenty four minutes. It was a really good chat with my old sailing partner. We wondered at the passage of time, at her daughter's fourth birthday and at the achievement of my dreams of sailing to Spain. All the times we'd voyaged together in the grey North Sea we were practising for an eventual voyage to Spain - some day. I told her how I felt her presence as I sailed alone and how I spoke aloud comments which I would have said to her and then found myself creased with laughter and was with her at the point of laughing aloud because I knew the moment would have had her bent double in stitches as well. Sitting in the 'Café - Bar La Barra' I pondered the events leading up to the single café con leche in front of me. I failed to trace the choices and processes which had led me there although I knew it was what I had wanted so much for so long. The day became pleasantly hot and I carried a bag of shopping including a new tin of diesel engine oil back to the boat. To attempt to explain life as a whole is like dragging up jellyfish tendrils on a fishing line and then trying to describe a jellyfish. Somehow I struggled into a position from which I could continue to move south.

With oil in the engine, a decent weather forecast and food on the boat I sailed out of La Coruna on a misty morning. The oldest lighthouse in the world, the Torre De Hercules, was the last thing remaining in view after two hours.

Three hours further on and the coast had disappeared in fog, but out at sea it was hot and clear. A new period of small journeys; around to the Ria De Muros surrounded by pine clad mountains and fishing villages; meeting good friends and new faces, sailors all. There were islands, the Islas Sisargas, a villainous looking cape, Cabo Villano on the way to the Ria De Camarinas. Camarinas, a village harbour in a glacial estuary, contained two major sources of joy. There was Peace Four, the catamaran from Bristol marina with Anne and Nev aboard. I was quickly treated to home cooked apple cake and a square meal. In the morning I was taken for a trip to the local supermarket and supplied with local cheese, chorizo, apple juice, butter, nuts, fresh local bread and a load of delicious fruits. I felt thoroughly looked after and I had reached the end of a distinctly lean period. My debit card had arrived at the Camarinas Yacht Club. So now I had friends and cash. Both friends and money build in intensity if nothing is drawn from them. I had not spent any money since leaving Wales, apart from about sixty pounds I'd had in my purse. My bank account had been untouched for over three weeks. Neither had I been with any friends for the same period.

SP was stocked with delicious local food, scrumptious peppery chorizo, a whole soft white cheese with a will to be eaten and 'Maria bread', a circular, rustic loaf, tasting good with the first two. I had fruit juices, butter, tins of lentils with sausage, fruits to rival the Coruna peaches and vegetables enough to feed a viking.

Peace Four left Camarinas making for Finisterre. I stayed because the

Radio Four shipping forecast for sea area Finisterre had me alarmed. It was for easterly winds of force 6-7, occasionally eight. Anne and Nev had a much larger boat which could stomp along through force 8 winds. SP was tiny in comparison and winds of force 8 made really heavy going. Anne and Nev also knew from experience that the UK Shipping Forecast regarding Spanish waters was more representative of the area well offshore, rather than the coastal regions. They left and I felt empty and disappointed in my own conservatism.

Two hours later I reasoned it would be safer to make southing than getting increasingly weather bound in the northern regions with October just a few weeks ahead. With carefully prepared self, boat and navigation I motored out of the protective estuary. The wider scenery of the coast peeled open to each side as I crept intrepidly out to sea. The mouth of the ria was a couple of miles wide. Cabo Villano stood like a black organ to the north and high mountains slumped away southwards. Inland rows of wind turbines on the mountain tops churned the heavy clouds. Some were stopped for no apparent reason, others obscured by thicker cloud coming over the ridge. In my peripheral vision the wind was visible in the cloud movement and the wind turbines like sentries looking out over the sea. I was concentrating on getting offshore efficiently and safely. The wonderful scenery was fearful and beautiful. I caught up with Peace Four in the Ensenada De Sardineiro, a small bay sheltering in the lee of the great Cabo Finisterre.

To have rounded Cabo Finisterre was to have reached the real west coast of Spain, from now on the coast plunged southwards right down to Cabo Sao Vicente. After Cabo Finisterre Anne and Nev seemed to relax and begin real cruising. We moved south in easy day sails of 20 or 25 miles. Warm placid seas swarmed with fish, fishing boats and sea birds. We entered a region of mountains covered in pines, rocks and wind turbines. Occasionally a cloud filled valley gave the scene drama and perspective. The coast of north-west Spain, Galicia, is known as El Costa Del Morte - the coast of death. High rugged cliffs and offshore reefs of rock and sand banks make for challenging pilotage. The Rias Baxios are on the west facing coast, they are littered with small harbours but also many rocks, sometimes 5 miles offshore and unmarked by buoys or lights. Sailing past such reefs was awe inspiring. Swell bursting upwards in sunlit white and small fishing vessels much too close for comfort. Fish collect around rocks, where there is food, oxygenated water, plants, shelter and bird life. A constant presence on the Spanish coast was terns, either common terns or sandwich terns, I was uncertain, probably both. They bounced along on sharp tapered wings. Seen close by perched on a buoy or fishing boat they can be quite tiny, not much bigger than a swift. They dived in an instant from fairly low over the waves. Gannets plunge from much higher and head straight downwards with wings in a W shape. The birds at sea drew my attention and gave me endless pleasure with their dives. The sight of a shear-water wheeling through Atlantic swells with its wing tips tracing every nuance of the heaving waves was unforgettable. The fulmars approached, made four or five complete circles around the boat then landed in the wake to feed. I saw storm petrels.

Biscay came back to me in tides of awe. I remembered it as a series of separate scenes: A picture of endless crests on mountainous swells; giant grey ships butting towards me or, earlier in the journey, carving their way across a smooth morning sea; the gps indicating hundreds of miles yet to go; my resigned stance at the tiller accompanied by real fears of not getting back to land; nights with various lights of ships and fishing boats around the horizon, all potentially threatening; golden and blue sunrises along with mare's tail clouds emanating from the south west, a repeated warning of stronger winds. Anxiety and joy were harnessed into blunt effort at continuing southwards. When I was just 60 miles from La Coruna I sailed the boat so fast it was luck which prevented one or both sails tearing. The final 30 miles had me careering along at 6 knots, crashing through the occasional cross sea in the dark. Winds had blown force 5-6 for three days and SP took me through the ocean scene as long as I could steer.

In the stronger winds of the second half of the voyage I was unable to make the steering sail work and I stopped to sleep under the watch of a kitchen timer. SP averaged 3 knots, 24 hours a day for 7 days. I managed 5 hours sleep per day, taken in 15 minute snatches and controlled by the battery powered kitchen timer. If I took out the hours spent heaved to, the journey proceeded at 3.7 knots. This was more or less what any yacht will average on a long passage. If I had been able to use proper wind vane self-steering the journey may have been shortened to under 6 days. Peace Four at 46ft long had four people aboard. They made it in under 4 days.

Catamarans are fast sailing boats and their average speed was over 6 knots for the whole journey. Ann and Nev were very pleased with the boat they had spent the past four and a half years building. Cruising in company with them I had the chance to watch Peace Four rising and dropping in the Atlantic swells, sweeping along like a great bird, a wonderful sight. One June day I had cycled into Bristol Marina with vague plans to sail the Bristol Channel. When I saw a long thin boat on an articulated lorry I thought, 'What a narrow beam for a yacht?' Then I saw another one like it on a second articulated lorry and realized it was a Wharram catamaran in-build. Little did I know the way this boat and her builders/owners would touch my sailing career. It was amazing to see the same boat anchored next to SP, in a wild Spanish ria and think how dreams can become real. Amazing.

Portosin is a small fishing village on the brink of development as a leisure area. I crossed the Ria De Muros to anchor there because the last few days of wind and rain had left me frustrated. At least the anchor held as the squally gusts swept over the mountains. It was not cold, even when thunder and rain bucketed down. At night the temperature was sweaty. I lit a coal fire after I decided I would no longer need the sack of coal I had carried from Bristol. I could not just throw it away, so hoping to dry out some of my rain soaked clothing I prepared kindling and fire lighter and lit it up. I had a number of wet socks from using the dinghy to run ashore. In windy weather the dinghy butts into wavelets and they curl over the front, soaking bum and shoes. I then spent an extremely uncomfortable evening waiting for the coal to burn away and the cabin to cool down again. We may have been having unsettled weather but it was not cool enough to burn anthracite. I sweated until midnight when I gratefully slept with the slightly cooler night air soothing me.

Being at anchor was free of charge and I loved the thought of saving all my money for myself and the boat. Spanish marinas charged around 10 Euros per night. I could not afford to go in them apart from once every couple of weeks to do some laundry or have a shower and charge up a pile of aa batteries. Washing was all done each morning before breakfast with a bowl and a kettle of hot water. I was clean and hopefully not smelly. There was however the chronic problem of frequently wet shoes and warm weather - they ponged. The café I chose to rest in, contemplate and just be off the boat, overlooked Portosin harbour. It was quite a wide area of water walled off for protection of the hundreds of small to medium fishing boats. Fishing was the only industry in town - the sole concern of most of the coastal communities all the way from Coruna. A poster depicting a portrait of a bearded man with a naked figure of a woman cleverly worked into the facial features advertised the café. The words, *En que pensa o home* over the top meant, *What's on a man's mind?*. At the lower edge was the name 'Sigmund Freud'. The face with the woman incorporated was one I had seen before. The poster would be more apt if there was a fish, instead of a woman's figure knitted into the face to represent the unconscious desire of Galician man. Perhaps Salvador Dali had already done it. The poster was a gift in 2001, to the 'O Noso Bar'. The bar was quite new. The owners family and friends noisily enjoyed themselves around a table in a private section with a television and sideboard, part of the house. They passed a camcorder around and laughed as the youngsters, out of sight but clearly audible, performed songs and joked in front of the camera. The view from the bar went 4 miles across the ria de Muros. Mountains of 600m lay behind and around the ria.

The weather was dry and hot and the sky clearer than recently. Being in a relaxed mood I decided to buy and write several postcards. I saw a small newsagent and went inside to choose cards. Postcards were not available. Portosin was so ungeared to tourists.

The gecko index remained at zero. A tiny church lay in a small wooded valley which met the port. Walls of rough-hewn granite made me look for the movement of lizards in sunny patches. But alas, none were to be seen. In Muros there was an iguana in the front window of a pet shop, bright-eyed and clear-skinned it was fairly young. The price was ninety Euros While this sighting sent reverberations through the gecko index, there was yet to be a sighting of a wild reptile. The gecko index would tell me when I was far enough south to stay the winter months. I would not be really happy until I saw a gecko.

On a table nearby a small newspaper had a picture of some important person. Behind his head were the red and green colours of the Portuguese flag. There was an interesting separateness between Spain and Portugal and I wonder how interested the Spanish were in what happened in Portugal. I was going to buy a Spanish mobile phone, but realized the cost would be very high if I used it in Portugal. I would be on 'Roaming' and paying as much as my UK mobile cost on Roaming. The border with Portugal was only about 40 miles to the south, yet it had a different feel entirely, the language, music, politics were all distinctly at variance with Spain.

The geography changed exactly at the Spanish Portuguese border. The coast lost its mountains and cliffs, flattening out to hundreds of miles of low lying sand. There were no rias to explore. Instead there were either artificial harbours with marina berths for yachts, or river estuaries. The latter were hazardous in onshore winds due to swell. As the Atlantic waves reached the shore they steepened and broke, or rolled heavily. Most Portuguese harbours had some sort of 'bar' at the mouth making them dangerous with heavy swells.

I thought about calling my dispatches, 'El Gecko', notes on how it feels to tenuously cling on to the wall we call life. My mission would be to find out, through the medium of 'El Gecko', whether there exists an easier and more enjoyable way of clinging to the wall and whether a bit of winter sunshine would be the answer to life's woes. I was called away from the Freudian poster café by a text message. A large trimaran was swinging with the wind shifts too close to SP. The other boat was already anchored when I arrived and so it was my responsibility to sort out the risk of the two boats contacting. Peace Four was at the Portosin anchorage too, arriving before me, having been driven out of Muros by a mixture of boredom caused by days of wind and rain, and, a too shallow position. Since we had arrived the tides had moved into a phase with increasing rise and fall. It would be a full moon at the weekend. A change was as good as a rest and even Spanish coastal cruising can seem tense and worrisome if the weather closes in. I arrived back at SP to see the large trimaran busy with anchor adjustments, but well clear of SP. I dinghied over and greeted the Portuguese single-hander and apologised for inconveniencing him by anchoring a little too close.

A trimaran has three hulls with the main one in the middle. One of the outer hulls is always clear of the water, similar to the sponsons of a flying boat. The anchoring method is a little more complex than with a single hulled boat. There is the need to have brace ropes attached to the amas (outer hulls) in order to prevent the large, light boat ranging around on its anchor. They use rope instead of chain to hold them due to its lightness, but it needs to be very much longer. This fact was what I'd neglected to observe when I carefully chose my anchor spot. Pulling thirty meters of heavy chain out of the Spanish mud and moving the boat made me hungry. For tea I tried the local tinned shellfish, called 'Mejillones', mussels in a rich orange coloured oily sauce. They were harvested by large boats with hydraulic grabs. These worked amongst the hundreds of 'Viveros'; floating rafts with ropes hanging vertically downwards to which the mussels attached themselves and grew.

One of the major coastal features was crowds of viveros in every spot with some shelter from the Atlantic, throughout all of the Rias Baxios.

Viveros are about the size of a medium sized garden. Gulls squawk the days away sitting on the flat islands and occasionally a heron rests amongst them, looking miserable and outnumbered. A cheerful, uplifting sight were white egrets which chose quieter, more charming locations to gather and fish. Always back to the fish. The fish seem to be enchanted by their own abundance, they swim casually by in groups, some flap on the surface and they reminded me of those in fairy tales which flip themselves onto the shore in order to be rescued by a princess. Anne, Nev and I watched a number of them right at the surface. Their lips were projecting out of the water and opened, they were like a silent, pouting, choir of synchronized swimmers. Terns were happy here, unconcerned if they happen to be sandwich terns or common terns and diving for enchanted fish. The gulls lived entirely from the detritus thrown from returning fishing boats and amongst the sun dried nets and pots on the quay they picked out the dead eyes and lips of disenchanted and unkissed fish. The designs of working boats changed with each different ria we entered. La Coruna was a hotchpotch of adapted pleasure boats, urbane and capable of sweeping past and leaving a tea spilling wake. In Camarinas they were most attractively shaped, traditional wooden open boats with a sweetly curving sheer from stem to stern. They had a flat bottom, like a dory, to get onto a plane in order to make speed out to sea through the long ria. In Muros they had much broader sterns and less sheer. They were all painted in bright colours and looked very well maintained. Ninety nine percent had newish Yamaha outboard motors. The Spanish boats here had evolved in accordance with the warm climate as well as the ever present Atlantic Ocean.

In the UK I had often seen decrepit, rusting, unkempt fishing boats put to sea. The disenchanted waters of the UK were made greyer by political perturbations and it was not only the cooler, wetter climate which shaped and rusted away the UK coastal fleets. I felt so much happier in the warm settled weather which had taken the place of the strong winds and rain of the past few days. A low pressure system was situated in sea area Finisterre, recently renamed in the UK shipping forecast to Fitzroy, after the Admiral who started weather forecasts for shipping. The barometer was rising, the wind had veered to the north-west and the sun was out. I was optimistic and the fish once more flopped on the surface of the water, inviting kisses to turn them back into princesses or princes. I watched a smartly kept vessel painted bright blue with a bold white stripe along the sheer leave Portosin harbour. It had a brand new hydraulic grab and ploughed out of the harbour entrance at speed. The crew hollered and laughed with the occupants of a small open fishing boat as they bounced and leaped in the wash. Long after the voices had died away the bow wave scrolled into the distance of a warm evening.

The gecko index remained at zero, but I had seen dolphins swimming and blowing near the boat. I had seen prickly pear cacti laden with fruit. I would not have the confidence to attempt to eat such viciously defended fare. I had seen a large grasshopper which flew rather than leapt, with turquoise wings. A satisfying day's observations even if no geckos. I was now ready to leave again with a fair breeze. Portosin - I always liked that name. It was the port of call for some friends I met while on my previous boat in Falmouth and I associate the word 'Portosin' with those two friends who sailed off to the Caribbean aboard a twenty four foot sailing boat on their way to New Zealand.

I relaxed deeper into the Spanish experience, rowing ashore, always a more satisfying way to get along than using the outboard motor, I landed on a beach of white sand. I pulled the dinghy up above the high tide mark and walked into the outskirts of Portosin. I found a steep road towards some woods. The woods were eucalyptus, very tall thin trunks with high leaf canopy, thin pointed leaves, the size and shape of a banana. I walked into an unfenced area on the edge of the eucalyptus wood. Rocky outcrops and ferns interspersed with patches of gorse. The ground was a mixture of black peaty wet soil and drier parts covered in viney sticks. I sat on a hunk of granite, watching a pair of crows and letting the place settle down around me and me relax into it. The crows were displaced by a cackling magpie. The sun disappeared and reappeared as large cumulus continued out of the west. The ria and distant Muros glittered and the further mountains were bright with sunny patches on rock peaks. It was a point of arrival for me. I looked at Spain and thought, 'I'm here, I did it'.

Soon the Rias Baxios would be a rich source of memories and I would be negotiating with the slightly worrying coast of Portugal. Sailing along endless sandy beaches is not as simple as it sounds. The problem can be actually seeing the shore and knowing when one is too close. With large Atlantic swells most of the Portuguese coast must be given a good offing. Sailing 3 to 4 miles offshore solves most of the problem until a port is approached. Most Portuguese ports are artificially built out of the beach with a couple of enfolding harbour walls. As I sat watching the Ria De

Muros in its splendour I was a mixture of calm satisfaction at making it this far but also the desire to go further was working strongly inside. The cruising life sounds idyllic and it sometimes was, but there were many concerns and sources of anxiety for the sailor. I wondered sometimes about how much I really enjoyed sailing, with it's harshness on body and mind. Sitting grounded on that rock, the scent of eucalyptus flowing past on warm breezes and crows just being crows nearby, I asked myself whether it was going sailing I liked or arriving in new places and regaining land. If a sailing boat was merely a way to move ones stuff around and a place to sleep, it would seem a very inconvenient and uncomfortable way to travel. Again I headed to the 'O Noso Bar' to write and enjoy the peace of my solitude. The picture windows held views as good as the café Caldy in Tenby. I noticed a sheet of strato-cumulus cloud moving in from the west and thought it time to get back to the dinghy and row out to SP. Changes in the weather were critical when at anchor. I moved without haste or worry, but I moved, back to the boat.

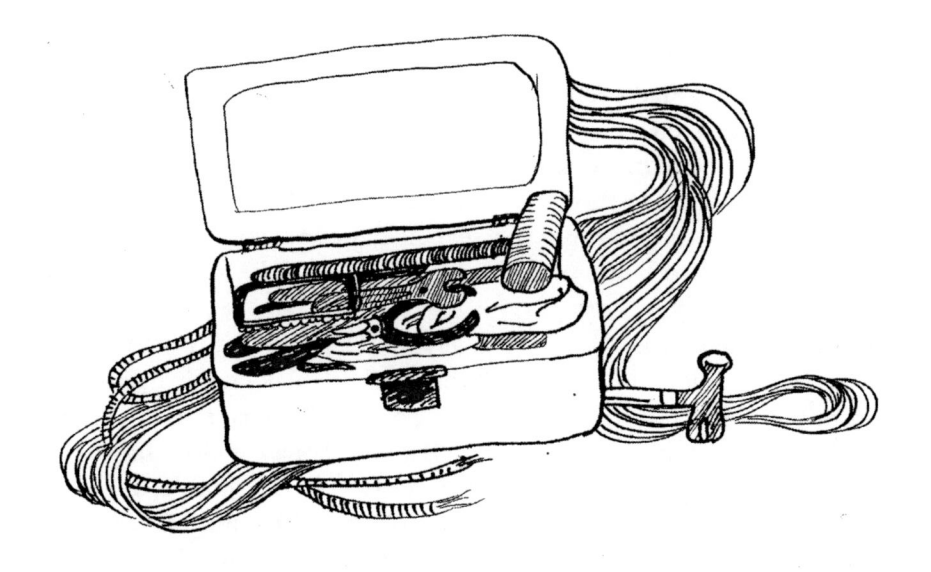

The day became like a toolbox full of wrenches, to open stiff nuts, grips, to take a strong hold of reality, a cold chisel, to break apart stuck situations. There were operating manuals and a plane too, for some plain speaking.

Group Think in Low Pressure

The Isla De Ceis were three islands stretching 5 miles along the Spanish coast. The Spanish Tourist Board had provided my pilot book with an aerial photograph showing Bayona with the Isla De Ceis in the background. Beaches of white sand and high cliffs with a narrow isthmus between two of the three islands. A very attractive anchorage promised white sand and I had planned a route which would take me past the beaches on Isla De Ceis, so if the weather was suitable I could spend a while in some of the most exotic scenery, as cruising folk say, this side of the Caribbean. But a low pressure weather system had been situated west of Spain, out in the Atlantic, for several days and so I felt an urge to make best speed to a more sheltered anchorage. The weather was not settled.

I left Portosin with a bank of foggy cloud flowing down the valleys and over the mountain tops around the ria. The thick cloudy mist flowed in from the north and followed me for 10 miles as I made out to sea and turned southward in the direction of Bayona. I managed to stay ahead, although it was gaining and now there were rolls of thunder in it. The diesel engine poppoppoped its way through the hours and I bit my lip as ragged fragments of low cloud began overtaking me. The weather forecast had told of a low pressure system but assured me it was 'losing its identity'. I reasoned it would do all the worrying things which low pressure systems do, but with a declining energy pattern and therefore nothing seriously concerning for me and SP. The sky went uniform grey and the coast disappeared in murk, but I sensed the thunder was the dying groans of a disturbance, rather than a building storm. Sailing wing on wing, with the sails on opposite sides of the boat and let out as far as they would go felt like a bird gliding downwind with wings held out to catch the breeze. White foam spread out in front and to the side as each wave accelerated us forward. The hiss of aerated water seethed momentarily and then passed astern as the next acceleration came with the next wave. I left the Islas De Ceis well inshore because the mist and murk persisted throughout the day. As I headed offshore I was a bit concerned about the low visibility and scooting ragged black clouds. The decision to miss out the splendour of Isla De Ceis was well founded because the visibility was worse inshore and around the islands and rocks. Offshore I sailed along and was joined by dolphins. They dived under the boat and played in the bow wave. I laughed and whistled at them. They seemed to hear my excited yelps and whoops. My mood was lifted by the wonderful company they gave and I felt safer in my decision to take the offshore exposed route to Bayona.

The summer wind along the west Iberian coast blows mainly from the north. Northerly winds of summer had largely deteriorated by September and the conversation amongst all cruising boats concerned the wind direction. Everyone was waiting for it to become northerly. The day I arrived in Bayona twenty cruising boats had left to head further south. The same weather situation which had encouraged me to leave Portosin gave them the opportunity to sail. They had, apparently, been waiting up to a month in Bayona for fair winds. I did not like to be involved in 'groupthink', where the tendency of individuals is to modulate their opinions so they are more alike when they are gathered together. It is a theory in social-psychology and has been used to explain why, for instance, Nazi concentration camp workers carried out inhumane duties without question.

I preferred to make my own decisions about the weather and whether to sail or not. From my perspective, arriving in Bayona seemed a real achievement in my push towards the warm south. The very word 'Bayona' sounded much warmer than grey sounding 'Muros' and I could certainly imagine winter snows cloaking the mountains around Camarinas. Bayona was the southernmost of the Rias Baxios and the last significant port in Spain before Portugal. One depression does not make a winter and I knew there would be hot sunny days in Bayona, before I too felt the urge to flee south again. The day after arriving saw me taking a siesta with all the hatches open, sweating in the heat of mid afternoon, with my clothes discarded on the bunk opposite.

A single-handed sailor must make her own decisions and this gives the satisfaction of an intense and personal form of experience. Most single handers are very open to communication with other sailors because there is always something to learn, such as, 'There's a deepening low just off the west coast of Portugal,' or, 'There are free showers in the yacht club'. The single-hander prefers individual communication rather than the mass movements of cruisers under the shadow of groupthink.

Santa whoever was being celebrated by various noises erupting in the sky above Bayona. They were not fireworks; rather they were maroons similar to those used in ports in the UK to summons the lifeboat. Rising above the Spanish maroons was out of the question. They were not calls to lifeboatmen, just big bangs. Some were so heavy they made my head ring. There were either groups of eight moderately ear splitting cracks, or there was one, two, three, or four mega bangs. This went on for over an hour, leaving everyone with ears so numbed we all just grinned at each other wordlessly when it was over. Conversation had been cancelled out in a ring of newly generated tinnitus. During the bangs Annie on Peace Four lost patience and began reacting to every 'CRACK!' with a 'YELP!' which itself became doubly intolerable.

I sparked ashore to see some of the goings on, wandering up into the older streets where plenty of people were coming and going. A line of market stalls led up to a church. Offerings of local foods, cheeses and preserved meats with flies liberally crawling on it all. The other goods on sale were things to wear which all had either a cannabis leaf or an alien head motif. The sellers on the food stalls appeared to be locals. The sellers on the cannabis leaf or alien head items all appeared Peruvian. A little figure with shiny long black hair in a pony tail begged at each stall. She looked Peruvian too, half my height and quite old. I do not think she even saw my face, only my long fingered, big palmed, bronzed, hard worked hands hanging at the hips of my jeans. I suppose I was just another tall Nordic type on holiday from the rich northern lands. These well off tourists were pleasant and polite to local working people, but despite their sensitivity to rural and poor people they clearly came from a world where north is up, above, and higher, in economic status than the south. Simplistic I admit, but, I in my threadbare jeans and shoes rusting at the eyelets, could return to my sailing boat in the harbour and I had several months food supply as well as fuel and oil to last me several hundred miles, so I was rich in a sense. I ignored the blue alien heads and the cannabis leaf motifs and the old lady begging was similarly disinterested in my face. I might as well have been an air brushed alien hovering over her. As she passed my hands remained impassively limp at my sides and this was enough to turn her toward the next stall to ask there instead.

Other sellers in the street market were African, They offered a range of leather wrist bands, handbags, *'Iron Maiden'* bum bags. Aha! just what I wanted, not Iron Maiden but a place to carry my passport and debit card away from my shoulder bag. So I searched the fly speckled aisles for a bum bag to suit my need. "Very nice" the stallholders suggested solicitously. Others simply clicked their tongues which meant, 'Look at my goods, buy something you rich b******d'. I found a bum bag small enough to fit inside tight jeans. I was pleased with this because it would be a much safer way to carry a money card on my lizard walks. For six

Euros I had a well made double zipped pouch with a quality webbing belt and strong plastic click fastener. Thanks to the sainted one whom the day was devoted to and who blessed me with a bum bag.

Doughnut shaped bready things were on many stalls. They were called 'Cristalleiros' and I bought some at the last opportunity after being undecided as to how pleasant they would taste. I got entangled in the purchase by my confusion, cleverly managed by the chatty sellers, over the price. I made the mistake of asking the difference between one brand of Cristalleiro and another. The one was more, 'flavoured', more tasty, than the other, the women sellers assured me. They took my money and I was sure they would retain the change, despite a lowering of the agreed price from 2.5 Euros to two 2.25 Euros. I disengaged from the chatting stallholders a bit unhappy about the cost of Cristalleiros, but the bright eyed, rounded seller, with her black hair back in a long ponytail gestured strongly with her fruit picker arms and handed me the change with a smile. I was pleased they had taken my money by agreement rather than by fudging it.

All seemed good until I tasted the Cristalleiros. There were about eight in a pack. They looked like ring doughnuts and the wording on the packet stated these were the best Asturian Cristalleiros locally made by skilled craftsmen who have been making them all their lives. Asturias is the region east of Galicia famous for food. They were like rings of bread which had been left to go stale in the hot fly ridden sun and then been dribbled with a paste of white sugar, maggoty flour and water, not at all pleasant. The packet of saintly sweetbreads cost as much as a third of the bum bag. I had been pleased with the bag and wanted to appease the saints after the luck of getting what I had wanted. Occasionally one makes a real discovery by trying new things, not with cristalleiros though.

Hungry still, I chose a small stall with a large apple picker sort of woman who was offering pastry savouries. There was meat or tuna. I chose tuna and batted away a few flies as I paid a round Euro for it. Not expensive for a large golden coloured, fried savoury, just what I fancied. It was delicious as I stood in the shade of a eucalyptus tree watching the festival market being gradually depleted by Spaniards, Peruvians, tourists, sailors and flies.

Later out at the anchorage a collection of sailors drank, played music and chatted on Peace Four's large expanse of deck space. Wharram catamarans are sold with the promise of becoming sea people and the brochures show attractive naked sailors populating wide deckings. We all enjoyed the gathering of international sailors and musicians, like true sea people, but we kept our clothes on. We played music ranging from Eric Clapton's, 'Layla', to Swedish folk songs. The latter were done by a single-hander with a large white accordion. The former was sung and played on a nice steel strung guitar by a Swedish sailor whose partner looked like Billy Holiday. I closed my eyes and sent swirling phrases in amongst the anchored boats and katabatic plunges of notes down through the wooden slats.

Later we ended up on a large red Swedish ketch drinking coffee and Danish bitters, a bit like an evil version of Schnapps. The bitters were so strong as to sober one up suddenly followed by an unstoppable drunkenness. "It is gooood for your body," claimed the Billy Holiday like singer, rubbing her belly and torso sensually. We all tipped a Danish bitter down our throats and the cabin briefly glowed like a bar scene in a Fassbinder film. The accordionist apologised for his serious expression, saying it was because he had been a judge. He added he had also been a go-cart driver. Now he was a single-handed sailor. He chatted in Swedish to the host as she mobilised another round of bitters. Another Swedish single-hander picked up a comment I made about geckos, "I had one on the boat once," he said. I was suddenly sober again, marvelling at the thought of a live-aboard gecko. "It came aboard when I was alongside a quay. He stayed for several weeks but when I sailed back to Europe I did not see him any more," my sad eyes reflected the thought of a gecko lost at sea, "when I cleared out the boat the following winter, I found the gecko dead in a locker, he had all dried up".

We drunk rich Swedish coffee and more Schnapps which was a heady mixture after wine and song. "Dreenk up! Iss gooood foer you," she said again. A German sailor did the torso rubbing this time, "It's goooed foer you." he said parodying the host. We were getting drunk and so several people made their way up on deck into the cool starry air. Cruising sailors think little of descending from a boat, five feet down into a wobbling dinghy, in the dark, when they are drunk and the water is around ten metres deep. Somehow we all found our boats and boarded them with little more than a wet bum or shoe.

Bayona was a very pleasant anchorage. It was the beginning of a community of cruisers, all with similar ideas about sailing, life and boats. Peace Four had their sea people hats on. The marina, where we all left our dinghies while ashore, was most pleasantly and politely managed. There was an old reputation of Bayona being a snobby, unhelpful marina.

However this was not true any longer. The other cruising folk, many whom had been there before, agreed it was impeccably run.

Bayona provided a usefully stocked chandlers and I walked several times along the long street which looked out on the anchorage, to the 'Automar', for engine oil, outboard motor oil and a Portuguese courtesy flag. I even bought a Spanish courtesy flag because I had not flown one yet. I bought tubing for a refuelling system suggested by Annie. I got some pads which are meant to soak up oil but not water from the bilge. I bought two spark plugs for the dinghy engine. It was good to have spent so long without access to my bank account, for now I could afford to buy spares and maintenance items. The impression I had of Portugal was of a place where spares would be hard to find. It would be like going into the Congo, or up the Orinoco. It turned out that advice was more out of date than the country.

When I arrived in Portugal my first impressions were of a more subtle character than Spain, somehow both cooler and warmer metaphorically and literally. The scenery had more detail and more colours. Portugal smelt of new shoes, non leather ones. I was using an old sailing pilot book, well, I assumed nothing much would have changed as I entered Viana Do Castelo harbour. I made my way through various inner entrances towards the yacht marina, indicated on the harbour plan. A policeman was suddenly gesturing from the quay wall at me. He was telling me yachts were not permitted in this bit and to go elsewhere. He indicated with a curving sweep of his hand. As I did a 'handbrake turn' in an old lock I thanked the official for his help. "Gracias!" I called and then remembered to try not to speak Spanish to the Portuguese. A universal trait of English tourists was to speak Spanish phrases at Portuguese people and then embarrassedly correct them as if they had insulted them. The trouble is, English people speak awful Spanish and their Portuguese is non-existent.

Portugal changed the second language from French to English several years ago. Films were subtitled in Portuguese and so the English (read American) was heard. I found most Portuguese knew a lot more English language than I knew Portuguese language. After travelling a kilometre around the harbour complex I found the new yacht marina. This gave me time to reflect on my existent knowledge base of Portuguese. I could think of only two words. 'Thank you' - 'obrigada', and, 'yes' - 'sim'. I then remembered 'please', because it has such a variance in the pronunciation of the s's. 'Faz favor' is spoken softly and the z is blurred into a 'jzsh'. A 'galon' is a coffee with milk, very different to the flavoursome, provocative Spanish coffees, a galon tasted like any cup in the UK made with instant coffee. What I liked was the glass tumbler, small white saucer and spoon which came with it. A galon was a long drink which left time to sit and think. A galon tasted pleasant even when it had cooled right down although it never tasted wonderful.

Note on the galon: Spelled galao later in the book because the way it was written on menu boards. Local accents also varied.

The marina cost six Euros for the night and this included water and electricity. The plug was a standard 'marina' type and I was pleased to be able to connect without hassle. The battery charger filled the ships batteries and I was able to charge a growing collection of flattened AA batteries. I had taken to purchasing cheap AA batteries because there was not sufficient power to recharge AA batteries without a mains supply. I had been away from any alongside services since I left Bristol, seven weeks previously. I regretted not buying a solar powered AA type battery charger in the UK. I had thought it would be too slow for practical use. However, there had been ample sunshine in Spain, enough to make one of those useful. I decided to save up for a proper solar panel which would be mounted over the stern deck between the twin back-stays A good enough solar panel would be expensive; several hundred Euros but I would be best saving money for that.

A postcard shop in Viana Do Castelo surprised me by displaying pictures of nude women erotically posed in froth and surf on a beach. After the Catholicism of Spain the images were daring and they were not discreet, being openly displayed on a rack in the street. Other pictures were rural scenes photographed in what looked like studio settings, depicting 'peasants' with deeply sunned and lined features wearing traditional clothing. Some people strongly contrasted with Spaniards. Men's hair was longer and more styled, or cropped and fashionably neat, like advertising designers wear in the UK. I noticed clothing was worn more casually, even men in suits looked relaxed and unhurried. Portuguese people showed a confidence which reminded me of Britain. I bought some pegs for a Euro All this way from the UK (a long way from my perspective) and I was buying pegs and browsing in a hardware store. Some things never change.

Oporto

Walnuts and bread in a black plastic bag. The bread was the colour of muscovado sugar and had a massive crust, the taste was similar to malt bread but not sweet, just succulent and firm, like savoury Christmas cake. The shop sold olives, nuts in their shells and soaked white beans in big round baskets. A grey kitten peered out onto cobblestones as a collection of men huddled around stockings and underwear on display in a small, dour, shop. The River Douro was a deep grey colour. The scene at the quayside in the centre of Oporto was as different to Spain as a view of the Ganges would be.

The huge bridge, designed by Eiffel of the French tower, carried trains and vehicles towards the south, through a great bow of iron. I was almost peeing myself after having a Swedish coffee on a Swedish yacht with the Swedish guitarist and café singer in the morning prior to visiting Oporto. I was glad to have not had a second cup, as I trundled and swerved along in a bus. The next couple of hours were spent walking down to and along the quayside. There were alleys with washing hanging out over the balconies everywhere. Very old tired fascias held wrought iron rails on which washerwomen and cat owners leant, looking out at change scouring their city.

Grand municipal and palatial buildings, statues of horses and soldiers reared on plinths of light cream stone, surrounded by the greenest grass since Wales. I found a café, or bar, I was not certain, and used the loo, to my relief, after the strong impressions Oporto imported. After Viana Do Castelo, just a small city, content to tell its story over and over, and proud of its role in the past, Oporto reverberated with cultural history and the forces of change and modernity. Muted, anal colours, brown, cream, stone and grey were bound together by an unseen, but writhing colour which I shall call Brazilian Emerald Green Tree Boa. This snake of the Amazon jungle sleeps on a bough in a perfectly symmetrical coil tapering at each end, with the head at the middle on top. The emerald green is picked out with unblinking, gold eyes and nearly pink, diagonal body slashes. In my childhood the idea of Brazil was wrapped in the coils of the Emerald Green Tree Boa. When I eventually heard the language of Portugal and Brazil I was driven further into a fascination with that vivid, vivacious green. I loved the music of Brazil, the intricate chords and breathless rhythms of Bossa Nova. I once met a Portuguese guitarist who described it beautifully simply, 'It is jazz, but tropical jazz,' zithing his words on the tip of his tongue. The small parks and bunches of trees in between the hassling traffic were verdant green. There must have been ample water supplied to keep it so lush. Or perhaps my impressions were exaggerated with emerald tree boas and Portugal conflated in such a green passion.

Oporto was a very fascinating city with an old river flowing through it, the Douro. I was pleased to have stopped in Leixoes, pronounced 'leshshwoish' and meaning 'little rocks'. Portuguese people were extremely polite. They showed a self-confidence which was reminiscent of Englishness, always on the edge of egotistic, but remaining warm and helpful. A most attractive trace? ran in the faces and where it frequently surfaced in an individual they made the most of it with clean lined and subtle coloured clothes, often in the browns, golds, creams, stones and greens of the land. The language was, like bossa nova, evocative of the beach, tall palm trees and Atlantic sunsets endlessly promising more again tomorrow. The sound of the Portuguese language in music is one of the most expressive for the soft edged, zithing vowels. Spoken Portuguese has a 'swishing' sound, as if little waves break on the tongue. I was exaggerating again, but the Portuguese were moved to exaggerate about their land too. A leaflet described Viana Do Castelo,

The sea is also there, offering outstanding colourful sunsets and far blue horizons, as well as the wide open valley, sprinkled with green, ripping the sunrise. Visiting the city is meeting a living history museum. From the medieval era date the small and mutilated Old Hospital. Open to both river and sea Viana crosses the new IC-1 and extends over ripped spaces, where one feels like living in.

(Thanks to Francisco Sampaio - leaflet author).

One of the funniest moments of my life was during a previous visit to Portugal. In a restaurant with two friends while choosing from the menu we became disabled with laughter by two items on the menu, 'Chicken in house art' and, 'Bailed eyelid'. The proprietor noticed our mutilated composure and attempted to illustrate the two items by making chicken noises while flapping his elbows and none of us were able to look at him as he indicated what 'Bailed eyelid' was. I remember a series of farmyard animal noises, his red podgy face, and just crying with laughter.

...the bright eyed, rounded seller, with her black hair back in a long ponytail gestured strongly with her fruit picker arms and handed me the change with a smile.

Later we ended up on a large red Swedish ketch drinking coffee and Danish bitters, a bit like an evil version of Schnapps.
The bitters were so strong as to sober one up suddenly followed by an unstoppable drunkenness.

Bayona provided a usefully stocked chandlers and I walked several times along the long street which looked out on the anchorage, to the 'Automar', for engine oil, outboard motor oil and a Portuguese courtesy flag. I even bought a Spanish courtesy flag because I had not flown one yet.

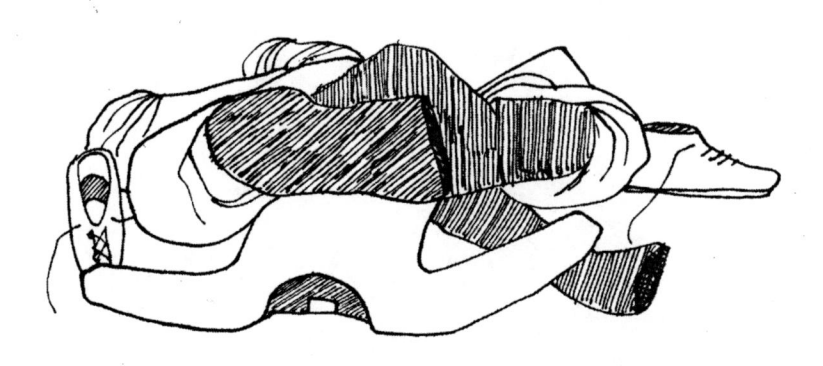

The day after arriving saw me taking a siesta with all the hatches open, sweating in the heat of mid afternoon, with my clothes discarded on the bunk opposite.

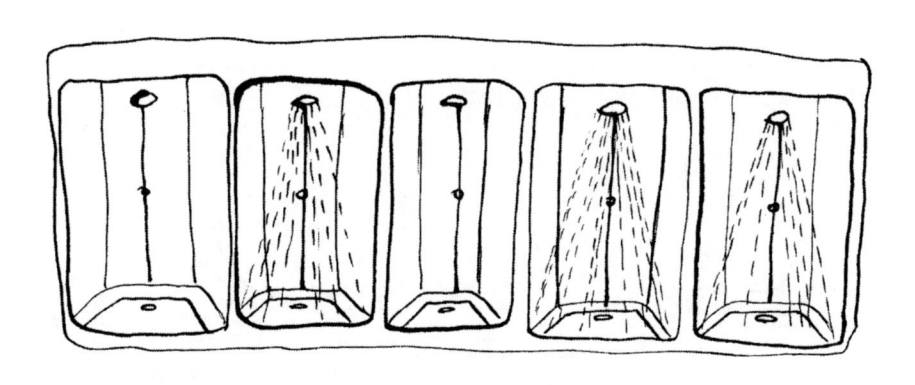

...single handers are very open to communication with other sailors because there is always something to learn, such as, 'There's a deepening low just off the west coast of Portugal,' or, 'There are free showers in the yacht club'.

A single-hander with a large white accordion. The former was sung and played on a nice steel strung guitar by a Swedish sailor whose partner sang and looked like Billy Holiday.
I closed my eyes and sent swirling phrases in amongst the anchored boats and katabatic plunges of notes down through the wooden slats.

Gracia

...I thanked the official for his help. "Gracias!" I called and then remembered to try not to speak Spanish to the Portuguese.

...perhaps my impressions were exaggerated with emerald tree boas and Portugal conflated in such a green passion.

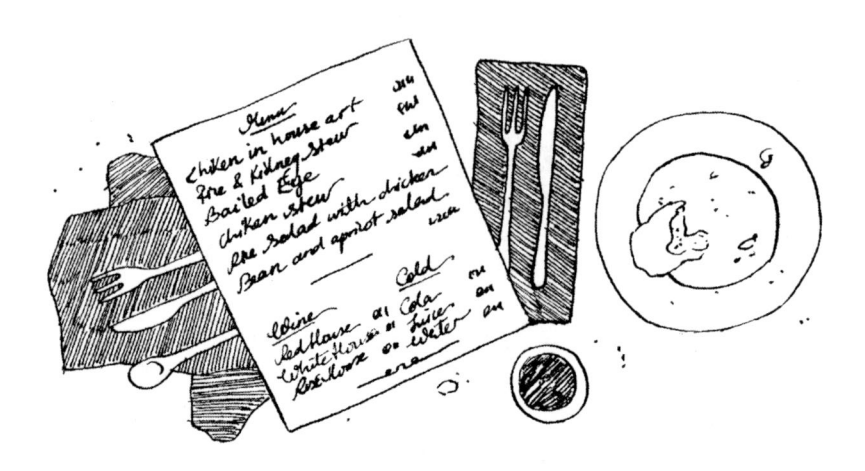

Disabled with laughter by two items on the menu - 'Chicken in house art' - and, - 'Bailed eyelid'.

Walnuts and bread in a black plastic bag. The shop sold olives, nuts in their shells and soaked white beans in big round baskets. A grey kitten peered out onto cobblestones as a collection of men huddled around stockings and underwear on display in a small, dour, shop.

Chapter 2

Nazare and Peniche

I set out from Leixoes on impulse at 4pm, in a hurry to make southing. A friend on a lovely steel boat ran along the pontoon calling, "Where are you headed?" I made a long passage overnight and throughout the following day, 100 miles, past all those difficult harbours I'd been warned about.

I arrived at Nazare and met Captain Mike, the casual harbour master. Mike was British, a retired oil tanker captain. He smoked a Popeye pipe. He lived with his wife Susan on a large steel yacht, they'd sailed in from the UK several years previously. The harbour office was overrun with kittens. I nearly decided to stay the winter in Nazare but when I noticed the heavy knitted socks, jumpers and ponchos on sale along the seafront I thought I'd better go even further south.

Nazare was inundated by rain and wind. I waited for a gust and heavy shower to be spent, under the office of the marina. A policeman stood nearby sheltering and we watched a tall French sailor carry her daughter across the wind swept patch of grass towards their boat. Suddenly hail stones racketed down. The French daughter hollered at the blustering wind and the policeman amusedly exclaimed as we exchanged a surprised laugh at the force of the weather.

I peered through the window into the marina office but it was closed, there were several cats asleep on chairs, piles of paper and computer printers. Some of them were kittens and I had been offered one to keep. They were all strays which had been rescued locally. Many single-handers have a ships cat, I was informed. I explained I was after a ships gecko and asked if there were any available. There had been one a couple of years ago. It was aboard the boat of a well known yachting writer who had been to Morocco. On his way back to the UK he had decided to leave the gecko in a suitable climate and let it go somewhere nearby. I listened with interest and was only mildly disappointed to hear there were not resident geckos in the area. Further south, further south. What surprised me was the fact of there being turtles in the region. A turtle is no more than a wet, hard gecko without the ability to run up walls. The gecko I once had as a pet, called 'Gecky', had golden eyes and could run up the vertical glass sides of a vivarium. Gecky had a continuous smile and attractive sand-coloured skin.

The red zest of Spain contrasted entirely with the green zing of Portugal. Bamboo grew in great green clumps near the harbour. The sticks were used as pot markers by fishermen. I tested the strength of a washed up cane on the beach. It was two meters long and slightly curved, light and springy and it bent without breaking. I selected a café carefully and with considerable wandering. The one I chose had a small beige dog on the pavement outside. I politely walked around the dog which seemed happy enough and this small event had me entering the doorway on a hunch, plus it was light and spacious while most appear dingy. I ordered a galon, which being made with boiled milk, lacked the intense espresso coffee hit of Spain. A bamboo plant on the window sill next to my table had a label written in English, *Lucky Bamboo*. *How would you like to be luckier?* I thought I would like the four tourists at a nearby table to stop staring and grinning at me. I know I am tall, elegant and blond especially so after days being buoyant out in the shadeless ocean under hot sun, but I was doing my best to ignore their crass interest. Oh well, perhaps I reminded them of someone they knew.

To buy extra café time, I tried a couple of snacks. A delicious almond sweetmeat rolled like a pancake had me thanking the bamboo for bringing me luck. Then a muffin which was pleasant enough. Outside, a large palm, the shape of a giant pineapple, thrashed about in the wind and restaurant canopies flogged themselves onto the winter maintenance schedule. Great waves poured onto the strand of beach in a constant rolling boil. Every so often one larger swell would send a white tongue of foaming water over the brow of the beach. Here it would lay trapped by the slope it had mounted and then drain into the sand leaving just an edge of spume. People watched in awe as the unstoppable met the immovable. Some of the energy dispersed as white noise, while most turned into white foam, white being the surprising result of the confrontation. I often wondered at how gulls kept their beautiful white feathers when they spent most of the time squabbling over fish offal and harbour rubbish.

As usual there was a low pressure weather system to the west of Fitzroy which was predicted as moving south east into Trafalgar. I was now in sea area Trafalgar. The low was said to be deepening. This was the reason for the sudden hail stones, the thrashing palm and probably the inane grins of the tourists as well. They had likely spent too much time confined by bad weather in hotel rooms, cafés and cars. The result was they had become a bit bored with the road, a little tired of cafés and most likely a touch weary of each others constant presence and chatter. Their days were full of yet another café, in yet another seaside town, for yet another snack. All they could do was stare out of their own tedium at others, most of whom were holidaymakers too. I was raw from lack of sleep during my one hundred and sixty kilometre sail from Leixoes. I was vulnerable and outnumbered by four to one. I was probably making all this up and making too much of it. By the time I had fended off a couple of grinning stares by ignoring them, the coffees had been slurped and the tourists gone to another part of their holiday. They had drunk their coffees in the way one does at a motorway services stop, quickly and without pleasure. I imagine they would be looking forward to getting home so the photographs could express what a superb holiday they'd enjoyed. Their return would be followed by a couple of weeks of funny Portuguese cigarettes, cheap and triply unhealthy.

Fairly quickly the routine of regular work would annihilate the Atlantic from their auras. The Brazilian emerald green tree boa which had stirred them while on holiday in Portugal would coil up again in symmetrical patience. Or, perhaps the boa would slither out of their lives in search of deeper forests. Next holiday they would opt for a warmer climate, more in season and with more colourful local characters to grin at. The Brazilian emerald green tree boa might be coaxed back into their natures if they truly sought the exotic and the exciting.

The green in the hills around Nazare was a soft, mossy, jade, tone. It made me feel curious as to what coiled and ran in it. But was I so different to the tourists? A man called from a car as I walked along the sea front. I ignored him, but he drove out of the car park and parked ahead of me along the road. I thought he would be unable to head me off on the beach because walking on sand is like walking in a dream as ones feet slip away with each step and he looked fat. I was wrong he approached, grinning, and asked me if I was on holiday. I told him I was working, as if it may give me an excuse to be busy and therefore unapproachable, but of course it was not the best reply and he produced more questions until changing his mind and suddenly walking away. When I reached the town I sat next to the lucky bamboo with a black coffee. The 'galon' was too insipid for today. Unfortunately the black coffee was so strong I began to feel indigestion after the first few sips. I asked for some hot milk to be added, but would have been happier with a 'galon' after all. Not all days are ecstatic bows of wandering.

The waves breaking onto the Nazare beach had been fantastic. Four metres high, much bigger than any I'd have seen on UK shores. After a night of thirty knot winds from the south west, waves exploded and fell on the beach in bursts of white spray shooting upwards twice that height. I photographed them for an hour, but I knew the pictures would look unimpressive. A telephoto lens would make the most of the swells piling onto the beach, but the photographs would then be hyper reality, like photos in surfing magazines. What shocked me was I sailed to Nazare intending to anchor and run ashore in the dinghy. People who cruise long distance had told me how they anchor off surf beaches. The way to land was to wait for a lull in the wave train, run in quickly, beach the dinghy and hop out as you drag it up beyond the surf. Fine I thought, but the bay around which Nazare clusters is particularly deep. The sand beach is steep and the swells arrive untrammelled and become unstable within a short distance of the shore then quickly plunge into white noise and surf. In Nazare there was no question of landing through the breakers in a dinghy. It would be fatal, not just wet.

A man, obviously a tourist, by his clothing and posture, stood grinning with his feet in the licking white surf, transfixed by the magnitude of noise and height of the rollers. I watched him being seduced by the boiling mass in front of him and he stepped closer, further towards the tumult, gaining courage but losing judgement. He got to a point at which the incoming waves were hitting his legs and shooting straight up his front in a fountain. He turned and grinned at me several times. A local elderly man walking by called to him and gestured to come away from the waves. The local indicated with his hands pointing steeply forward and downwards how the beach was steep to. The tourist only grinned at the local, who shook his head and made a gesture which cast away his responsibility and walked away along the beach. The Canhao de Nazare is an under-water canyon which reaches right into the bay from the Atlantic depths. I realized the local man would possess a mental image of this geological feature, based on hearsay and the talk of fishermen. The beach in his minds eye would likely be the very edge of a pit as deep as the Atlantic itself. The local man's warning to the tourist would have been based in this mental picture of a precipitous canyon edge forming the beach of Nazare. The Canhao de Nazare was 100m deep within half a mile of the shore. Within 5 miles the canyon dropped 450m. It was an impressive feature reaching into the bay of Nazare, but not precipitous. It did present an extremely difficult anchorage in fifty to ninety metres depth if one wished to gain shelter in the bay as well as keep clear of the breakers.

When I told other sailors I carried 80 metres of anchor chain they exclaimed, "80 metres! That is, er, around two hundred and fifty feet!" I grinned, deeply satisfied with the profundity of my anchor chain. The next comment was generally, "Don't ever get that lot straight up and down, you'll never be able to pull it up." That shook my confidence because I knew the total weight of my chain was too heavy to lift, certainly with the anchor itself adding 15 kilos. Practically I could only ever use just over half of it. I reckoned one could not have too much though. If I ever had to cut it away because it got caught on a wreck I would still have a fully stocked anchor locker. In addition I had two spare anchors. Really good ground tackle was a strong feature of a cruising boat. Meanwhile postcards on sale along the seafront showed the beach crammed with bathers and sunshades, while waves lapped quietly ashore as children stood wonderful and amazed in the Portuguese summer. Now the marinas were all on low season rates and the Atlantic swells, born of hurricanes thousands of miles away on the eastern seaboard of the US, as well as low pressure systems within sea areas Fitzroy and Trafalgar made the beach an awesome place. When the sun shone though, the temperature was as hot as August in the UK, most pleasant.

The end of the beginning of the Narnia Voyage. I was exhausted and needed to pause for the winter. Even in southern Europe the weather closes the ports for days at a time. Several days ago I'd arranged a winter berth in Nazare but after visiting Cascais, by bus, I quickly rearranged my plans in favour of sailing the 60 miles further south to Cascais. A glimpse of Lisbon while passing through en route to Cascais had impressed me much. It looked lively and cultured, a fine place to have nearby for a longer stay. I needed to reflect, to find out whether or not I had fulfilled my objectives: *To sail south 'til the butter melts; to sail to Narnia; to see geckos.*

Having reached Spain I found an open ended dream. But that was fine. There were a number of reasons to spend the winter in Nazare Marina. It was well protected from all weathers with pontoons to moor the boat to and locked security gates and electricity and water supplied to the pontoons. There was a toilet and shower and an office where I could receive post. The marina was run by a friendly British couple and the marina office was full of charming cats. The gecko index was given a latitude of 41 degrees north. Even a gecko bought in on a sailing boat from way down south and never having been seen since would do. So far the geckos I'd failed to find had given me much pleasure.

Things in foreign countries have to be more impressive, mountains must be twice, no, three times higher and steeper, animals must be exotic colours or really big. Instead I saw miniature ants on a whitewashed wall in Sitio, a town on top of the cliff overlooking Nazare. They were almost too small to recognise as ants. I was loving the view from the high point, wondering at the way altitude appeared much greater from the top looking down than from the other way. A crowd of surfers moved silently in and out of the white spread of waves in slow motion. People from this height were as small as the ants on the whitewash. And there was a lizard with a grasshopper in its jaws. The 'elevator', a funicular railway, carried people up from Nazare to Sitio. On the shortish incline the cliff sides were covered with aloe vera, thick green soft spiked leaves. Occasionally a trainer shoe, a piece of car bumper, a grubby nylon cardigan or a carrier bag of rubbish tied tightly had tumbled to a halt from above. In Portugal rubbish was often seen in beauty spots. The people who threw away rubbish saw natural settings as unoccupied land and treated it as a dump.

At the top of the sloping terminus of the elevator I emerged almost immediately onto a terrace with a couple of cafés, a couple of cars, a couple of cats, dogs and a man selling nuts. I bought a round, sweet biscuit thing, covered in nuts, for a Euro It was rather good, not too sweet and full of protein. There were nut sellers dotted all about the place. Another common sight was racks of drying sardines, gutted and opened out flat with heads and tails intact. On the beach down in Nazare fishing nets covered the rows of racks to keep off the gulls. The gulls were mad for fish when the trawlers arrived in the port each night. I often heard a 'BRRRUUNNGGG!' as one flew into the rigging of SP. There were so many they flew carelessly around and around in great whirls, joining in a circular flow like a carousel. Their shadows, like phantoms, projected from the trawler deck lights onto the quayside warehouses. I found a flat cornice to sit on where nobody hassled me.

The nut seller threw a plastic sheet over his stall to have lunch. Then I strolled amongst the whitewash alleys, looking for geckos, but saw only the occasional dog turd and graffiti. Someone dressed in loose fitting, sandy coloured corduroy trousers with a thick check shirt and a flat cap, the typical wear of local fishermen, beckoned me to the shady wall where he stood with a box of dried sardines. His fingers eased some flesh away from the line of fine bones and he offered me a taste which I was pleased about, having seen the local speciality but not tried it. As he offered me the morsel his hand and head came together slightly in a brief eating gesture. I reciprocated by bringing the fish meat up to my mouth and he nodded encouragingly. Portuguese sun dried sardines were obviously going to be the savoury equivalent of the peaches of La Coruna, a discovery of immanent Portuguese taste. My teeth closed onto the morsel with a taste of strong salt. The next chew brought strong fish. The next even stronger salt with even stronger fish. I even thought I might blow it all out of my mouth as a cyclist would a fly, but he was smiling and nodding next to me. It was really nasty. I felt like a spaniel which had found a rotting herring on a beach, chewing the rancid morsel in a neurotic act of self denial. To tell him I was dubious about the fish I held my hand out flat, palm down and tipped it side to side, trying to convey polite uncertainty towards the flavour. Misreading my signal he shook his head, saying "No, no" as he made the movement of fish swimming with his flat hand held on its side and wiggled it forward. "No, no" I said, trying to make him understand I was not saying the fish was a flat fish, like a Dover sole, but that I was in wavering about the flavour. He insisted by showing me again the swimming fish of his hand. I walked away disappointed that the pleasant taste of the nutty biscuit snack had been displaced by rancid fish. The fingers of my left hand which had taken the piece of fish smelt like a piss soaked alley on a hot day.

Dozens of tourist buses fed the souvenir shops and stalls. People shopped off handedly, buying mass produced clutter from typical locals who sat in typical stalls. There were sunglasses, typical crafts of the region, metallic sparkle multi-windmills and other rubbish. The locals seemed a little tired of playing the typical local. I observed tourists stooping to read price tags, sitting locals and small sleeping dogs. Dog shit was everywhere and the tourists spread it around until it combined with sand blown up from the beach and crumbled into dust. Lines of plastic dolls held fishing nets to catch tourists who seemed to prefer the practical jumbo knit socks and zipped sweaters reminiscent of clothing from the high Andes.

It was now the beginning of the long passage of winter and the weather unsettled. After a few days of cloudy rain and cool temperatures it turned as hot as mid August in southern UK. In the evenings, which were now dark early, one could spend time with very light clothing on and sleeping was stuffy and hot. Other nights were much cooler. Other boats I'd met before arrived in the warm spells. The Swedish couple from Bayona arrived in their beautiful red ketch, still with stocks of Danish bitters aboard. A UK sailor who had built a boat I found to be one of the most appealing boats I have ever seen, turned up from Leixoes. He was full of sailing and told me, "I approached Aveiro entrance but it was getting dark, I could not work out the lights and I didn't fancy attempting to enter". I knew the swell of the last few days would make Aveiro a really tricky place to enter. The Swedish couple came via Figuera da Foz. They told me the entrance there was closed until the swells abated.

I'd come from Leixoes in one leg, a 100 mile passage, because of those factors. The pilot book warned against using those two harbours with heavy swells running. I felt I had made a wise decision to rest in Nazare and I had taken the initiative rather than following the herd. I was sure it would be interesting, peaceful and pleasant for a while. A French single-hander was aboard a small scruffy yacht. It had so much gear lashed on deck it was impossible to walk around. I was told he sailed to Dakar each winter for his job as the head of medicine for Senegal and he sailed back to Portugal each spring, to attend conferences in Europe. The boat 'Phoenix' disappeared north west of Spain in spring 2005 and he was never seen again. He had made the voyage between Brittany, or Portugal and Dakar each year for twenty years, delivering medicines to the Casamance region of southern Senegal.

October 27 2002. Peniche was a port sheltering under the rock cliffs of Cabo Carvoeiro. High on the cape a lighthouse looked out to a group of small rocky islands. The nearest, Ilha da Berlenga, was 5 miles out to sea and designated as a nature reserve. I found the protected species of the island a little mundane; A poster advertised the islands with pencil drawings of a lizard, a seagull and a cormorant. A resident gecko population or whales to be seen from the farther cliffs of Ilha da Berlenga, or even better some funny cat like creature rarely occurring in

Europe would be worth a visit. Seagulls, cormorants and common lizards would fill the tourist trip boats but as a confirmed gecko hunter I would not be booking in. Islands are best viewed from afar, as an island, as separate and out of reach. There was a special type of gull there, the Gaivota-argentêa (Larus cachinnans). My *'Sea birds of Northern Hemisphere'* did not have a Larus cachinnans. However I did not know how this one differed from a regular seagull. My bird book was chosen for its price of £1.99p in a discount book shop in Bristol. When I reached the till to pay for it I was told it had been reduced further to just 99p and I almost put it back as if there just had to be something amiss with it at that price. My preferred choice of reference book of sea birds was priced beyond my budget. At the point of leaving Bristol the days were pock marked by new expenses, so I refrained from buying a proper *'Sea Birds of the World'* book, at £20. At that stage I could not be sure the voyage would reach beyond the Bristol Channel. The cormorant was a Corvo-marinho-de-crista (Phalacrocorax aristotelis) which was a catchy name, but if I saw one I would be guessing as to whether it was a standard cormorant or the Corvo-marinho-de-crista. Actually the Latin name showed it to be a regular cormorant.

The information board offered coordinates of Farol da Berlenga, the lighthouse on the main island. They were stated as: 39° 24, 99'N 009° 30, 47'W. The Portuguese seemed comfortable in 'knowing' and I felt a Spanish tourist office would not be concerned with such formal detail. The signboard, in my eyes somewhat temptingly, described an, *interessante população de répteis,* which did not take much linguistic imagination to understand. I was so wrapped up in the urge to flee south, there was hardly a moment to ponder the interesting local population of reptiles; A real wasted opportunity. When on earth would I come this way again? How? Postcards showed small inlets around Ilha da Berlenga crammed with anchored boats and little beaches swarming with sunbathers. There were hundreds of such places along the mainland coast, but people will always be fascinated by the idea of going to an island. Instead of peace and solitude Ilha da Berlenga looks to be as busy as a car boot sale on a Sunday morning in the UK. Ilha da Berlenga was a main economic input of Peniche and a fleet of tourist boats kept a dedicated portion of the harbour. It was similar to Lundy Island off Ilfracombe in Devon, UK. I expected to find a poster pointing to 'www.Berlenga.pt - visit virtual Berlenga' as Lundy Island has. There was an opportunity for a budding internet designer to work up a cyber-tour of the cormorants, lizards and gulls. At least Lundy Island had puffins, those parrot like sea birds of northern climes.

I remained fascinated by the sight of the little wall lizards wiggling, stopping, wiggling, then gone into a crevice. I wondered what it was I found so joyous about lizards. As a child I kept a pair of South American Green Iguanas. One was named 'Iggy'. They lived harmoniously for a couple of years, but one day the larger one almost killed the smaller. Big Iggy, the bully, was given to a school with an enlightened biology department with a spacious cage and thus awarded the larger kingdom he had bloodily clawed his way toward.

October 28 2002. There was perhaps a part of myself which I recognized in reptiles. Perhaps the clawed 'will to power' of Big Iggy or the smiling face of Gecky the Gecko, or perhaps the wiggling aliveness of wall lizards in the hot sunshine on dry European walls. Meanwhile, I found myself walking next to crumbling walls in the southern European midday sunshine and feeling the sudden joy of noticing the movement of one of those glittering little creatures. When I was little I wanted to work in the reptile house at London Zoo and maybe I should have been a herpetologist, with three fingers missing and an eye wound from some angry monitor lizard. Monitors are larger, heavier, and live far, far away. It is an inversion of preconceptions to learn the monitors will take and eat a chicken, or a chicken sized creature. Usually the sad scene of a chicken pecking up a poor little lizard. I did not lose any fingers during my herpetology phase, but I once pulled a hungry polecat ferret off, which had it's teeth clamped into the end of my finger and the little carnivorous incisors ripped my flesh as they clenched it as food. Plunging the polecat into a bucket of ice cold water would have got him off, apparently.

All of the ports I had stayed in down the coast of Portugal had leaflets containing a map of the town, a list of telephone numbers of local services and government departments, photographs of the must see sights and a few paragraphs describing the place, written and signed by a local, significant person. The covers of these promotional leaflets always had a smiling woman dressed in traditional costume. The leaflet describing Peniche differed by having a picture of a dramatically overhanging rock cliff edge. A man cast a fishing rod close to the edge against the azure Atlantic Ocean. Slightly less touristy and more of a working town, Peniche had fishing as the main industry besides the trip boats to the Ilhas da Berlenga.

I'd sailed around Cabo Carvoeiro, the rocky headland depicted in the brochure, with a huge sunset stretching from the south eastern horizon to the north western sector. The light was falling quickly and an astonishing number of small boats materialised from all quarters, as if out of nowhere. Like an invasion force suddenly they were all headed at full speed towards the harbour mouth, most of them without lights. There were forty or fifty boats, from little open dinghies with a seven horse power outboard motor, to sports fishers with a pair of ninety horsepower outboards clamped on the stern. One or two went very fast, their lights crossed the armada like a peregrine falcon through a flock of sparrows. A fast rigid inflatable boat with young and handsomely bearded men aboard sped past very close. They looked like divers, or surveyors, or maybe they worked on the nature reserve of Ilha da Berlenga. There was a trace of challenge in their passing so fast and so close and SP's red ensign glowed deep bloody red in the colossal sunset. Peniche was the scene of a landing in 1589 by an English force. Perhaps this history was being alluded to in the challenging way the fast boat rushed past. The older fishermen in the mass of boats approaching the moles made no such comment with their wakes and their courses, they simply took the most direct route into harbour. Once through the outer entrance the boats around me slowed to a similar pace and settled fairly close to each other in the relatively narrow space between the two stone arms of the harbour. I spotted a sports fishing boat showing just one white light coming out of the harbour, against the incoming horde. I swung over to starboard, to pass it on the left hand side. There were dozens of boats ploughing right towards the departing one. The unfortunate boat had come to a dead stop obviously unable to compute a safe course out to sea. As the incoming boats spotted the contrary one, hollers and shouts went up amongst the skippers and they all worked around the wallowing vessel in a rolling, boiling seamanship.

I found the visitors pontoon and moored near a French yacht. Later I met Jean Charles, from Loctudy, near the Iles de Glenan in Brittany. He was an architect. He made me aware of the interesting buildings in Portugal, particularly Oporto and Lisbon. There were buildings put there by the Phoenicians, Moorish forts and various colonial style residences, which looked like film sets for Pink Panther movies (i.e. where diamond thieves would live). Many derelict mansions overlooked the ocean where old money had lost it's hold. Stainless steel railings edging the cliffs near Cascais were described by a Swedish yachtsman as, 'Euro money'. We all knew what he was saying and what he meant. Running a sailing boat brings acute awareness of the cost of anything fabricated in stainless steel, it does not corrode and when polished it looks smart for years, it is very expensive. However, none of us quite knew whether Mat's observation was a critique, or a celebration of the European project. When he said it, the phrasing was in the style of a Texas oil man pointing out recent urban development, saying, 'Oil money'. If the comment was a critique, then it was a subtle dig at the way European money was being spent on regenerating smart railings for tourists while the rest of the world continues to fall off the cliffs.

October 29 2002. A fly landed on the edge of my coffee cup and then on my snack. I wafted it away with a hand, careful not to send the coffee flying, but the fly was persistent and I wafted it right away from my table. A miniature annoyance arose in me so I decided to attack the fly if it re-entered the air space above my table. It could do what it liked in any other part of the Pastelaria (a café selling sweet things to eat, more a bakery than a café), but if it bothered me again I would deal with the fly with extreme prejudice. My hand contacted the dozy insect and it responded by curving back swiftly to briefly alight on my hand. Disarmed by this tactic I paused while considering whether the fly, in landing on my hand, was making a point, trying to tell me something, but then it flew straight for my coffee cup edge, landed and did it's nasty feeding routine, which was to throw up onto the food, and then suck the combination of fly sick and nutrition back in. This happened in the two or three seconds it took me to wonder why it had landed on my hand after I had swiped at it. I reasoned it was because my hand was the nearest point to the coffee cup and I was, or my hand was, just a stepping stone to food. The fly had contravened my 'no fly zone' over the table, followed by a direct approach and landing on my coffee cup rim. I was maddened as the fly flew off, leaving me to a violated coffee cup rim and diminished anticipation towards my pastry. Turning a blind eye at recent events, I sipped at the coffee and savoured the pastry. Waking up can be hard sometimes.

One day I found the north side of Cabo Carvoeiro, where there were large fishing boats being constructed from sawn timbers. Whole trees sliced into planks were laid out on trestles to dry. The beginnings of a sixteen meter boat in the form of a single baulk of timber ended in a high prow at one end like the skeleton of a dragon. Ribs had been fixed, which were made from Y sections cut from branching trees. It was beautiful work, the joins between the planked hulls were closely fitted along the entire length of a boat. I was told, by a friend whom had taken me to this wonderful site, the planked hulls do not swell when the boats are launched, because they do not let water in between the planks. With a good coat of paint the boats do not soak up water and swell, as the ones in UK do. In the UK a wooden planked boat almost sinks for the first few days while the wood swells until the gaps close tight. I suspected this information to be hyperbole, but with language difficulties and busy boat builders I doubted I could ask for any clarification. The boat building was done on a sandy beach, a far cry from the working environment in Bristol, UK. John Smith, a Bristol shipwright, would often answer my technical queries while laying on his back in the soggy, boatyard mush. The mush was a mixture of the UK winter rains and the pressure washed coatings, paint, barnacles, slime, sawdust, rotting wood, rusting fixings and cigarette butts of hundreds and hundreds of vessels. John Smith turned many a forlorn ship back into a dream boat. I imagined John sitting in the hot clean sand under the Peniche fishing boats with his caulking mallet and helpful comments where he would be a far happier and healthier working man than in the Bristol winter.

October 30 2002. After searching around Peniche for the post office I went for a coffee in a new café. The girl serving seemed nervous with the language differences between us. An old woman came up and demanded change, holding out a ten Euro note. The young girl serving me dealt with her early onset xenophobia by opting to deal with the older customer. Anything I said was multiplied by several orders of complexity by the young pastelaria girl. When I pointed at a bolo (a doughnut type thing) and held a finger up, nodding, it seemed she thought I was asking whether the eggs used to make it were corn fed, organic, or free range. When I pointed at a cake and tried to ask for a bit, it appeared to be as difficult to her as it would have been for me to find out the subtleties of baking. The cake knife wavered around the cake like a broken second hand on a clock, jumping this way and that, back and forwards. I just wanted my cake and eat it. A small black soft eared dog broke the faulty clock once and for all by standing up against my hip and licking the finger I had been pointing with. The second, not quite so young, pastelaria girl jumped into the language gap between the cake and myself by rattling off a stream of words at the dog. Pleased with the attention, the dog ran behind the counter, reappeared smiling in the way only dog can, went back behind the counter and was finally chased through the doorway to the street outside.

Young women said "Chao" while holding well dressed kids in expensive Gap clothing. One little boy wore a brand new, well cut, denim jacket; corduroy trousers; cotton rich shirt in a deep green, and, blood red t-shirt with trainers of soft tan dyed suede. The boy grinned and squirmed in his tall, slim mother's arms, pleased by the attention of her attractive friends who fluttered big make-up eyes at him, blowing ironically flirtatious kisses. I avoided the eyes of these women, they were so good looking and freshly made and I did not wish to ground the buoyant mood of the café, by catching the almond shaped eyes flitting between themselves, the pastelaria staff and me the foreigner. It was Friday morning and we were all alive and well.

November 1 2002. On All Hallows Eve, cars paraded out to the end of the harbour wall and back. People walked, laughed and shouted good naturedly. I had noticed witch dolls hanging in souvenir shops, with hooked noses, a cursory wart, pointed black hat, astride a broomstick. No language problems there, just a regular witch. A psychoanalyst might claim the intent, or meaning, of a spell is received unconsciously, therefore, any spell in any language would work on anyone, assuming spells do work. The idea of an unconscious is bizarre and psychoanalysis is just as strangely unbelievable as witchcraft.

Small children came into the pastelaria carrying plastic bags. They addressed everyone, "Bom dia!" They collected sweets as part of either, Halloween, or All Saints Day. I was unable to establish the exact day as the day before I'd lost track after changing my watch, thinking I had set it wrong and then I did not know for sure what day it was. Teenagers were rejected for being harder, and vaguely extortionate in their approach, like bands of clown gangsters asking for treats so they would leave without mishap. They got nothing while the pre-teenagers received kind smiles and sweets. They wore the colourful, urban attire of well kept families; Rich colourings and attractive well designed fashions.

I had been fortunate since leaving the UK with nothing breaking and only minor sail repairs and engine maintenance needed. Then the water-tank in the bow burst and filled the bilge with eighty litres of water and my laptop computer failed seriously. The water-tank was made by Crewsaver, the same company who made my life jacket so I hoped the same thing would not happen to the life jacket. The laptop seemed simple after a PC specialist company told me they would save all the data and reinstall Windows, then reposition all my data in the new operating system. But the hard drive would not give up any data, despite having a proper data reading application attached to it. I went home that night depressed at the thought of losing loads of personal files, photographs and music files. The next day the company had extracted all my data and they then fitted a new twenty gigabyte hard drive for one hundred and twenty Euros

Peniche museum was a massive fortification originally built to defend the coast against pirates and foreign invaders. Locals called it the museum but it was a castle. It enclosed a cove into which the Atlantic slurped through a stone tunnel, onto a tiny rocky beach. A stone bridge arched over this enclosed inlet linking the outer with the inner wall. Stretching over the warm flat slabs of the bridge I looked over the edge into the cove. A tide line of plastic bottles, seaweed and offcuts of fish nets lay in a small crescent. Green waves entered, echoing, through the tunnel. A pair of dark coloured lizards twitched below me in foliage and another lizard half way up the wall leading to my spot slipped into a crevice. A security guard approached through an arched wooden door cut into the massive castle doors at the inner end of the bridge. He stood watching me through dark brutal sunglasses. The castle had been a high security prison during the dictatorship of Salazar. I left the lizards to their sunning and fly hunting in their sun trap, where winter would be held back for weeks. The guard stood in the foyer behind the main doorway to the inner courtyard. A woman visitor suddenly stepped back and exclaiming, "Waah!" A piece of plaster had dropped from the domed roof onto the stone flagons in front of her. The security guard just laughed and prodded at the fallen plaster with his black shoe and then, unconcerned, hands behind his back, continued to pace about under the entrance lobby.

Some pleasant sculptures were propped against the castle walls. The inner area was open air with several other buildings set inside it. The five meter thick walls were inset with cannon firing gaps, splayed out to give protection inside but width of view to the outside. Below these bulwarks sheer cliffs fell vertically to the sea. A white painted rectangular building had been the anti fascist dissenters prison. A guard house looked onto around twenty iron barred windows in two storeys. I peered through the rusting bars and broken glass cell windows. Cells were regular sized prison rooms with a round spy hole in a heavy door and a compartment for the slop bucket. Floors looked to be of wood. I could not see but imagined below the window there would be a sleeping bench. Several cells had been utilised by artists. Model fishing boats were being constructed in wood in two cells. A third housed a sculptor working in stone and wood. One cell was derelict and covered in salacious, fluorescent, graffiti. The actual museum cost one Euro to enter and I paced around the first room enjoying photographs of Peniche school classes from the nineteen thirties. The person who sold me my ticket apologised, saying, "The museum closes in twenty minutes, and, there are three floors". I wanted to see the anti-fascist resistance part on the top floor, so decided to come back for another visit. I signed the guest book and left.

November 2 2002. Three pumpkins lay on the ground near some waste-bins. They had been hollowed and carved with eyes, nose and teeth. One had been used as a football by children. Halloween had come and gone in Portugal. The harbour was shrouded in grey drizzle. I repositioned the mooring lines of SP as they were taking a lot of wear. Peniche was a well protected harbour however there was a constant surge to and fro as the Atlantic swells worked their way in. I was given the daily print out of the meteorological forecast for Portugal from the marina office as I passed along the quay. Relations with people remained on a very superficial level due to my not knowing the language. In Spain I would improvise freely and often get completely confused. In Portugal the language was more difficult to simulate.

I got to my regular café and ordered a coffee with milk and a bolo as usual. The English speaking man about the place asked if I wanted something in my bolo. A bolo was shaped like a jam doughnut, textured like cake inside, with a pleasant crusty outside sprinkled with coconut. I had enjoyed several on consecutive mornings. Today I was invited to try butter, ham and cheese in it. I wondered whether April the first had a different date in Portugal. Or, maybe I was being welcomed into the local scene by being harmlessly deluded into eating a sweet pastry with a savoury filling. I sat down and tasted the bolo. Of course the sugary coconut, ham and cheese was discordant. I persevered, but it remained odd as the sweetness went to one part of my taste buds and the savoury to another. The coconut melted into the cheese but then the deeper note of the ham left the mouthful unresolved right down into my stomach. If the two people serving and the patron were having fun then they were being extremely dry humoured. There was not a trace of a snigger or hidden giggling. I plodded on through the bolo, but with an uneasy feeling of being the day's entertainment. The patron was impeccably pleasant as he explained it was a Portuguese speciality. I wondered whether this was an insight not into Portuguese snacks but rather into Portuguese dry humour and I was convinced the pastelaria would erupt into laughter when I had gone.

The Bay of Biscay came back into my thoughts sometimes. It had left deep impressions on me. I was glad to have sailed across a part of the ocean for I had always wanted to experience being properly offshore for an extended period. To have sailed 530 miles in one go was an experience which had altered my conception of sailing. I felt I had the psychological tools to decide to sail more or less anywhere I wished in the world. The calmness of the seas way out in the western approaches to the English Channel had surprised me. The route from Wales had taken SP 20 miles to the west of the Isles of Scilly to avoid the shipping lanes, which lay 15 miles beyond the Scillies. Light variable winds meant SP ambled about on a generally southwards course, but her sails slatted to and fro and I could not sleep. I could not motor with the huge distance ahead, there was not enough fuel. La Coruna was another world, one I'd often enthused about as a destination in high spirited rants fuelled by single malt whisky. Sea area Sole, was calm. I was over 100 miles to the west of Ushant, the top left corner of France. Sole was named after the fish which used to flap about on the continental shelf there. Just one hundred metres deep, give or take forty metres, sea birds were on every horizon. Early one morning I passed to the stern of a huge trawler. Behind it a line of turbulence was exploited by thousands of sea birds. I cleared about a mile astern of the trawler. It rumbled with a massive diesel engine on very low speed and listed to starboard under the horrendous drag of a huge trawl net, which I hoped had passed already. Thousands of herring gulls flew after the trawler, picking up anything which appeared in the wake. Smaller sea birds swam in the moving path left by the trawler and its net. Then further behind as the wake closed over and fish swam in to feed on the droppings of gulls. Hundreds of gannets dived in close succession into shoals of prey, bam!, bam!, bam!, bam!, bam!, bam!, from 20m up, they dived into the same patch of sea, sometimes 2 hit almost the same spot. A white explosion of water occurred as the large strong birds plunged in. They disappeared for a few seconds and then reappeared manoeuvring something in their long bills. Gannets had long wings and were a lot bigger and heavier than the herring gulls.

A few days before I left Milford Haven I had gone into a chandlery to buy a passage chart. 'The Bay of Biscay' sounded dangerous and writhed with disastrous tales as the chandler warned me, "Hmm, it's a bit late to be crossing *the bay*." A few weeks later and 700 miles south of Milford Haven, I was in Nazare. On a concrete wall a German yacht crew had painted:

Steve & Stefan, Yacht 'Greenfly', 1963 & 2001, They said, "You left it too late", we said, "Biscay is just a bay".

People hold fixed ideas about the best time to sail. People who have sailed further are pragmatic, looking at weather forecasts rather than received wisdom circulated by yacht clubs and chandlers. The voyaging reference book, *'Ocean Passages of the World'* describes the UK as an area in which: *...passages can be made all year, however the temperature is colder in the winter months than in the summer.* That's it. Real knowledge leaves out unnecessary information and drama.

November 4 2002. A Monday morning and I had a list. Armed with a list I intended to make the day productive. The last few days had seen drizzle and a cool north breeze, although there was not a hint of the autumnal scent friends in the UK were commenting on. An email from the Cambridgeshire fens was titled - Hello from carrot land, so I replied with - Hello from sardine world. With my list I found the post office and sent an overdue library book back to the UK. It was a sailing pilot book of the western French coast, which may have been essential if I had been embayed by strong westerly winds while on passage, although I had not been within 60 miles of France. With my list I repaid a loan a friend had offered me at a time when my mobile telephone company made errors and presented me with a horrendous bill. My list then ordered me into a supermarket to get a couple of five litre spring-water bottles. These would suffice as water supply bottles while I got around to replacing the flexible eighty litre bow tank. I was amazed at the efficient storage of the flexible tank. To stow eighty litres in solid containers would take three times the space because the gaps between cannot be filled. I was in a quandary as to whether to keep the spring-water which was very heavy to carry back to the boat, or discard it. The bottles weighed almost nothing and it was only them I wanted. The water would be topped up from taps. Wondering if a little spring-water would do me good I struggled home with the bottles and their water. Besides I felt embarrassed about pouring ten litres of water into the road, or someone's driveway. It was a ridiculous feeling.

My list got me to do two loads of washing. The marina had a machine which costs just a few Euros The cost of a winter berth in Peniche was extremely cheap because storm waves frequently broke over the harbour wall and threatened boats in the marina. I was shown a video clip on the marina office PC of the harbour in a storm. The waves were very impressive, but not as impressive as the price of mooring there, just under sixty Euros a month included a pontoon berth with secure key card access, electricity, water and shower. One of the best points about small boats is the reduced running costs. It was explained the harbour does suffer a persistent surge, as the Atlantic swell works its way in, in the form of pressure waves. The effect was a to-ing and fro-ing of everything in the water, giving ropes and fenders a very hard time. I was warned I'd have to replace mooring lines and fenders regularly.

November 5 2002. I bought a new shoulder bag in a soft mousy colour with a zip and a long adjustable shoulder strap. It was elegant in a simple, practical style, not posh or dressy. I had used a black furry bag for years, which was a bit cock-a-snoop at convention and the new bag was more respectable for a small, far away place. The old furry bag had a tail, a black fur tail, like a cow's. I sewed the bag from scratch to my own design. One of the first things I did when stepping ashore in Spain was to hide the tail. I felt it would pull too much unwanted attention and I was vulnerable on my own. It would give an inroad to someone who wanted to pester me, they would comment on it or pull it.

One sunny day I would probably dig out my old furry bag, unveil the tail and stride out in full confidence again, but I felt like blending in a little. The sun was bright and warm and the sky a clear blue. The weather forecast gave northerly winds for three days. I was very tempted to sail down to the Algarve with the favourable winds, but the price and facilities in Peniche were highly attractive. I could go further in the spring, although I worried I would find the south of Portugal too hot by then, but apparently the blood thins. Sunny weather certainly made things easier. I worked on the boat, removing the radar reflector and a damaged aluminium bar from between the twin back-stays. I could hang the paraffin lamp on the back-stay, using a rolling hitch which would slide up or down but grip like mad, also known as a camel hitch, it is possible to climb a wire stay if each foot is placed in a loop attached to a camel hitch. The lower one is slid upwards while standing on the upper. I never attempted it, but used the knot for adjustable steering lines, flying the ensign and attaching a paraffin lamp to the wire back-stay and if I ever meet a camel I shall know how to hitch that too.

Lunchtime in the pastelaria was relaxed and quiet, free of the brash energy of morning. Sunshine slanted across the blue and white tiled floor and gulls laughed on the roofs outside. I ate a proper savoury croissant with ham and cheese, much better than the previous day's sweet and savoury mix of bolo with ham and cheese filling. When the sun shone things felt so much better and my list lay in my new bag almost completely discharged.

November 6 2002. The computer consultant went to lunch halfway through installing a new hard drive. I was hungry and went to the big supermarket nearby to buy food. A flock of women alighted next my table. I hired a mountain bike for three Euros as I had a fair amount of to-ing and fro-ing to do. The bike was wonderful, I needed to go back to the boat to pick up a Windows boot-able disc, then I had to find an adapter to use my laptop with European electric sockets. The latter was difficult to find and I was glad for the bike as I went to a number of shops in the search. I learned another Portuguese word, 'adaptador'. My laptop had been loaded up with Windows, however, the whole operating system was in Portuguese. I had thought it was simply a matter of changing the language in 'settings', but not so. The whole system had to be reinstalled using my own disc. Of course it was more complex, because there were several extra drivers which needed to be added from the web. I was glad someone was doing it for me as I would have found insurmountable difficulties in doing it myself.

A very warm and sunny day with a lovely cool north wind made me think seriously of sailing to Cascais, near Lisbon. Despite feeling comfortable in Peniche, with its hardware stores and the very low marina fees, I had an urge to carry on cruising. The gecko index remained unfulfilled. During my stay in Nazare I had gone on a coach to visit the catamaran, Peace Four in Cascais. At the time I was thinking seriously about staying the winter months in Nazare and I wanted to visit Cascais to help me make up my mind. Nazare was simply too rural for my long term needs. Whereas Cascais had swift and cheap access to Lisbon. Cascais itself was a substantial town with tourist facilities. I liked urban spaces with shopping malls and 'Cascais Shopping' was as big as any I'd ever seen.

Cascais Shopping was a cluster of hypermarkets and superstores under one roof. I went to experience a bit of shopping and first went into a vast music and video store. Listening posts with headphones allowed me to bathe in an aural feast of new music. A gallery of photographs set in a semi-circular space with a comfortable leatherette settee allowed the visitor to sit looking at the images, and listening to a soundtrack with complete visual and aural screening from the rest of the store. The images were of the Burning Man Festival held in the Arizona desert of the US. The people captured by the images were astonishing, tattooed, plaited beards, silver space costumes. The vehicles these freaky people drove had bizarre body adaptations which made them look like spaceships, or seed pods. It was a celebration of individual creative spirit and diversity. There was not a fisherman to be seen, nor a sardine.

November 7 2002. Riding through Peniche on a mountain bike, hopping kerbs and occasionally dropping off steps, I felt so much at home. It was just like being back in Bristol, where I would so often ride my bike in search of an outlying non-ferrous scrap yard or somewhere such as an reinforced tubing supplier. The months leading up to departure from the UK were memorable for the intense and relentless effort to reduce the length of a to-do list. The to-do list would grow each day as departure became imminent. As I added more gear to the boat, spares, raw materials for running repairs and more and more food every day, the bows dipped downwards and the blue water-line disappeared under the surface. One of the most important things in a boat is to keep her buoyant and being 'nose down' is not the best trim for handling large seas. So, as well as making, fixing and altering the boat and equipment, I was also discarding things. I gave away bits of spare anchor chain, a stainless steel chimney, a dinghy inflation pump, a roll of headlining material, alloy poles, stainless steel sheeting, plate, bar and tube. I was the gift horse of the boatyard, my offerings eagerly accepted as the poor old boatyard denizens added them to the pile which would anchor their hearts for yet another year. To leave a marina after several years was a great effort of will. Such interesting stuff comes along from people passing through, or from the occasional sailor who leaves. To travel is to reduce clutter. Only at a critical point of lightness will a journey commence.

Peniche was a practical town where I could maintain the boat with shops and engineering works to support the fishing industry. I began looking again at wind vane steering methods. A UK sailing boat came in which had a type of wind vane I had based mine on. My one had never steered the boat because it was stuck on the lower part, the pendulum servo oar, which was more complex and had a high requirement for both strength and very light responsiveness. Many different devices were used by the boats I had seen but I rarely saw self built ones, however, it seemed the effort and time needed to design and construct a working version would be too high. It seemed better to spend the time working to earn the money to buy a new one, rather than spending months fiddling with something which may not function. Long distance sailors said, 'Why don't you make one?' as if it was a simple decision and an easy process. Invariably they had a 3000 Euros 'Monitor', or 'Aries', or one of the other proprietary models. If it was so easy why did they cost so much, and why didn't more people make them themselves? SP had a part-built wind vane on her stern, ready for development and refinement, or a replacement which actually worked. I had originally attempted to design and make it too complicated. The main problem was getting sufficient strength in the section which interacted with the water. It needed to be massively strong while the wind sensing vane, the top part, would only work by reducing friction to a minimum at the same time as having a vane which could work in most wind strengths, from light to strong. I was reluctant to attach, with substantial fixings, something which would turn out to be an early model and need to be developed and attached in another way, needing more holes in the boat. All this led to the conclusion that it was probably best to save up for a proper wind vane self-steering device and be done with it.

November 8 2002. Blowing hot and cold about staying in one place or sailing southwards for the next three months. My instincts were telling me to snuggle down and take advantage of the shelter and friendly character offered by Peniche people and their harbour. A few days of strong winds and cloud made me content to accept the encroaching winter and just rest awhile. Then a beautifully sunny and warm day would make me wish I was sailing southwards and experiencing the changing scenery of travel. I knew the winter would be much cooler and with strong winds, but I was unsure about the actual climate of Peniche. I was twelve degrees south of Bristol in the UK and I hoped for a significant improvement in climate but accepted it would get fairly chilly by January. I read an account by an American sailor who voyaged around the world. His writing consisted of fairly short paragraphs and I made a note to myself to try and be more direct. I had sailed and written previously in the Bristol Channel for six weeks in 1999, when I found a pleasing wandering narrative style to suit the Welsh and Devonshire coastlines. Then too I had been alone and I found the same style again.

Ann of Peace Four enthused about 'micro economics'. Her idea was to save the seemingly insignificant amounts of money we all spend frivolously every day, coffee in a café, postcards home, a chocolate bar here and a packet of crisps there. All those add up, over a month to more than insignificant amounts of cash. The UK population spends a huge amount of money on chocolate bars, more than any other European country. Ann would save those small amounts and then help people she wanted to. Before I left the UK in SP, Ann had pressed a ten pound note into my hand, saying, 'If, or when, you get to Spain, buy yourself a bottle of whisky as a celebration'. Often while walking with Ann through the streets of Spain, I would suggest sitting on a sunny terrace to drink a tasty coffee, but she would resist, saying, 'How about we have a nice cup of tea aboard the boat?' She would add temptation, 'and we can study that book about sailing in the Caribbean'. Ann had a knack of nurturing and nudging people's dreams into reality. Tourists spend at every step of the holiday - a coffee - all round ice creams for everyone - entrance fees to entertainment - gifts for those back home - sun tan lotion and on and on. A large number of the people sailing long term on well maintained yachts would be unable to afford the cost of a conventional holiday, even though they spend whole summers living in the places holidaymakers dream of.

November 9 2002. My argument against Ann's economics was the value I personally got from sitting in cafés. The coffee was a contract which allowed me to spend time writing. I wrote easily and with pleasure in cafés because there were people around to stimulate thoughts and ideas. My muse heads for the busy morning café, or the laid back afternoon terrace and I go with her.

I strongly wished to sail further south and catch up with Ann and Nev on Peace Four, but I seemed to have decided to stop for the winter. It was still possible to sail towards the Canary Islands where I would gain winter sunshine far beyond the weakening rays of Portugal. If I only had a self-steering wind vane, then I would be able to go Plus Ultra - more further, and head towards the African shore and the Islas Canarias. It was cold in the UK by now. A friend emailed from Bristol telling me she spent bonfire night in some park, shivering in damp mist and with chilled hands. On the same night I was strolling around Peniche in a thin jumper not at all cold. I remained typically British; always talking about the weather.

November 10 2002. Friends asked for photographs of me looking sun kissed and ravishingly slim after all the exercise of sailing and the days spent at sea in hot weather. I had an image of myself with long golden blond, sun kissed hair and skin the colour of almonds, a blond Girl from Ipanema. In reality I was only a little more tanned and sun kissed than usual. The photographs I sent depicted my usual, partly stressed, partly uneasy self. Two towels hung over the railings on the quay. Two German travellers broke pieces of bread to eat as they sat on the decking outside the marina office, showers and laundry. They were waiting for the agent of the Ilhas Berlengas to sell them a boat ticket. They were camping and travelled on trains with rucksacks and the dusty, casual look of contentment travellers can have.

In the café where I sat a television showed a chat show host previewing her show. She had 'big' hair and often contracted the muscles around her eyes in an effort to appear warmly attractive. Instead she looked manic, as if she would bite off your head in a nightmare leaving red lipstick around the severed neck. Television weather forecasts said it was a lot warmer here even than in the north of Portugal. The temperatures increased from north to south. In the north, 17 C was usual for November. In the central area including Peniche there was 19 C and in the Algarve it was often 24 C. I talked each day in the Capitanaria using the weather bulletin as a language lesson. It was really pleasant to have conversations which I missed in general. 18 C. was most agreeable, it did not drive me into the shade, yet it was easy to be warm with a light sweater. I was told the climate would not fall much lower than this apart from the chill of strong wind and rain. March and April would be really warm again.

Each day I talked with the marina man about the meteorological predictions for the next three days and we both acted as if I was waiting for a weather window to sail southwards. But we both know I was quite happy to remain in Peniche for the time being. I learned the Portuguese for fog, high cloud, strengthening wind, morning mist, early frost, storm, depression and the whole range of variations. Early frost had me worried but I was reassured it would be brief and would soon burn off as the sun came up. I was being superficial in my weather obsession, as if I had nothing better to worry about than whether it was going to be sunny, like some hyper-tourist who refusing to go home, wandering the holiday resorts in search of a bit of sun.

I went again to the museum. Within the fortified walls there were little corners where the sunshine was unsullied by November breezes. As I came upon one such space a little lizard sped across the stone floor like a tiny clockwork toy, it's tail flailing as it ran between some sculptures. I stood stock still aware that the shadow of my head was laying quite close to where the reptile had hidden, but there it was again. Eager to soak up the sun in the short days of late autumn, the lizard came out again in little spasms of movement, to rest in the sunshine. It's black tongue minutely smelling the ground. I left it to it's sun patch and went to see the cells of political prisoners under the dictator Salazar. There would have been little sunbathing lizards in those days too, when fascist guards patrolled the stone flagons of the fortification. On 25th April 1974 the lizards would have hidden in their rock crevices, alarmed by the mass gathering outside of celebrants of the end of that dictatorship. Drawings made by a prisoner of the time were pencilled figures and faces. Finely drawn with singular strokes, clear curves and perfectly round circles, each line was a boldly executed trace which suggested a highly artistic temperament with a carefully expressive hand. Sketches are often smeared images with indefinite form, true to the experience of being an observer. Reality blurs and pulses in front of us in an indefinable flux and artists often portray this uncertainty of the visual field by applying several lines for a single side, or shading and blurring to give uncertain depths. However, this prisoner had drawn beautifully with bold, curvaceous commentary and innocence of thinking outside the political regime which had imprisoned him.

Cafés are less about coffee than rest. Reading a newspaper, or watching people go by, come in, or leave was endlessly banal and wonderful. Occasionally a café failed to be either banal or wonderful. A free internet facility financed by the Portuguese government was closed for a two hour lunch. The day was very warm, I had walked for an hour, making a detour to an outlying shop to buy credit for my mobile phone and I was looking forward to sitting in a café for a bit of dream-time. The bolos looked bland. I ordered something which looked filling at least, and a teeny weeny cup of coffee. I chose a seat with a view onto the town square, giant pineapple like trees, zebra crossings everywhere and a busy, soothing liveliness. The bolo was as bland as it looked. Half of a yellow cream filling ended up on my fingers and the sugar coating scattered across the table and my lap. There was no plastic tissue box as there usually would be in a self respecting pastelaria. I reached for one on another table, glad to be finished with the messy, unexciting bolo, but I needed a sink with water and a mirror to remove the yellow slurp from my chin and fingers. I did my best to clean up and swept the sugar off the table onto the empty plate. Looking forward to the intense espresso coffee taste I was disappointed with a bitter cup lacking pleasure. The waitress was young, pretty, and employed only for those traits. She wiped my table but this was most unusual, not to be left to relax amongst the spoils of consumption at my leisure. My coffee cup was removed and I felt stripped of the one minor pleasure left so I indicated that I had not yet finished my coffee and the waitress looked at me as if I was dumb, for the coffee cup was all but empty. I just wanted to savour the final sugary grounds at the bottom of the cup and in my own time. Once the table was cleared there was only one choice, to leave. The pastelaria was obviously owned and run purely for profit, not the friendly family businesses I usually found. The fly killing machine was vicious. A pair of ultraviolet light tubes attracted flying insects which were then sucked through an aperture and shredded by a high speed fan. I just about enjoyed the last drop of sugary coffee in the bottom of my cup and so the visit was now complete. I would not revisit this place where the other customers too looked miserable and angry at life.

Where the harbour mole joined the fortification of the castle dozens of cats lived in small holes in the high walls. They were fed with bowls of food left in a nook. Nearby where the road ran past the base of the castle wall, old men sat in a line. They looked like retired fishermen, chatting and watching over the harbour activity, leaning on walking sticks or standing, with flat caps and muted, worn clothes on. One of these men approached with a plastic carrier bag. As he hollered the cats reacted immediately, peering around rocks, waking from slumbers higher up on the part cliff, part wall of the castle and running down to his feet. The man walked to the sea wall, now followed by four black, four tabbies, two gingers and some pale coloured cats. They ran around, tails in the air and rubbed against his legs as he reached the feeding spot. More and more cats came out of the fortification wall and ran across to the man as he emptied the bag. On the wall above the line of men was a collection of household objects. Several telephones were placed into notches in the rock and a television set had been set on a ledge, as if it was in a café. Painted letters declared,

'THE SOCIAL CLUB OF PENICHE'.

As the man fed the cats I thought how sad it would be if 'health and safety' rules prevented this scene. In the UK twenty or so feral cats would be removed for there own and the public's good. The man's voice as he hollered to the cats was unrestrained and carried the joy of bringing twenty cats running to his feet. A cream coloured cat walked over to the castle wall and disappeared into a small opening. It was sheltered from the westerly storms by the massive walls. The cats doubtless suffered a lack of veterinary attention even if those which came running looked bright eyed and healthy. On a walk in another region, while visiting Cascais, a cat living in the sea wall next to a cliff top restaurant had kittens which looked very unhealthy. They had running eyes and one was almost blind with infection. The difference between the two populations of cats was the attention and protection offered by the retired men who treated the cats as pets, whereas the sick kittens were in a place which was busy with tourists in the summer but almost deserted in the winter, a cliff top road several kilomeres out of Cascais.

Peniche was very busy with fishing boats at all times of the day and night. When a large boat arrived a siren, like a war time bomb alert, whined and brought workers to the fishing quays. Orange flashing lights on fork lift trucks sped about and the sound of diesel freezer compressors echoed over the water. A boat pushed hard between the red and green lights of the harbour entrance and continued at full speed across to the waiting buyers and handlers, for an instant auction of fresh fish. At night I stirred in my sleep at the sound of a boat arriving and within two or three minutes a wake reached SP and tossed her up and down against the fenders. My fenders were tested to their limits by these unrestrained fishing boat washes. When one split open I bought a bigger replacement. I did not mind lurching and bouncing against the pontoon, as long as no damage was done to the boat. I hardly noticed it sometimes, when I was absorbed in a burgeoning new design for a wind vane steering system. I had been spending time with the muse of self-steering system designs and I had a new version to work on. It was extremely simple compared to the over complexity of previous approaches. The new version would result in an emergency rudder.

One night was distinctly chilly. The weather forecast spoke of frost inland on higher ground. I missed the hot sunshine and the friends I made when we were all making way southwards from northern Spain. In the ports along the way we would always meet again, which was quite funny sometimes. Alone and exploring a forgotten alleyway leading to some enchanted town square with cicadas buzzing and caged canaries singing, there would appear 'so and so' from Sweden, or 'what's their names' from Canada and they would be just as surprised to see me. Greetings, information about the recent sailing trip to get there a, 'We'll pop over later', and then alone again to wander back into the enchantment of solitary exploring with a route carefully set away from the other cruisers. For they too had to discover for themselves the lovely view of the sea if you walk up to the saintly statue or, the old stone public washing house found by walking just up the hill from the supermarket but those experiences would be ruined if someone else insisted you go there. Telling cruising people about all the best spots and experiences around a new harbour would force them to sail somewhere else and discover things for themselves, in peace. In Bayona a couple with two children would appear at the window of almost every café I found to hide in. The children would call, 'Hello Clarissa!', through the sunny doorway. A joy to encounter, every time, although we all looked forward to a time when we had all become truly lost in our travels. The family sailed to Madeira, on their way to Australia. They were self educating the children who gave me drawings of SP and a fishing boat and a paper chain of little storm petrels flying across the sea. Meeting again after travelling several days was always pleasant and at sea there was plenty of time for solitude.

In the café where I sat a television showed a chat show host previewing her show. She had 'big' hair and often contracted the muscles around her eyes in an effort to appear warmly attractive. Instead she looked manic, as if she would bite off your head in a nightmare leaving red lipstick around the severed neck.

A Storm was Coming

Winds of 60mph were forecast for starters. I moved SP to a more protected berth inside the pontoons having been warned Peniche suffers from surge in strong south-westerlies. Worse would be a violent storm from the south and that was forecast. I purchased a new fender to replace one which had split. The new one was bigger than any in my set of eight fenders. Usually I picked up flotsam fenders after storms and as long as the boat which lost it was not obvious I added it to the collection, such as a fender found in Boulogne, France, and named 'Big Bertha' because it was huge. But Big Bertha was sold with a previous boat, Juggler. SP was twice as heavy as Juggler and I needed to add several more large fenders. In twelve years of cruising I had never purchased a fender.

Now I was a long-distance, deep-water sailor (gulp!) it was impossible to tow a dinghy behind and I kept an inflatable dinghy deflated and rolled up on deck at the risk of not being able to use it in an emergency. This was one of the ongoing dilemmas and I strongly wished to have a dinghy to get into at short notice. Twenty minutes was far too long to be confident of saving myself in the event of a sinking. This was what winter was good for, a time to sit back and reflect on the way I had been doing sailing. I read the accounts of some cruisers whose attitude towards cruising was very down to earth, such as when a gale prevented progress one day, it was described as, 'We had a force 8 blowing against us for 9 hours which slowed us down'. If I met with such heavy weather I would fill several pages with descriptions of the waves and the struggle to keep going. When these cruisers encountered really adverse conditions they simply closed the doors and sat inside, playing cards until it blew itself out. The wisdom is rugged, *All storms have an end.*

The wind in Peniche reached around 60mph. Yachts moored on the marina pontoons leaned in the gusts as if they were sailing. I chatted to the marina man and he told me five years ago a section of the harbour mole was breached by the sea. Also the main pontoon of the marina was destroyed by waves after breaking over the top of the mole, plunging across the car park, slipping down a concrete slope, across seven meters of water and finally smashing the pontoon: a distance of approximately 60 metres from the massive sea defence: rows of interlocking concrete shapes, with three prongs, like 'Jacks'. Low scudding clouds eventually ceased and the sun shone warmly again. The forecast was for strong winds again. A French single-hander heading north wanted to sail to

Brittany, his home. I thought it madness to consider such a voyage in the winter and I would not even wish to be so intrepid. Other cruising friends talked of sailing throughout the winter, with plans to go to the Algarve, then spend a month in the Rio Guadiana, on the border between Spain and Portugal. A yacht could get 50 miles inland and reach Seville. I loved the thought of cruising on a river for a long way inland. I needed to build a successful wind vane self-steering, then I could do things like that when I got under way again after the winter storms.

On a ledge in the wall of the castle above the retired fishermen who sat there everyday was a television. In the rain, a tabby cat curved around one corner and raised its tail in a homely manner. It was as if the television and the cat had been abstracted from some domestic sitting room and plonked there on the ledge in the castle wall. Around the corner a pair of dogs, an Alsation and a heavily built Labrador cross were hunting a tabby cat on a ledge of the castle wall. Where the sea enters a little cove surrounded by the fortification the cat fled along a dead end which petered out to a sheer rock face above the green glooping waters. Ears pricked forward, tongues lolling made several inroads to the ledge as the cat peered about for an escape route. The big dogs were unable to approach the cat closely due to the narrowing shelf. A third dog arrived, a much slimmer, lighter hound and began to explore the ledge towards the cat. I told myself I was the dominant animal and after several days of rain and gales I had gained a certain pent-up aggression which was looking for expression. I drew closer and stood taller, "Pssst!" I told the dogs, "I am coming". They turned towards me, the two larger ones sensing my body language and sauntered away. The thinner dog was still on the ledge with the cat which was peering nervously out of long grass at the point where the shelf turned to a precipice. I told the dog, "Pssst! Hey! Come on now." The dog looked between me and the cat, confused and then came back off the ledge, probably realizing I was going to place it in the very same position as it had the cat.

I went for a coffee. Heavy rain came. A young child in the pastelaria was rewarded with a tube of Smarties, for being funny and chatty, by the woman serving. Someone passed a strongly egg scented fart. The rain stopped. The butcher came in from his shop next door.

I visited Cascais for a week to stay on Peace Four. A seagull deterrent consisted of a sound recording of a herring gull's alarm call, broadcast at unbearable decibels every five minutes, almost twenty four hours a day. At some point a captive gull must have been tortured to make the recording. A single bird abused and recorded as a sacrifice to the thousands of gulls which would be harmlessly driven away. The sound became terribly aggravating and I wanted to broadcast a horror movie soundtrack, with blood curdling screams, outside the home of whoever invented the gull repellent. The Peniche feral cats could do with a similar system. They could have the sound of a dog being beaten, continuously played at high volume. The gull deterrent was a main reason not to go to Cascais Marina. There were pleasant things in Cascais too, such as free bicycle hire, courtesy of the town council, while Cascais Shopping would offer endless browsing in the music store. Peniche was over-run with gulls. Occasionally a large flock flew overhead, moving between feeding grounds. There were thousands and it made a wondrous spectacle in the evening light and their cries were from real gully beaks. The pontoon beside SP was a night roost of a hundred or so herring gulls. I did not mind the droppings, as the rain washed them way and the sun baked them to white powder. When I slid open the hatch in the early hours the flock of gulls made a panicking screaming, warning noise amongst themselves and then took off with the noise of their feathers pushing the air and their feet shoving away from the pontoon, very quietly and very closely.

Two French boats arrived. One was a type which I have been interested in when looking for a cruising boat, an Arpege by Dufour. It had a wide hull with narrow ends, typical of 1980's cruiser/racers. Looking at it again though I was less keen on the overall design, which appeared more suited to weekend cruising, closer to home, a thin, fin keel and unprotected spade rudder hung on a narrow skeg would be vulnerable to damage if it hit a reef or a container from a ship and those were significant risks for a boat doing long offshore passages and entering unfamiliar areas.

The second French yacht was a small, light weekend cruiser built of plywood. It had been sailed to Madeira and was heading back to Brittany which I considered near madness in December. The north of Portugal and Spain during the summer were mostly calm and forgiving, with fishing boats bobbing about on the swells easily netting shoals of lazy sardines. A yacht could meander southwards full of dreams and canned food from Asda, but the winter was cold, windy and dangerous.

Sailing across the Bay of Biscay was a great personal achievement, but it had to be a triumph of understanding, rather than of hardiness. A feat of self awareness rather than any form of conquest in the wilderness. At the point where I understood, or reasonably expected, the conditions on the journey and the readiness of the boat would not prevent me from completing it, I set off.

The preparation period was simply a matter of ensuring I had enough resources to keep sailing long enough to reach Spain, with some basic safety considerations, such as having an inflatable dinghy available in case the boat failed to keep the ocean out. The risk of being run down by a ship was calculated and a kitchen timer used to allow fifteen minutes of sleep. This was widely accepted as the time it would take a ship to travel from the horizon to your boat, as well as the minimum sleep period to be effective over a week or so. Each time the beeper sounded I sprang out of my bunk and looked around the horizon for a careful couple of minutes. If the light of any vessel was visible I remained on watch until it had passed over the horizon. If the light was a fishing boat which often would remain in the area, I would sail the boat away until I was alone again. In the shipping lanes there were dozens of ships in sight at any one time. They passed in a line, each one a few miles behind the other, in both directions. This was a most difficult situation because the track of the ships was very similar to my own. I wanted to be away from the shipping lanes but everyone was travelling between the same two corners of France and Spain.

When the weather forecast warned of stronger winds to the west of my course, I veered further east into the Bay of Biscay which was where I joined the straight line with all the ships. When I got to within 170 miles of Spain I felt close enough to be able to spot the mountainous coast, but it would be a couple of days before I saw land. With just 60 miles left I felt close enough to touch land and I was accompanied by an imaginary line of cliffs as I closed Spain at an angle. Each time I plotted my position on the chart I realized land was still out of sight, but still I could not shake a mental model of the sea and land in which I was running along the coast quite close inshore. I reached a position 14 miles out to sea from La Coruna during darkness. This was ideal because it would enable me to safely approach land by daylight. However I felt so near to the shore I continued sailing towards the enticing harbour. I was overtired and became confused as to the exact position of La Coruna. My mental map and the chart did not seem to match.

The gps was indicating one heading and my senses were saying it was wrong. It was easy to believe the gps was wrong because it only indicated the precise position of latitude and longitude which had been entered into it. It was an easy mistake to plot a position incorrectly on a chart and then enter the incorrect latitude and longitude. As I sailed all the doubts weaved into the sureness which I felt in what I was doing and this web bound me to the Spanish shores. It is doubt as much as competence which carries one towards a goal. The last of seven nights alone on the ocean saw me confused and overtired, but how could I resist sailing to that Spanish shore, now just 14 miles away.

I spent a day altering the self-steering wind vane, borrowing a round file from a Dutch boat and searching out my electric drill. I changed the wind vane pivot to reduce friction by making it swing on a stainless steel tube around a stainless steel stud. On the old version the stud itself pivoted in the support pole. The fact the centre of balance of the wind vane and counter weight were not over the pivot point meant there was too much friction. Moving the pivot to a tube right between the vane and counterweight significantly freed the pivot. A new plywood vane was cut to a shape resembling the wing of a world war two Spitfire fighter air plane. I knew little about aerodynamics only that the Spitfire functioned particularly well. A rectangle would probably work as well, but also lack elegance and the wide outer end would be vulnerable to damage in gusts. The Spitfire wing provided an aesthetic form which was proven to be aerodynamic and durable. I re-drew the rudder and trim-tab design, simplifying materials and fabrication so the whole thing could be built by myself with local resources and without buying outside help. I was offered help with stainless steel welding but then the Danish shipwright was unable to use a gas welding torch when the wind was strong and then when the wind became light he was anxious to get off towards the Canary Islands.

The rudder could be hung on lashings. Peace Four, the Wharram catamaran, had two large rudders hung on lashings with a clever figure of eight which gave easy, chafe free movement with stability. Low technology can work very effectively and cost almost nothing. A number of holes and some lengths of light rope were all that was required. They were easy to make and a sense of freedom from clearing away the usual way to do things and finding a simple method which works equally well and for almost no cost.

A woman in a tweed jacket and a stylish hat spoke as she leant against the pastelaria counter smoking a cigarette, "Why doesn't she speak Portuguese?" I told her it was a difficult language for me because many words did not sound at all like the English, or French equivalent. 'Table'

- 'La table' and chair - 'chaise' were easy to spot in French and in Spanish 'mesa' is table so it can be remembered as 'the mess', but in Portuguese a table was something like a 'cetheedra' (spelt phonetically), while a 'mesa' was a chair to go under it.

In the gate house of the commercial fishing port there was a bored security guard who told me the language was quite easy for English people to learn, but Chinese people had problems producing the sounds of the words. He demonstrated a Chinese person by squinting his eyes puckering his nose and drawing back his cheeks to make him appear to have just two large buck teeth. I could not help erupting in laughter at the facile racial stereotype.

For several weeks my breakfast bun was only known as a 'bolo', but gradually I learned to produce strange sounds by running difficult new noises through my mouth and throat until they became easier. The bolo was promoted to an 'ergfada' (phonetically speaking).

Note on bolos: A 'bolo' is a 'treat'. An 'ergfada' is a specific treat I took a liking to, being cheap, simple and easy to down with a coffee. I refer to the ergfada with various spellings as my impressions altered from town to town with different local accents. Sometimes I describe the way ergfada was written on menu boards which also differed with locality.

The pastelaria girl was teaching me well, "Bom dia, um ergfada y um café con laite, por favor," (Good morning. A round sweet bread coated with coconut and a coffee with milk, please). The Penichenses liked to communicate, it was part of their 'joie de vivre'. A woman pointed at my coffee and ergfada as she left the pastelaria, and told me not to let it get cold. I was absorbed in thought and had hardly touched my breakfast in twenty minutes. Older people often leaped the communication gap between strangers, saying, "Bom dia!" and a passing face beamed with existential joy. On the way to the library, a man was always on his tiled balcony, 'Bom dia!' he always called over the road and I was lifted out of a state of civil inattention into a warm greeting.

Fishermen and ex fishermen clustered around the bars along the road by the tidal river, eyed me sceptically, as a foreigner, alone, female, a yachty. Yet there was often a greeting if I caught someone's eye, or the sun was out. The sun burned off recent rain and a cold wind carried the rain clouds down towards Lisbon. Many days I noticed the weather in Peniche was very similar to that in Faro, in the Algarve. The sea was just one degree colder here, the air temperature was the same at 15 C. and there was rain forecast in both places. A full moon must have put the muse of self-steering wind vanes in a good mood. I made good progress with improvements. Also in attendance was the muse of geometry who brought ideas to solve problems with angles and forces.

Reducing friction to the minimum and increasing power transmission between the wind vane signal and the big part in the water would eventually make it work. Having started building it in Bristol meant it was relatively easy to improve on now. The lower part was more difficult because I had not seen any plywood for sale. I had been told to visit the large fishing boatyard on the far side of the harbour. This was a hike so I waited for clearer weather to go there. I had reservations about hanging an extra rudder because I was aware of the extreme forces which affect the hull when waves hit the stern. If the rudder failed and became twisted into a bad position it would cause difficulties I would rather do without, so the rudder had to be a success by building it strong enough and getting the design right.

A French yachtsman set off southwards making for Sines, 100 miles south. He had a proper wind vane self-steering device. Darkness came early and the nights were long and cold. A long trip would be safer and more likely if I was able to sit under the spray hood and keep watch without having to sit steering in the cockpit.

On a map Cabo Carvoeiro looked like a large wart attached to the occidental coastline of Portugal. I walked out of the internet café into very warm sunshine. It was so warm I took a right turn instead of the usual left to go back to the harbour. I wondered about the chance of seeing a gecko. Past the usual urban sprawl of flats and housing interspersed with patches of neglected homesteads from an earlier period. Dry stone walls tumbled in sections to reveal tall thickets of jade coloured cane. The ruins of tiny cottages rested amongst these small holdings and piles of dumped household waste spread out from the broken sections of boundary. I dared not go gecko hunting inside these annexed territories because they were amongst residential areas. Children sat on doorsteps accompanied by little sharp faced dogs. Old fishermen passed by on scooters, always with carrier bags hanging from the handlebars. Fluffy clouds moved inland from the Atlantic, gazing down at Portugal, a new shore after 3000 miles of ocean. Wall lizards waited in torpor between lintels and king stones for hotter months. The road became dishevelled, with deep drains left uncovered and fine cream sand encroaching on everything. Cars hurtled past, scurrying towards Cabo Carvoeiro, or away from it, for I was on the road leading west to the point. I bought food for a picnic in a dark and cluttered grocery store. Goats cheese, a bottle of water, a packet of crisps, two tomatoes, biscuits and a couple of bananas came to 5 Euros and I repressed the thought I had been overcharged for the sake of respect for the locals. The bananas and tomatoes were weighed in the same bag and an arbitrary price conjured up. I was wary of becoming paranoid in thinking I was being taken advantage of when perhaps I was mistaken. The Portuguese had never given me reason to distrust them and seemed more apt to pride themselves on being fair and reasonable.

In hot sunshine I reached a wide area where buildings and spaces for cars lay scattered amongst swathes of sand and patches of ice plants. Occasionally kerb stones had been laid off into scrub, where building development had been started and then forgotten. Always there was dumped household rubbish, particularly where it could be thrown downwards, such as into an ancient well or blow hole in the cliffs. A breathtaking view of blue sea drew me onwards across springy ice plants onto a cliff path leading downwards to broken rocks. Cliffs separated into pillars made of layers of eroded stone, like piles of giant pita breads. Herring gulls hung in the wind over the crags and the sea broke heavily around the bay. Through the stacks of eroded rock the Ilhas De Berlenga lay 5 miles to the west. All too salty for geckos, but perfect for a picnic and I chose a spot away from the smelly niches where fishermen and visitors went to the toilet. Below were strewn boulders, to where arches and rifts in the cliffs passed through to the churning white sea. The stones faltered in scale, as my eyes pulled into and out of focus on the variable terrain. Sometimes a particular boulder seemed massive, as big as a double bed. But then it shrank to a mere stone, such as one might carry home for the garden. I ate my picnic and flung little bits of food into the rocks for creatures who might live there. The road leading to Cabo Carvoeiro had spectacular sheer drops with fishermen using long beach rods, casting out into the swells from a height of seventy metres. I saw the same scene as in the photograph on the cover of the Peniche tourist map, a precipitous drop with the azure Atlantic beyond and someone fishing at the cliff edge.

Right by the road were caverns where the sea had produced caves and blow holes. They dropped straight down to sea level and were largely unguarded. It would be very dangerous to arrive at night and park a car just off the road. As usual there was household waste strewn down the sides of these geological wonders, bleach bottles, polystyrene foam packing, worn out espadrilles, plastic squash bottles, breakfast cereal packets and used nappies bobbed far below in the shadows. Waves spread under the cliffs churning and gurgling the rubbish into smaller and smaller bits. Plastic bottles last for hundreds and hundreds of years like this. In five hundred years time there will be a new type of sand consisting of billions of plastic containers reduced to smooth granules of matter. Animals will have adapted ways to utilize this product of late twentieth century humanity. There will be shore crabs which exclusively live in bleach bottles and travel on the summer winds in their plastic shelters. They will reach the Sargasso Sea, at the centre of the clockwise Atlantic currents to breed in great mid ocean rafts of plastic and waste. Further around the scenic roadway there were several buildings with signs declaring them to be a military zone. The road was accessible to the public and I found my way to the very tip of Cabo Carvoeiro, marked by a viewing platform, the roof of a café built into the cliff itself.

Two lovers embraced at the disastrous furthest corner, the female sitting on a white wall with nothing but giddiness behind her. The male stood pressed into the corner almost appearing to be pushing her towards the vertical space. A cormorant flew by in a straight, self absorbed flight, fifty meters below. A coach load of visitors stood in the accelerated air around the bluff. They stood against the Atlantic and the Ilhas Berlenga, smiling, to make photographs. Then they alighted back aboard the coach, via the loos, which were hidden underground. The coach had its engine revved to supply the air conditioning and as a signal it was time to carry on to the next spot. A cliff path led towards Peniche past a series of coves between the cliffs. The path went from cliff top down to beach level several times before going amongst housing again as it entered Peniche. It was only a couple of miles back and as I walked across the road onto the harbour car park the same coach full of visitors swept around the bend. One of the observant tourists did a double take as she noticed me and obviously recognized me from an hour ago. Coaches make a whole days touring around a very limited area, stopping at each scenic place and moving on to the next, via some church or bridge or whatever. In this way a full day trip can be enjoyed without going more than 20 miles. If the tourist does not look at a map, the blur of scenery and beauty spots spread along the route would appear to be a long distance, until one spots a walker and realizes the coach has only moved a couple of miles along the coast.

Back at SP I felt very tired and as I lay down I felt sick with mild heat stroke. The day had been very hot for November, but I could not understand why this particular day had affected me. I drunk water and slept for a couple of hours. On waking I felt better again. The Portuguese have a term for this sickly autumn sunshine. It was the 'Veráo de Sáo Martinho', the summer of Saint Martin and renowned for making people sick.

The wind vane self-steering significantly improved by adding a plastic tube inside to bear with low friction on the stainless steel studding. The real problem was the rudder arrangement and I had decided to make an auxiliary rudder with a trim tab attached. It was impossible to put a trim tab on the SP's existing rudder because it was under the transom and so there was no way to run control lines to it. It would be possible to fix tubes through the hull, but the boat would need to come out of the water and the tubes would be vulnerable to damage. An auxiliary rudder could be used as emergency steering if needed. It needed to be easily demountable, to service the parts or adjust the control lines to the trim tab. After several days looking for ply wood, I'd learned only what it was called, 'contraplacado'. Numerous directions led to little dark workshops where chairs and tables were being discretely constructed. Each one of these minute factories had a piece of ply leaning against the wall amongst the sawdust, but none of the carpenters would sell me any ply. "It is very expensive," they apologized, adding, "for the carpenter only". This occurred in deep Portuguese, but I understood the message due to repetition because 'plywood' (ubiquitous for me while in the UK) was as rare as geckos in Peniche. The trail of directions and suggestions led through the rarer parts of Peniche and I treasured the opportunity to step through corrugated doorways into the smell and dust of wood yards. The bigger factories had chipboard and hardboard for making household furniture, as well as hard woods in great slabs a couple of inches thick and three meters in length. Plywood remained elusive. An elderly couple who sold hardware and carpets tried to help, scratching their heads and gesturing this way and that. I repeated the word, 'contraplacado' at intervals, while the shopkeepers failed to think of a supplier. A teenage girl swooped in to try out her English, she knew somewhere, she said and as I followed her away the defeated shopkeepers resorted to warning her to be careful of strangers. She smiled at their old fashioned advice. On the way to the centre of Peniche again, she met several of her school friends and showed me off to them, but they were unable to mobilize their English language in the face of a real English person.

Eventually we entered a store which sold bathrooms. In my mind I pictured the panels which fill the spaces alongside a bath and hoped they may be plywood. But no. Eventually, after walking a fair distance, I found a proper building suppliers. There were tools and materials, things I needed, and things I could change my world with and I immediately purchased a round file, but I could not remember what specifically I would do with it, I just knew it was the kind of thing I would be glad of in the near future. There were electric grinders on special offer. Twenty one Euros seemed a very reasonable price. An electric grinder will meet almost any material and reduce it to dust in an instant, they are a phenomenally vicious tool, the sailors chain saw. I wanted one but decided to focus on what was needed first. They had sheets of ply. Trouble was I could only buy a whole sheet, which measured two and a half metres long, by one and a half metres wide. It was huge, but it was meant to be because the Clube Nautique de Peniche offered me the use of their workshop and I was certain they would be pleased to have the surplus. I purchased a sheet which was going to be delivered to the sailing club the following day.

A westerly swell thundered on the mole but the wind remained light. The difference in speed between the waves and the disturbance meant the waves were arriving before the wind. Even though the wind may be blowing at 60mph, the storm itself may be travelling at 8mph. The waves, a third aspect, spread outwards from the windy storm centre like sound waves from a washing machine. During its fastest phase, the spin cycle, the noise of a washing machine is loudest and can be heard right at the end of the garden. *BOOOOOOOMMMMMM*, a huge wave reached the mole, *SSSSSSHHHHIIISSSHHH*, a white tongue of sea-water spilled onto the car park. These spills were occasionally heavy enough to damage a car and there were barriers preventing access while big swells were arriving. The Portuguese for 'waves' was a beautiful word, 'rafagas'. The perturbation which made the present rafagas was 600 miles to the north-west. An entity without awareness, an area, a system, hardly a thing, and not at all an organism. As a storm it was illustrated as a spiral shaped whole. It had dangerous and safe sectors, which defined the actions a vessel may take to gain a safer position when cornered by one. The idea of being caught by a storm suggests an angry mind, or malicious intent, an angry god or goddess, inside, driving it along with a will. Ocean meteorology maps show the paths of these storms, like the routes taken by migrating animals. In the northern Atlantic a storm will usually travel to the north east after being born on the eastern seaboard of the United States to travel over the Atlantic to western Ireland, then pass to the north of the United Kingdom. Reaching northern Scandinavia and the Arctic under the high atmospheric pressure and cold of the polar regions the storm weakens and finally withdraws into itself. There, with just enough energy left to flutter a snow goose's tail, the tired old storm inscribes its journey from the equator to the pole in arcs and circles in the snow, drawn by the sharp tips of sea grass in the cold breezes under the north star.

In the southern hemisphere storms revolve about their centre in a clockwise direction. In the northern hemisphere it is anti-clockwise. This fact is one of the prime reasons the United Kingdom has a fairly high annual rainfall, a low passing to the north of the UK has winds revolving anticlockwise around its centre. This causes prevailing westerly winds over the UK. A low pressure system covers huge tracts of geographical space, so when the swells are crumpling onto Peniche harbour mole, the low itself may be centred over western Ireland, or south of the Nantucket Shoals off Newfoundland. The wind strengths are higher nearest to the eye of the low, the centre, because there is the lowest atmospheric pressure and the winds are the result of air rushing in to fill the hole, or eye from the surrounding regions. Due to the Coriolis Effect the in-rushing air mass spirals, in the same way the water in a bath runs out of the plug in a twirl, the result of the spinning world. Water or wind moving towards the axis of rotation is deflected by the amount of the vector of the rotation. A potter's wheel has splashes of slip which lay directly outward from the centre, but the path they took relative to the potter was a spiral. People move with the surface of the earth, as it rotates under the winds and so we have a relative wind caused solely by our movement along with the earth's surface.

A sun trap down in the cove where the sea comes through a tunnel onto a stony beach surrounded by rock and fortifications sheltered a baby wall lizard, wiggling itself across the sunny rock face. My heart gasped, 'They are still here'.

Cod and Tar

'All around us the water slips And gossips in its loose vernacular, Ferrying the smells of cod and tar'.
From: *'A Winter Ship'* by Sylvia Plath

A monthly gypsy market set up on the wide space in front of the castle. The scene reminded me of a photograph I'd seen in the museum, of the day the Salazar dictatorship stepped down with the whole of Peniche gathered in defiance of fear and triumphant effervescence. It was the 25th April, 1975. The gypsy market was a re-enactment, with a chorus of "Cinco Euros, todos, cinco Euros" (5 Euros, everything 5 Euros). Life's woes could be driven back by spending five Euros on a new pair of slacks. The word "Euros!" rolled around, like trapped thunder, under grubby white tarpaulins. Guy ropes were attached to stakes hammered deep into the tarmac road. Everyone seemed angry and urgent, demanding attention, barking into the masses. I had not yet had breakfast and found the market draining. Some women were extremely elegant, dressed in elegant black dresses, shawls, and low cut tunics with exposed belly button, their skin a sensuous olive-brown and where exposed decorated with necklaces and jewellery. Calf-length black boots with stiletto heels set them as tall as I, at one point eight metres. Men wore dark suits with trilby hats, both softened by daily wear and a little dusty from use. They had free flowing beards, blue eyes and both women and men were deadly serious.

Asians with microphones held close to their mouths looked like a cross between Krishna, the young, blue-skinned deity, and, Elvis, the young white-skinned deity. Bored, one of these sellers flicked his microphone on and off, making a feedback whistle which made a change from "Euros, cinco Euros CINCO! Euros". There were south Asian sellers with electrical goods, phone chargers, packs of alkaline batteries and absurd novelty toys that made me laugh aloud. A dancing Barbie-Doll with gyrating hips, in a pink frock held a microphone and jerked it back and forth in front of her mouth. It looked about as suggestive of fellatio as a toy could possibly be. My laugh drew the sellers and I briefly wondered about sending one to my sister and family. I asked the price, "Cinco Euros, cinco Euros". Of course, it was 5 Euros.

I escaped to a coffee and a bolo in the latest pastelaria where the ergfadas were so much more coconut moist and the coffee had more strength. It was near the Espaco Internet, which I visited each morning.

Portuguese people did not eat ergfada with cheese and ham fillings and I was pleased because it meant I had been the butt of a joke, which meant I was embraced by the humour of the local people and I felt bonded to the pastelaria with the ham and cheese filled doughnuts. To be part of local humour was to be part of the community. I felt this again in a café I visited one evening. I rarely went out in the colder, darker evenings, because the only option would be to sit in a bar with men watching football on television. Café Mystic was a trendier and non-traditional place. I sat down and watched music videos, resigned to almost total exclusion from the social life but I was content to enjoy a younger place. Then, in walked Carlos, the harbour master and he walked over and greeted me warmly so I suddenly felt like a part of the Peniche social life. Carlos sang in a band called 'Nautillus' and he loved the sea. His grandfather had been a fisherman in Nazare.

Carlos had introduced me to the Peniche yacht club who had offered me use of their workshop with benches, power tools, two vices and a scrap material store. Soon I found myself happily tripping back and forwards from the boat to the yacht club, carrying rudder shaped pieces of fibreglass and other bits of the self-steering. Fishermen, unlaying lengths of damaged hawser into smaller ropes, would eye me curiously as I passed, carrying the part completed steering device, "Eh!", one said to another, "Al Capone". I must have been holding it like a machine gun and it had holes drilled in it, for the rudder hinge lashings which had the appearance of machine gun bullet holes.

News broadcasts on the television had been showing Spanish beaches covered in oil from the tanker Prestige which had sunk off La Coruna. I grieved each time I saw the damage, covering hundreds of square miles around Camarinas, Muros and the other rias of north west Spain which had been obliterated by crude oil. I thought of the magical, clear waters seen under my rubber dinghy as I motored around exploring Camarinas. The fish lolling around in ecstatic abundance gave my fresh, recently arrived perception of a paradise, a world where the process of creation was yet to decay to a point at which the order of predators appeared. Fishermen hollered at each other in songs of plenty, in voices shaped like fish and the fish they caught were adventurers, cheerfully taking the route to market like Sunday congregations. There were synchronized swimmers, puckering lips above the surface, kissing love hearts onto the tabular rasa, the surface tension, of the living waters. At least the migrating sandwich and common terns had departed because they were here in Peniche, 240 miles south of the oily conflagration. I pitied the cormorants surfacing into a slow death of clammy fuel oil, beautiful reptilian faces, with yellow markings standing out like warning signs around cooling tarmac. Thousands of herring gulls would be perturbed by a sudden halt in the fishing and go hungry in the harshening winter climate. The search for other food sources would lead to inland rubbish tips with all manner of household waste and many would feed on unsuitable substances, which would hurt them in new ways. Young brown herring gulls would be learning the first lessons of winter, not sensing a blackening of the shore as a threat. So far everything had either nourished or escaped them. Oil just clung relentlessly, turning the never ending story of a young gull to tragedy. I feared the story lines of creatures in the rias baixos, discordant developments in the lives of dolphins, rolling around amongst shoals of prey and starfish spreading tentatively on the sandy sea bed three metres deep in sea-water, now crudely clotted. Mullet hanging like airships in groups underneath anything floating which offered shade. Shore feeders, too small and alert to be identified, small chirruping flocks of sparrows, waders, squawking herons, singular reedish, peevish, and delightful white egrets, nothing but white, and, all that signified. Feral cats of La Coruna, living among piles of rock along the harbour wall and all along the Digue de Abrigo Barrie de la Maza meeting thick clods of oil. All life forms badly affected by the sinking of the Prestige, a ship full of oil. Newly arrived in Gallicia I wondered at the flora and fauna and saw the world as a beautiful place through them. It seems I was not looking at reality.

A Swiss family aboard an aluminium sailing boat set out for the southern Atlantic ocean. Their previous sailing adventure involved an astonishing beat to windward sailing from Tahiti in the Pacific Ocean, around Cape Horn in an easterly direction, past Argentina then, still to windward, traversing the Atlantic not only from west to east but also from south to north, to arrive at the Canary Islands. A non stop beat to windward lasting 3 months. Their boat had been a very basic model known as a Hanse, built, somewhat economically, in east Germany. The trip they did was remarkable for any boat, but with two boys under six years old, and in such a modest craft it was a tremendous feat. Sabina said she wants to do all the difficult things in life, because having done such things already she had realized she could do anything as long as it was approached a little bit at a time. She gave the example of sailing a long distance, where setting off seems so tedious and the boat moves at just 4 knots, so it feels even longer. She said to only look at the present and live in the moment. One minute may involve seeing a dolphin, or making a cup of tea, or changing the set of the sails, until minute by minute, step by step, a whole day passes and the boat has travelled 70 or 100 miles. Sabina, Patrick, Stephan and Luca added to the set of human beings who made my world a fascinating place.

Since the 'Mare Negra', the black sea of the Prestige oil hazard, I questioned my tendency to want to make everything wonderful. How could I expect to go through life in wonder when it included oil spills? Sabina and family restored my optimism by sailing vast distances with such light attitudes. It made me realize that looking at reality was not the same as perceiving truth. If there was a place called Narnia and a road which led to it, it was within and as difficult to catch sight of as geckos in Peniche. When I eventually caught sight of a gecko it was the most natural thing in the world to see at that point. Narnia was a philosophy, a lightness of mind in unlimited terrain. Setting foot in Narnia was not occupying or possessing a place, it was observing a wall lizard in the sunshine, which in a second could be gone, but glittered with green speckled energy.

A French catamaran, a huge vessel costing two million Euros and brand new was being delivered to the Caribbean by three French sailors. For a week there was a pleasant social world on the pontoon in Peniche with meals of freshly caught dorada, bottles of Portuguese Vinho Verde, green wine, and some single malt whisky. After both the Swiss boat and the luxurious French catamaran left for the Canary Islands I became fired up with energy, doing all sorts of maintenance jobs on SP, throwing out loads of stuff and buying white paint for the cabin. I resumed the process of cleaning the cabin roof and sides of old glue with foam stuck in it, using a heavy duty stainless steel scouring pad which would appear a quick and easy task, but with fittings, lights, curtain rails, navigation equipment and the confined space, the job had not been completed before. I promised SP a nice white coat of paint on her cabin for Christmas. I installed a replacement flexible water tank in the bows, from a local supplier with a catalogue from which I was able to select the right one at a reasonable price and delivered from Lisbon the following day. The connections matched the existing pipes with only a few minor alterations. I filled the new tank via the deck filler and it was satisfying to freely pump clean tasteless water.

I looked again at the blocks of peat fuel for the wood stove, given to me in Bristol after I was so enthusiastic about the smell of the smoke from it. Les, an artist who lived in a ramshackle van had unfortunately died the previous year and his son had given me the peat during a conversation about the trips his dad made to Ireland to draw sketches of farms, churches and coastal scenes. They were done in pencil on artists pads and transferred to copper plates to be etched. I spent hours sitting in Les' van with the wood stove stinking out the whole boatyard and moaners moaning about what I consider an essential scent of life. He had racks of drawings and prints, some of which were displayed in the van windows. He would drive to places such as Valencia, the northern tip of Ireland and sell prints to tourists, making a good income. At eighty odd years old he said he wished he had discovered his lifestyle twenty years ago. Les and I enthused about wood stoves and he had several French ones, tall cylindrical and embellished with art nouveau curlicue, set off with enamel. Made by a firm called Godin, these stoves had the power to make anyone play the accordion in no time. I was given two peat blocks which were dry and shiny like bricks made of black plastic. One I had burned on midsummer eve last summer, in memory of Les. The other peat block I still had aboard and intended to burn it on the shortest day as a second commemoration to someone who knew the way to Narnia and took it often. I had to use up the peat block because it looked like a large block of hashish. I sensed the Portuguese customs officials would get very excited if they found it and I could imagine the difficulty explaining it away. I liked the smell of it when it was burning I would say as the customs became even more suspicious. Even if tests showed it to be harmless dried peat there may be sufficient alarm to do a destructive search of my boat. After such dismantling one is not entitled to any compensation or help putting it back together. A Brigada Fiscal high speed customs boat was moored behind SP so I was sure the smell of the burning peat block would alert their senses, but as I had nothing to declare I had no need to worry.

The Mare Negra had reached Bayona, the last major port in Spain before the Portuguese coast, 120 miles away. If the northerly winds continued I would need to think seriously about sailing away from Peniche as oil would be highly damaging to the white hull of SP, not structurally, but it would be extremely difficult to remove. I had spent two hours scrubbing the water-line of scum, weed, grass, fish offal and barnacles and it was hard work. At least for the present SP looked clean and happy. I loved the working harbour environment of Peniche and the townsfolk had been wholesomely friendly and helpful so I felt as though I could remain there, to gradually blend in, learn the language and the humour. Fishing boats piled in from the sea, rocking SP catastrophically as the fishermen cried out, closing the fearful gap between themselves and the shore by hollering to each other. Fish wives and retired fishermen sat on nets sewing up damage, under umbrellas and plastic oilskins. Thirty men handed a net aboard through a hydraulic roller and when a snag occurred more hollering caught the eye of the ever watchful gulls. Little dogs chased folds in the net, barking and snapping at fishtails missed by brown herring gulls who had reigned the nets while they were spread out on the quay.

Retired and older fishermen held an ongoing protest about there being no centre built in the town for their use. Signs and symbols stated the matter while the retirees sat beneath smoking and looking at the harbour and the ever changing weather, in summer baking hot and through cold winter rain. One place of protest was the fortification at the root of the harbour wall where a broken television, a transistor radio and telephones were placed in nooks in the wall to make surreal scenes where feral cats rubbed around them as if they were in a sitting room. The other site of protest was on the north side of Peniche at the exact opposite end of the fortification which ran from one side of the peninsular to the other. Near a boatyard where fishing boats were constructed on the beach a wooden trawler had been hauled onto a lawn and converted into some sort of dwelling with a round door in its side. I really liked Peniche but also I constantly wished to move on. It was nearly the Winter solstice. Since the end of October when I arrived in Peniche there had been Christmas decorations in the shops and streets. Television showed pictures of children sledding in thick snow and building snowmen. Loudspeakers broadcast festive songs, Christmas carols and popular songs played by a soprano saxophone, which I actually enjoyed for the attractive tones of the soprano.

I went to Cascais again where dazzling fairy lights of a richer tourist town, an outlying suburb of Lisbon was doing Christmas. Lisbon was a grand city known as the city of seven hills. It had a palace, art galleries and museums galore. I needed the stimulation of a more cosmopolitan environment. I had been asked to sail with a couple from Peniche to Cascais after Nadine had badly burned her hand during a previous attempt to do the journey. She had a rope burn and her hand was wrapped in bandages and unusable. We enjoyed the scenery along the 45 miles of mostly high cliffs with breakers throwing up a constant salt cloud. Cabo Roca was the very western most point of Europe, so yet another end of the world, a dramatic cliff backed by mountains of five hundred metres height. More dramatic than Cabo Finisterre, higher, bigger and further west Cabo Finisterre was in Spain while Cabo Roca was in Portugal and perhaps political reasons made the Spanish 'Land's End' a hotter destination than the Portuguese one. Finisterre had an attractive little town nestled behind it, whereas Cabo Roca swung gradually northwards to reveal a six kilometre stretch of exposed low cliffs and beaches with surf. After Cabo Roca was Cabo Rasa, with a white lighthouse, a gated forecourt area, garden and sleeping dog which would bark at strangers. I'd walked to the lighthouse previously. From the sea the luminescent green backs of breaking swells which had passed under the boat like tilting football fields, huge, occasionally obscuring the land altogether and giving the impression the whole sea was rising up. Without distinct tops, just an upward slope, then a downward slope. Looking at the sea it appears fairly flat, but if a trawler or yacht is included it disappears from view and reappears revealing the passing waves. I always presumed the horizon at sea would be straight, it was not and I thought how difficult using a sextant in a small boat would actually be. I think the Peniche harbour Master was hoping to have a foreign visiting boat in his marina over Christmas but I felt the ambiance of Cascais was much more attractive, even though I planned on spending Christmas in solitude I would still enjoy seeing the effervescence of mass hysteria, as an outsider. I could always escape back to my cockleshell to listen to the BBC world service on the radio.

I saw more television in Peniche than during the last three years in the UK. Each pastelaria had one switched on constantly on a bracket up on the wall. On television I saw the phenomena of the Northern Lights and realized there had been a recent occurrence which was witnessed in Lisbon, the bridge in the shots was the big one across the Tagus, which looked like the Golden Gate bridge in San Francisco.

A strange tale from the harbour master seemed related to the northern lights. Apparently, a host of witnesses including policemen, reported a huge explosion on the summit of the highest mountain in Portugal, the Sierra De Estrella (The mountain with its top in the stars) was accompanied by a noise like an airliner crashing. Common conceptions of alien life forms seem to assume life develops along similar designs as humanity, so aliens drive vehicles, or craft, which make mechanical noises, hums or buzzes and do things such as crash, or fly away, or land. There is no reason why alien life forms should be anything similar to the world of mankind. They might be amorphous thought-like fields of consciousness and may not need vehicles or spaceships at all. I saw the northern lights in the UK once, in daylight and I thought there was a gigantic explosion in the upper atmosphere. It spread right to the horizon all around and hung there glowing with eerie, indescribable unearthliness, like a big eyeball looking in at the world from space. Whatever people think up to spice the world with, the real world is far stranger and even more beautiful.

A plastic Christmas tree on the counter of the pastelaria burst into life as someone passed. It rang with digitally manufactured bell noises and then sang a hilarious rock and roll version of a Christmas carol. During this sequence the tree gyrated around and back, lights flashing in time to the music. 'It' sang in English and as the song progressed the tree began to push upwards, getting higher and higher like a fireman's ladder and gyrating all the time. It reached a height of one metre above its original size and finally went quiet, telescoping back down to a diminutive little counter top ornament.

There were a number of Chinese shops in Peniche selling absolutely anything from scouring pads to plastic singing parrots, so much more amusing and novel than the Western goods I was used to. But I also wondered at the pollution output of the mass plastics production by unregulated Chinese factories.

In Lisbon a young girl was painting people's names on rectangular sheets of paper in Western script but Chinese motifs, little smiling suns, colourful birds, pagodas, flowers, all produced with deft twists of the hand. Paints were bright gaudy colours and applied with rectangular splints of wood with twine bindings around the tips. This skill had obviously been learned from a young age, probably to earn money in a toy or decoration factory and it seemed a pity that such skills would be replaced by mass produced stickers printed by machines.

I refused to tap out Christmas greetings to email courtesy of Microsoft, although I had sent digital birthday cards. I had no desire to take part in the mass phenomena of Christmas and planned to do what I did the previous year - have a quiet day at home and reflect on the turning of the year.

Over the years I have attempted to 'find myself' by reading spirituality and self-development books. One was called, *Positive Visualisation*. One positive visualisation was to imagine yourself walking across a bridge to an island and meeting some people in a clearing - meet each in turn and then return to the mainland across the wooden jetty connecting the island to the shore with intuitive knowledge. The persons on the island were actually aspects of the person doing the visualisation. Since reading that book I visited my island often as a way to address personal questions and look for creative ideas about life decisions. I visited my island one night after going to bed early when thoughts were ranging around in my mind. I was trying to imagine what sort of life I wanted to create for myself by asking - *What do I really want?*

I walked across a wooden planked causeway, to a tree covered island where a path led to a number of people sitting around a fire. Trees surrounded the scene, sheltering and containing the occasion which felt like a celebration of friends. The island and the people were always similar, but not exactly the same as in previous visits. I wanted to consider whether I could be more content if I lived like other sailors with big, well kept and expensive boats - and tight itineraries - while I drifted along, care free in wonder at where I had got to already, such as when I first boated to Wisbech from Peterborough, a mere 25 miles of inland rivers. The downside of getting maximum satisfaction from minimum effort was laziness and a scruffy boat. I was asking how other people generate the energy and willpower to keep their boats in top condition and their lives in successful grooves. In my imagination I saw a Swedish family I'd recently met in Peniche on a brand new Ovni, an aluminium, sailing boat, with exactly the wind vane self-steering I craved, and also a wind generator and liferaft - well equipped to sail anywhere on the globe. They were headed for the Falkland Islands and the Southern Ocean and their boat looked really good. Plus they were friendly, open and warm people. I fell half asleep in my bunk on scruffy SP after reaching the imaginary island, where I sat chatting with a female figure by the fire in the clearing, about what it would be like to own a brand new Ovni sailing boat and to be the sort of person who could manage to equip and maintain such a vessel.

A noise outside brought me back to SP - a propeller in the water - a boat had arrived. Cruising boats had become very infrequent in the cold, windy season, with hardly any yachts coming from the north where the oil hazard from the Prestige continued. The yacht was identical to the Swiss yacht of my friends, another Swiss Ovni. And it was exactly the same as the yacht I had been visualising in my mind's eye. The sailors were also Swiss, having sailed non-stop from France and taking a route which took them to seaward of the oil glooping wreck of the Prestige. They had sailed for seven days in cold and windy conditions. They had arrived next to me as I lay half asleep imagining a boat almost identical to theirs, including the precise type of wind vane self-steering and wind generator on the stern. They had arrived from 600 miles away to within 6ft of me in my bunk. The sailors were tired and so I went back to bed, leaving them to adjust ropes and fenders and rest. In the morning I met the Swiss Ovni skipper who was very impressed to see SP, saying, "I so admire you in your little boat with such modest equipment, coming so far".

He then helped dispel my being impressed by his much larger boat, the mast of which reached nearly twice as high as SP, by saying, "She does not sail well to windward, but she is a really strong boat". I thought to myself, at least SP sails well to windward and is a really strong boat too. The Swiss sailor suggested we meet later for a drink together and I spent the day looking forward to some rare socializing. Later on the Swiss Ovni had left for Cascais in a hurry to gain southing away from the winter storms when a boat can be delayed for weeks. I was hardly concerned at their leaving as I had only briefly met them. I arrived back to SP later in the day to find a bottle of wine left in the cockpit, a French red from Cahors in the Lot valley, 2000 vintage, Appellation Controlee, a good bottle. It could only have come from the Swiss Ovni. The only other users of the outer yacht pontoon were the uniformed and occasionally armed Brigada Fiscal and although in no way unfriendly, they would certainly not have given me a nice bottle of wine. The Swiss Ovni was a thought provoking visitor after arriving coincidently with my visualisation and the bottle of wine suggested a mutual appreciation between the Swiss skipper and myself despite only meeting for five minutes the morning after they had arrived, when we'd only discussed our respective routes from northern Europe to Peniche and the Swiss sailor had admired SP and the distance she had travelled.

The awe was mine - how could such a coincidence occur? As if there was a subtle yet structural connection between real events and my imagination - had I psychically seen the arrival of the Ovni? After seven days hard sailing the crew would be tired and highly sensitive, was it mental-waters reflecting on the real-sea? Had I unconsciously called the boat and could they have unconsciously responded? When they carried on their voyage after a brief pause and even briefer meeting with myself, they then thanked me, with the bottle of wine, for pulling them in from the restless sea and the opportunity to rest for a night and refuel in the morning. Mind and identity are highly reflexive processes. If the mind's eye concentrates on mental-waters it may see beyond the physical location of the mind. Perhaps it is no stranger than seeing the sky in the quiet surface of a pool.

180 miles out into the Atlantic ocean, towards Madeira, were three major sea mounts; under-water peaks rising up from depths of four thousand metres - the Lion, the Unicorn and the Dragon. They were nearly islands, but not quite, the shallowest reaching up to within twenty metres of the surface. In a storm huge swells would trip over those obstructions and break into cascades of dangerous foam. A small boat would be shrouded in green and white sparkling garlands as waves thundered around. On calm days the presence of the sea mounts would be barely noticeable - perhaps a moodiness in the sea surface. The trio of archetypal creatures made me want to sail out that far onto the mythical sea, likely en route to the Canary Islands via Madeira on the actual sea. SP had actually reached Narnia the instant I slipped the mooring lines and left Bristol Marina but then it took me 900 miles to begin to realize it, even so if the DIY wind vane self-steering was a success, I would keep going.

The gecko population in the Canary Islands was renowned. The Swiss sailor from the first Ovni cruiser, told me a story about geckos She had a friend, a German single-hander, who lived on a beautiful wooden boat in the Canary Islands and made a living by making gifts out of painted acrylic shapes and modelling clay. She was asked by a tourist shop to make geckos in the form of window stickers using a particular material with a peel off backing and which needed the painted surface to be hardened in an oven. After spending much effort and some expense the oven process failed and her geckos were all ruined but I found the story very very encouraging. It seemed there were significant numbers of geckos in the Canary Islands and that was where I wanted to be.

The day before the shortest day of the year bunches of yellow and gold flowers were carried by in the weak sunshine. Fish continued in breeding frenzies, gathering at the surface in bunches of thirty or more. Little dogs rolled playfully around with each other. The winter in Peniche had been gentle so far. I suffered in chilly north-east winds and frequent rain showers, but when the sun shone it was warm as a fine June day in the UK. I walked to the Espaco Internet to check email and browse. I liked the calm, safe environment with clearly laid out conditions of participation there. The spacious room was open plan with the computers clustered around two central nodes so everything was out in the open and each person visible to each other. I felt safe there and the occasional giggles of young teenagers when somebody sneezed or hiccuped were quickly put down by the person in charge.

Some of the young lads repeatedly printed copies of what they are looking at and slipped the paper into their bags to avoid the charge, levied after ten pages. The paper crinkled guiltily as it slid slowly into the bag. They only got away with it for a while, after which the youngsters were told off reprimanded? again by the person in charge. The Espaco Internet was a micro model of the kind of society which many who like the idea of being Europeans aspire to - a shared resource flexibly administered. If nobody was waiting one could continue using the PC within the opening hours. The positioning of chairs and desks made for easy eye contact with others using the computers which engendered a social feeling, even though there was rarely an exchange of conversation between participants. One or two serious faces had a calming effect throughout the room.

I sat on a wall outside the Espaco Internet, in warm sunshine, waiting for my turn. A large domestic fowl cried out as it was placed into the trunk of a car. It had plainly reached the terminal phase of its function. Soon it would grace the table of a happy family gathering over Christmas lunch. The bird made a sonorous call which seemed to say, 'No, no, no, no, no, no!' I reassured myself by thinking the bird would not suffer once it was dead. The strong hand of fate seized the scrawny neck of life and the Christmas turkey of time was hung in the garage of destiny.

After surfing the web for an hour and a half I went for a coffee. A moustachioed man wobbled into the pastelaria. He had four carpets draped over his shoulders. Nobody responded and he turned and walked back towards the door. It seemed normal for someone to hawk a few rugs here, there were often ad hoc stalls set up on the path by traders. People in the UK would look at that carpet seller with disdain. I knew it to be the case because I felt a gut reaction as I noticed the poor quality and dull design of the cheap looking rugs. However a more open and humanist part of myself would like to see him throw them on the ground in a flourish and using a combination of charm and willpower, sell them all while the pastelaria staff served free coffee to everyone. He did not and they did not. The noise of Christmas collapsed into a vacuum left by the undesirable mats and bakers slid trays of rolls about, cleaners wiped off tables. I left the pastelaria.

In the evening I watched the sun set on the shortest day and thought about my time in Portugal. Cats wended through the rocks and flecks of gold sunlight flashed from waves way out in the dusk. It felt significant and magical. Later I emptied a can of sardines onto the sea wall for the cats while aboard SP the single peat block was stinking out the whole marina. With fishy fingers I fiddled happily with my solstice fire. At the change of shifts of the Brigada Fiscal I heard a suspicious, 'sniff!', as the uniformed man passed. Lighting a peat block produces the smell of burning rubber, old socks, pipe tobacco, single malt whisky and hashish all in one enveloping aroma. I could still smell it when I walked right along the wall to where the cats were, to give them sardines.

No other foreign yachts had remained in Peniche for the winter, apart from a dismasted Dutch vessel whose owners lived in a house on Sardinia. When I told anyone my intention to remain in Peniche, they exclaimed and asked how on earth I would keep myself occupied in such an undeveloped port. I kept myself very busy with writing emails, reorganizing the boat and building the wind vane self-steering. Sourcing materials took much time and I almost wore out a pair of shoes by walking the length and breadth of Cabo Carvoeiro in search of plywood and stuff with which to make rudder pintels.

I fitted a water-proof electric socket in the cockpit to power a new electric tiller pilot. Despite trying I'd failed to buy a Simrad TP10 autopilot back in Wales before I left because it was a decision between fair winds and delivery periods. I had some extra money for Christmas and so decided to buy one now.

One morning after Christmas I lay in bed trying to work out which way the wind was blowing. The sun streamed through the windows and the wind was strong, but there was hardly any movement aboard. The fenders were not grinding between the hull and the pontoon, neither was there any noise of ropes banging against the mast. The only clue was a glooping slopping noise from the stern as wavelets hit the lower part which emerged at a steep angle backwards and produces those sounds. I did not expect there would be a firm wind coming from the north-west, but, watching a cloud move across the window left me no wiser because it was too large and high up to determine which way it was travelling as the boat moved backwards, forwards and side to side with the ceaseless surge. At the same time the breeze heeled it to and fro and there were small pitching and vertical movements which made judging wind direction difficult while remaining in bed. I eventually got up late in the morning and was pleased to see a bright, warm day with a whistling wind coming from the north-west. This explained how quiet the world had appeared as I awoke. Cabo Carvoeiro was sheltering Peniche from waves, nevertheless, strong swells continued to break against the harbour wall as usual. It was that time between Christmas and New Year, when people wandered about aimlessly, wishing, I think, to get back to normality as soon as possible, even if that meant going back to full time jobs. I felt distinctly excited by the clear warm weather as well as the thought of longer days and spring happening in a couple of months.

A black redstart fluttered away in a small garden where I always saw a family of cats lounging or playing and the days went by. New Year's Eve felt like spring. The Espaco Internet was closed but I enjoyed the ten minute walk to find out. I had washed my hair using the hose on the pontoon, something I like to do in the summer but to be able to do it in mid-winter was a pleasure. Last year in Bristol my hands would ache with the cold if I used the hose pipe. Occasionally the water would freeze in the pipe and I would have to wait until the sun had melted it by the afternoon. Flowers blossomed throughout winter, on waste ground, of which there was much, yellow flowers covered large areas. Red Admiral butterflies flopped about. The Pilot Atlas of the North Atlantic told me the average temperature would be just one degree less in January and February, than in December. The month just past had seen a series of low pressure systems which had brought strong winds and rain. However, overall the climate was frequently very mild with warm sunny days.

One night I was riveted by a book written by a friend, eventually getting to sleep at half past three in the morning. I was gripped by her story about becoming a Catholic priest, then working with oppressed and poverty stricken persons and communities. Meanwhile she fell in love, got married, had children, during which she was coshed by an Australian policeman, she was also visited by Mother Theresa of Calcutta to be told she was resisting the church with her pride. After this she went through a process of gender reassignment and was involved in an armed Aboriginal uprising against a corporation about to steal their land. Later her lifetime relationship with the creator, the god/goddess was developed in a beautiful exploration of spiritual living which drew on the theology involved in training as a Catholic priest, the experience of Australian aboriginal ways and eventually full circle to the Irish Celtic beliefs of her family ancestors. I met Jani and her dog 'Storm' in Bristol, several years ago and reading, *The Seven Days of My Creation - Tales of Magic, Sex and Gender*, I was in awe of her tremendous range of experience and the deep personal commitment she had towards her own and others humanity. Her book liberally offered wisdom which dispelled many, almost all, of the deep rooted assumptions of Christianity. If there was a book with which to free oneself from the spiritual discomfort engendered by Western Christian morality, it was Jani's. The bastions of state religion and religious/philosophical history were relentlessly bought into question with many institutions found to be insulting, damaging and often fatal to individuals and sectors of humanity. A deeper spiritual quest grew as Jani wandered around Wales in a Landrover, meeting Druids, dryads, guardian spirits and chanters on the beach. Jani's story was a reassertion of self knowledge as sacred and powerful.

A few weeks ago, after going to see the new 'Harry Potter' film I was wondering about evolution. As part of my thoughts I asked a friend 'which evolved first - spiders, or snakes?' His reply was so rational it was mildly depressing, he said, "It is only a fantasy you know, it is not reality and therefore your question is irrelevant". I found this strange, to think there can be a real world and, quite separately, an imaginary one. A Cartesian dualistic conception of matter and mind. This was why my friend was an architect, while I was just a dreamer and it was a while before my sense of wonder and open-minded questioning of what it was 'to be alive', returned again. It was restored while reading Jani's book.

Good weather came like healing as I put on my shoes - they were warm and soothing to my feet. I had spent over an hour trying to remember how to make an eye splice after a long rope chafed through. I sat in the cabin struggling with bits of insulating tape, scissors and multiple fraying ends, none of which seemed to want to be spliced correctly. As I spliced two big eyes into two lengths of rope the sun sailed upwards in an augmented arc, warming my legs and feet through the companionway hatch. A cormorant like bird preened at the edge of the marina, it had a white head with a dark face and was the size of a small duck. Occasionally it held it's head with beak at a steep angle upwards and this is what made me recognize it as a young cormorant, or maybe a shag. Shags were less common and a little smaller than cormorants.

The little dogs which lived amongst the criss-cross of old streets often lay asleep, or on guard at many of the crossroads with one dog in view of the next, although they never seemed to fight. In contrast a dog tethered in a garden jumped up barking and slathering at me as I passed. A small whippet shaped dog lived around where the retired men sat. This thin little beige coloured animal chased cats as they crossed from the fortifications to the slip. The good weather made more cats run about and more chases by the thin beige dog.

The subsoil in Peniche was sand and it gathered in sheets or waves over everything which was not washed down by the rain. The combination of damp sand and a frequent humidity level of ninety five percent gave the town a wet atmosphere. The reason it was taking so long to build the wind vane self-steering rudder was partly the damp - usually much too high to use epoxy resins. It was often quite hard to keep happy and healthy in myself. On some days frequent rain and the relentlessly restless harbour waters saw me sitting, staring into space, while being jostled uncomfortably by the surge. The constant pushing and sucking of the harbour water had damaged all of the high quality mooring lines, leaving them hardened and stiff from being unendingly yanked and tugged at. Knots I had learned to use while sailing over twelve years, were no longer strong enough in Peniche. The strongest bind I knew - a round turn and two half hitches - used the world over to moor fishing boats to quaysides - would, over a week of being wrenched and snatched, be pulled through to the ropes end. This left the rope so strained as to be really difficult to undo knots which I had in the past prided myself on being undo-able after any load had been on them. One of the lores of a sailor was any knot must be able to be freed quickly and easily. Now I had the experience to know the limits of even sailor's knots and I would see them from then on as more or less temporary arrangements.

On New Years Day I walked towards the usual pastelaria, knowing it would be shut, but giving my back some exercise with the walking upright. So many stormy days with short daylight hours had made me a little creaky. I deeply feared a recurrence of sciatica as of a couple of years ago. A pack of dogs surprised me with their barking as they passed up the middle of a busy road. Cars beeped their horns and queued up in front and behind as this canine rabble went noisily up the street. One small Corgi like dog trailed a length of chain, about four metres, and, had obviously wrenched itself free to join the pack. They turned off the main road and disappeared down a side street. I could hear the cacophony as they passed yet more dogs and raised more yapping. I took the pack as a passing wind and followed. They were not at all concerned with people and so were not threatening in any way. They seemed to be centred on themselves in a bunch of noise and kept running along in their own freedom. The way they went led me to a poor part of Peniche, a hillside with dwellings made from soggy hardboard, lean-to's, broken down caravans. Shadowy faces peered out and smashed up cars had children standing about on them. The dogs had dispersed and the Corgi trailing a length of chain panted by, heading back from the direction it had come, alone. The chain repeatedly tangled in four excited paws and a hot tongue lolled to the side as the little hound hurried past. Some others from the pack sniffed around a group of men and fishing boats outside a ramshackle yard offering boat repairs.

Beyond the poverty ridden hillside I recognized the Lidl supermarket and I was moving generally north, towards the other beach and so I carried on towards there. A noise caught my ears so I retraced a few steps and stood still to listen. There it was again, 'rraarrk', it was a toad, calling out for a mate. I wanted to see it and each time it croaked I moved into the patch of yellow flowers. I did not see it, for it stopped making any noise when I neared. Then I passed some tiny one story cottages, their uneven white walls bulging in great callouses of damp which in the heat of summer would dry out, cooling the interior. They had cane filled gardens where people huddled and rustled at work. Fishnet waste was everywhere, very fine light blue fibres bunched into wind blown balls just waiting to ensnare wild creatures and take their legs or lives. I reached a road called, 'Rua Boa Fonte' - The road of the beautiful spring - an enchanting proposition, but I carried on to the north, not wanting to be tempted back in the direction of Lidl supermarket. As I passed an acre of houses I saw behind them, on the Rua Boa Fonte, a swathe of thick canes growing twelve feet tall and enclosed in a falling dry stone wall. I thought that must be the location of the beautiful spring. The environment was so suitable for geckos but they were absent. All the gecko institutions were in place - the gecko services, puddles for drinking; gecko food sources, numerous insects; deep cracks and spaces in the dry stone wall and foliage for gecko housing and shelter. But no geckos. A kilometre further on at the edge of Peniche a surprisingly attractive coastal scene appeared. Stark cliffs, an isthmus with a stack surrounded by huge white rollers arriving in slow motion. I gasped at the visual treat and thanked the pack of dogs for leading me astray and myself for following them and then finding, Ponta de Papoa, a thin bridge across the broken stem of the isthmus. The Ilhas Berlenga were just visible in the haze, 5 miles offshore to the west. Fishermen with rods 6m in length stood close to the giddy cliff edges.

Small coastal and songbirds rested on hummocks against the sky or flitted out of sight into blow holes where the sea jostled around in salt soaked caves below. I turned to the east and followed the coast path to come upon an ancient ruined fort. The Forte de Luz stood at the edge of a sudden drop into a scene of great breakers around a high stack where seven cormorants perched. I could not share some people's fascination with old ruins, for it seemed they always had the stench of human faeces and I found no wonder in exploring the layout of a 'good place to have a poo'. Even so I noted with interest the Fort de Luz was circular and definitely ancient. After this I walked on a wet sand track, past a typical Portuguese windmill, with only a long pole sticking out of the roof and no sails attached. Thick areas of cane looked inevitably inhabited by all manner of gecko like creatures, but none were to be seen. I arrived at a place I knew, Peniche Cima, the north beach where wooden fishing boats were being constructed at the high tide line. It had been a particularly enjoyable stroll, made even more so by the thought of both Christmas and New Year, like two great headlands, having been passed by. Now I was looking forward to strengthening sunlight and, after January and February, sailing the sparkling Atlantic swells again.

I took my camera to photograph the little dogs which occupied each crossroads. The photographs I had set up in my mind did not match the actual scene in the streets. There were a few regulars at their postings, but I failed to get good pictures of them. They moved too nervously with my sudden arrival and focusing on them, in and out of strong shadows. I crouched at small dog height while locals looked, wondering if here was the first daft tourist of the season. A couple of small dogs tethered by a doorway looked like good subjects and I sat on my ankles to get a photograph. One strained towards me, smiling, saying, 'stroke me!' The other, a tiny black and tan breed with ears like feathers erupted into a cannonade of yelps. A third dog joined in from a roof terrace above and next the householder appeared at the front door wearing thick house socks. I blamed myself and apologized for making the dogs bark. She smiled and hushed them, muttering something like, 'Here we go, it's starting, daft tourists poking their cameras into our lives, they're early this year'. It was only the 4th January and the weather was gloriously warm.

Chapter 3

Ergfada

The bolo was a 'treat' and after it refined into an 'Ergfada' (phonetic spelling) I named it the 'Our Father' because that was how the word sounded. In the sunshine a song went around my mind:

Ergfada, which art in pastelaria, swallowed be thy form,
Thy sweetness comes,
Thy taste be won,
Today as it was yesterday,
Give us again our daily bolo,
And lead us not into abstention, for thine is the flavour,
And the good chew,
For breakfast and brunch,
You'll do.

A bitterly cold wind blew for three days and so I bought a piece of bacon for the thin, beige stray dog who lived on the slipway. The cold came off the freezing slopes of the interior of north Europe being carried here on the north east wind. I saw the little beige dog asleep one night with absolutely no shelter, not even a bit of cardboard to lie on. The thin little dog was pretty eyed but when I offered some fried bacon bits she eyed me very suspiciously. A bigger hound turned up and fawned at my feet. This submissiveness was rewarded with bacon and when the beige, thin dog saw the big sturdy dog enjoying bacon she tried it too. When I walked away both dogs followed close on my heels like bridesmaids. I went to a local food store to find a cardboard box and placed it where the beige, thin dog slept, then went home feeling pleased with myself for having shared my share of creation. The following morning the sun was delightfully soothing, despite a cutting north easterly breeze and the little thin beige dog was stretched out in the sunshine looking more relaxed and comfortable than usual and I hoped my attentions had warmed her little heart. The other larger dog was one of the ones I had prevented from worrying the cat and I wondered if he remembered me and if the humble bacon-getting posture contained reflections of our previous chat where I'd told him, 'Go on, now, leave the poor cat alone', while manoeuvring my 1.8 metre height, unarguably between the cat and the dogs.

Iraq had been shown to have no 'smoking gun', yet the US and UK continued to step forces into the gulf as if war was inevitable. I felt saddened by the rhetoric of pro-war leaders who were manufacturing most of the fear and therefore the consent to terrorize Iraqis. I resented the strong ideological floods of paranoia which were sweeping away respect for foreigners. Now it was difficult to look at anyone who appeared Arabic, without a vague mistrust. One thing I felt certain of was that racism would be worsened by the war on terror and that Bush and Blair were part of a global political shift towards the right and a generally diminished potential of humanity. The political right cannot succeed in flaying it's own demons out of itself using it's own leather belt, although it may continue to enjoy the process. Helplessly I went to buy bacon to feed my friend the thin beige dog and myself, as I'd found fried salty bacon sandwiches scrumptious.

January 12 2003. After carefully deciding on the optimum positions I drilled bolt holes for the gudgeons on the self-steering rudder. Stainless steel was difficult to drill, cut and file, but when the correct pressure was applied to a file, or a hacksaw, it was sheer pleasure to feel the gradual yielding of the metal. Drilling was the hardest and had caused resounding metallic shrieks and graunches in the sailing club for the past week. The heavy work was completed and I now had to seal the mounting holes with epoxy before bolting it all together and connecting up the control lines. The wind vane sensor had been functioning impeccably for a month since I'd made improvements and severe gusts had kept it swinging to and fro without damage or wear on the bearing. What took so long was the process of simplification, where ideas were given form and shapes were assigned to materials.

When I looked at the final drawings they looked so simple, so obvious, but the process which had led there was complex - a transformation which took much energy and many packets of chocolate wafer biscuits gone through. I was almost too pleased with the stainless steel and epoxy coated wooden structure, reluctant to hang it on the stern, half immersed in water, but also very much looking forward to setting it up and testing it under sail.

A large French yacht visited Peniche and I joined them one Friday evening to share chat and booze. They had a black cat from Martinique who was very talkative and even though actual sentences were not used, the pace of the cat's utterances were readily understandable, 'Stroke me, there, yes, more, stroke me' and so on.

The workshop with a heavy vice and big hammer enabled me to fold some stainless steel bar around 180 degrees to make rudder fixings. The building shook as I wielded a massive iron hammer, like some Norse god amongst the smaller, southern, dark headed people. I worked a second, larger stainless steel bar into a bracket to attach to the stainless steel ladder on the stern and support the whole rudder assembly. It was difficult to work up an idea which used the existing structure, without making it all too haphazard. One of the sailing instructors commented on the rudder and pintels, "It looks MUCH better". At first it had looked pathetic but that was back in December. The sailing club was one of my centres of activity and a life saver, providing me with a social resource as well as a practical space where I could use power tools, benches with vices and a pillar drill for making accurate holes in stainless steel. Epoxy resin was demanding of a space in which to work and leave items to harden. I felt so very fond of Peniche by now and could even sense a reluctance to depart. The little beige whippet was asleep under a street lamp in cold rain one night as I carried home a bag of wholesome food. I thought how happy this little thin dog was during the daytime, amongst the fishing nets and fishermen and how uncomfortable the place where it slept no more than a scrap of cardboard in the open next to the lifeboat station, under a street lamp. Peniche was working class and many older people were obviously hard-up yet they hollered to one another in greeting, across the road, or over the gap between a boat and the quay in sonorous voices let loose with vitality. In Peniche I learned to feel free with my voice, not to restrict, or curtail the sound of a cough and to clear my throat unselfconsciously. Around the harbour the people liked to be greeted in the mornings with, 'Bom Dia,' - strongly, 'BOM DEEEYYAAA' descending in note. And so life went along.

January 14 2003. The rudder and trim tab were bolted to the back of

SP and connected to the wind vane. It flapped oceanically in the water, but friction in the tubes carrying the control lines was much too high. Even so I had completed the major works requiring the workshop so I drew a notice for the sailing club - a drawing of a fluttering Storm Petrel, two photographs, one of SP, showing off her splendid full keel, one of myself gazing out over the serene azure Bristol Channel. In multi-coloured felt pens I wrote,

Obrigada to everyone at the Peniche sailing club. Thank you for letting me use the workshop to build a self-steering wind vane. From Clarissa Vincent (UK sailor). Storm Petrel of Narnia.

Then before the shops had a chance to close for the lunch break, I had the poster sealed in plastic to give it a long life in the damp interior of the sailing club building.

I decided it was essential to buy a back-up position fixing unit and while looking for a good deal on a Garmin gps I was delighted to find their new model was called the 'Gecko'. Obviously I was helpless in the face of such an appealing product, but I had to wait until February for it to be released onto the market. I had often worried about being half way to some far flung Atlantic island and standing on the Garmin gps, or it simply failing. It had given faultless service over the past eight years, which was why I wanted another made by Garmin. I would feel extremely anxious faced with locating a small group of islands with hundreds of miles of open sea to get lost in and no gps. I had a sextant, as well as the sight reduction forms and various instructions for different methods although I had never used it and it was a last resort, more suited to navigating over great distances when accuracy of 10 miles at best would be enough, whereas I needed to keep tabs on more local navigation, unmarked rocks and fog where gps really makes life easier, or entering a river estuary in foul weather when a sextant would be worse than useless. gps had completely revolutionized sailing, making it far safer by taking most of the guess work out of the most important question, 'Where am I'.

The small beige slipway dog was called 'Princess'. Carlos the Harbour Master told me. She was very pretty, if slightly grimy and an old fisherman had once taken her home, but she bit through the lead and ran back to the slipway to continue her life, unfettered. Princess now greeted me and one day, to my surprise she let me stroke her which she had never done before. A little white poodle was with her. I think Princess was a little tired of the poodles keen attention and used me to block out the nuisance.

'Islands in the stream, that is what we are', sang the Bee Gees on the television in the pastelaria, and Maurice Gibb had died a few days earlier. Several of their songs I loved, for the vocal harmonies and melodies but the Bee Gees were one of the most 'un-cool' groups when I was growing up. Now I was free to like any type of music I wished. A delicately primped, white poodle on a red lead walked into the pastelaria. A roguish dog with a foxy face followed the poodle in with nose to anus. A black shawled woman with silver hair hissed at the rogue, who skittered out looking like it expected an imminent boot. Another small free dog, black this time, entered to have a sniff at the perfect poodle and again the shawled woman hissed at the intruder, to send it too skittering out of the entrance. I laughed aloud at a piggy old black dog with a grey muzzle when it went curving off the pavement after a Zundapp motorbike passing slowly and noisily. Scooters and small two stroke motorbikes were ubiquitous, often with an old packing crate tied to the rear with tatty rope, to act as a carrier. Usually a supermarket carrier bag was looped over one handlebar, containing lug worms for bait, or maybe some scraps for the feral cats. The dogs which had free run of Peniche all seemed to have developed good road sense, trotting diagonally through a line of cars, anticipating the forward motion and cutting in close behind the moving traffic.

One day a fire broke out in the extractor of a sardine restaurant. Peniche was transfixed by the wailing signal calling the firemen to their vehicles. A hefty man sprinted past me up the middle of the road, coming from the slipway, passed right by the fire and headed for the fire station the large doors of which were open to reveal several red vehicles with blue lights flashing. The fire engines were waiting for the crews to assemble as the siren continued to wail and the onlookers gathered in clumps at each end of the street where the smoke billowed. A tiny chestnut coloured dog with a weeny little bat like face, skittered by in the direction of the fire and I could not help but laugh aloud at the sight of it, and then I felt guilty for seeming happy during an emergency.

A number of cruising boats arrived and it felt almost busy after such a long time without any visitors, apart from the odd delivery crew aboard a yacht who would be gone in the early hours of the day after arriving. The large, yellow, French, ferro-concrete yacht departed for Madeira. A tired old steel double ended ketch, also French, had rested for over a week. Two posh Dutch yachts came and the skipper of one admired the creativity of my wind vane project before leaving for Cascais a couple of days later. A UK catamaran stayed one night on his way northwards and a large, luxury, Swedish yacht refuelled and swished away again out through the harbour entrance. The French double-ender contained two remarkable people, both aged over eighty, they had sailed the boat for forty years. Helene needed daily hospital visits to control a health problem. I met Helene and immediately warmed to her because even though my French was poor I could understand her easily enough as we enthused over long keels and slow boats. She explained how cruising people in modern fast boats with fin keels were always so happy to be making quick passages and she laughed as she explained after an ocean crossing of several weeks a fast boat may arrive just one day ahead of a slow one. We agreed the motion aboard a long-keeler was so much more comfortable, but that the problem was the rolling, she said, "Good roll - good sail."

The French double-ender had a most intriguing wind vane self-steering. It was very similar in principle to mine, but much simpler. Helene declared they never steered by hand, the wind vane taking care of all points of sail and they had used this system for ten years, even carrying a complete spare device - which I was invited to study. Several of these cruisers had passed through the region of the Prestige oil hazard. It was described by a French sailor as clumps of black oil floating in an area of roughly 10 miles, but no wide sheets and only a little oil stuck to the rudder and hull of the boats. Three quarters of the cargo remained inside the sunken tanker and continued to leak out. The cargo was 70,000 tons of crude oil and so far, 20,000 tons had caused such a massive problem on the coasts of Spain and western France. The oil hazard had not yet reached south to Portugal, remaining just beyond the Portuguese border.

Three taxi drivers tended their time and cars on the town square. Taxi drivers look the same the world over - cloth in hand, emitting smells of polish, wearing boring trousers - persistently angry faces. Three lizards sunbathed on a tiny ledge of rock - duller coloured than the wall lizards - brown and dark greeny-grey and at first glimpse they were slightly fatter, which made me think they might be geckos, but no.

Friday, and the pastelaria on the town square was brimming with smokers, children, babies and dogs. Sunshine glued it all together and I felt I was seeing a preview of the high season. The wind vane was working, although I had not yet tested it under way, still the trim tab continued swinging in response to the wind vane movements day and night. I still faced the difficulty of making the lines slide inside the tubes connecting the vane and the trim tab, like bicycle brake cables. It took several days to find Teflon grease and it was horribly expensive - ten Euros for an aerosol can - worth it if it did the trick, but the only way I could find out was to try it out by buying some. I tested it but was quickly disappointed with the lack of results. The fishing line would not slide through the plastic tubing even with Teflon lubricant squirted down the pipes. I became depressed and decided to redesign the whole top part - the wind vane - to be the same as the one on the French boat, Karak. After all, they had sailed the Atlantic, the Pacific and to Japan and New Zealand.

The wind vane they used was completely simple. It was of the type described by wind vane books as not very effective. All the manufacturers of wind vane self-steering love to explain at length why their particular model was the only one which would work properly. I gained a fairly deep knowledge of the principles and in particular the evolution from the type on Karak to those costing thousands of pounds. Of these third and fourth generation models the cheapest on the market was £1,500 and the most expensive, £4,000. There was a huge difference between what was written about the subject and what was actually in use successfully on boats. The key to the Karak type was simplicity. Enthused again by the Karak voyagers I photographed and measured their wind vane gear and in view of my discoveries I bought a stainless steel tube to consolidate my intentions. In the meantime, having given up trying to make the present version work, I squirted WD40 down the tubes, which I thought would kill it by eating away the plastic line and tubing, but suddenly I saw it begin working much freer. It continued to move freely all night and the following morning. I pivoted the vane side to side and watched as the trim tab, a small rudder, worked to and fro in response. After a few adjustments of the line tension and tubing clamps I had a working wind vane, ready for sea trials. And that is what I did.

A fresh north-easterly made whistling noises in the rigging and the red ensign crackled, held horizontally by the breeze. I swept away the clutter of winter, started the engine (it took ten minutes to start) and took the boat into the middle of the harbour to test the vane. Very quickly at first, I wrote it off as useless because the effect of the trim tab was futile in the real swirl of water at the stern and even the steering rudder itself was ineffective too, so as I turned it this way and that the boat sailed forward without heeding the signal from the rudder which was just too small - I realized the whole project had been a futile waste of time. Firm gusts of wind came through the harbour making for a rumbustious first sail of the year. I headed toward the harbour entrance beyond which a big swell was running but with the wind in the north-east the sea south of Cabo Carvoeiro was gentle. The cockpit filled with a disarray of ropes and fenders as I reefed the mainsail to stop the chaotic rushes forward in the stronger winds. Two dinghies from the sailing club swooped by and the club safety boat came to meet me. Jose, who had done welding for me, looked at the waggling vane gear and somewhat sardonically asked, "Does it work?" In an understatement I said, "I have to balance the sails first". Jose grinned, and I knew he knew I had a lot of refinements to make with the steering gear. It was crucial to balance the boat almost perfectly, to make any wind vane steering work. Soon I was on my own again, in the distance Cabo Carvoeiro, hollowed out at the foot, bit at the waves and Ilhas Berlenga lay in a grey haze near the horizon. Occasionally a fishing boat roared past and the wash erupted at SP's bow, instantly washing the long winter months off the decks in a cleansing salt scrub. I fiddled with the vane after settling the sails and course along towards Cabo Carvoeiro.

With the mainsail reefed and the tiller lashed, the tiny bias from the wind vane rudder made critical corrections to the boats heading and suddenly I could not believe my eyes as SP held a fair course without my intervention. It really was working. Despite being minute, the corrections were in perfect opposition to the usual impulses which sent the boat off course, waves, gusts, lulls in the wind and my weight shifting around. The wind vane steering countered each minor course deviation in direct relationship to it. When the boat needed to luff into the wind, the vane gave assistance. Then when the boat was on course, the vane was in a middle position. The vane gave a positive bias to either oppose a course deviation, or assist any natural force which corrected the course. I was fascinated by the rudder swimming gently at the stern, which I had built, and which could potentially revolutionize sail cruising into real voyaging.

January 29 2003. In March a big carnival was set to happen. I wandered into one of those shops which sold more or less anything at very cheap prices to be confronted by vast arrays of novelty sparkle wigs - blond princess locks, as well as witches hats with long black hair emerging from underneath, elasticated hooked noses, clowns shoes, pirate masks and hooks and a whole gamut of accessories, such as giant inflatable hammers which squeak, swashbuckling swords, large plastic cleavages bulging over aprons and horrible rubber moulded brains which fitted on the head. March, it seemed, would be wild in Peniche. I wondered if it was linked to similarly animated celebrations which happened in the UK, such as Obby Os day in Padstow, or the Straw Bear parade in Whittlesey. They seemed to be about the exuberance of taking on new forms by wearing masks and costumes, but also they were linked to the turning of the wheel of the year - the Celtic festival of imbulc when the Ewe's milk began to flow with the promise of new born lambs, and in old Scottish lore it was the time when snakes came out of hibernation. For the voyage of SP the meaning was clear - there would soon be geckos

When I had first arrived in Spain I felt it wise to remove the 'tail' from my furry back sack In Bristol and London, this animistic accessory was just a fashion statement, and it said, 'I am a strongly individual person because I go against social codes. I wear a tail in recognition of the animal I am and as a reminder that humanity is not so far away from the animals'. In Spain I had tied it in a knot and tucked it up into the straps. Now I felt it time again to let down my tail, perhaps I was feeling at home in Peniche, or more likely my inner rebellious nature was irrepressible. A couple of local men watched me pass and then one burst out laughing as he saw the black furry tail jiggling along behind me. I thought how most Penicheans would find animal parts appearing on people quite shocking and taboo. In numerous folk tales the gateway between the animal and the human worlds is transgressed, such as Little Red Riding Hood, in which a wolf dresses as a grandma in order to trick the little girl into being eaten. I was certain similar story lines existed in Portugal so my tail was a bit attention seeking and so an impediment, however, I was confident enough to carry my tail with enough irony to get away with it. Maybe I liked having a target at which laughter could be aimed, so while my tail was grabbing all the attention, I was not. My tail was a fly paper, upon which the annoying flies of unwanted attention could get stuck. The tail came with a black, furry, back sack I was given as a present years ago. Since then I had made a replacement after the original was ruined in a tumble dryer, turning out like a worn out scouring pad. One day when I visited the Arnolfini modern art gallery in Bristol there was a very similar back sack with a tail attached in the very same manner, as a part of an exhibition of a New York artist and as I browsed the exhibits with my tail in its usual place, I was asked by the gallery assistant, "Are you the artist?" I should have replied, "No, but I have a tail to tell too". The question was a vindication of my ways. I have often wondered why the idea of wearing a tail was not widely used. Tails are fun, they can be playfully tugged and when I was in a good mood my bouncy swinging walk made the tail wiggle happily from side to side.

I decided to sort out the engine after it had lightly seized twice and was low in power when I came back from testing the wind vane. After doing some sincere enquiries a proper marine mechanic arrived and took off the cylinder head. It had very poor compression. The cylinder head gasket had signs of leaking, in the form of black marks across the compression surface. The valves needed grinding and a replacement head gasket set fitting. The rings needed replacing too. All this would cost me dearly, but the engine had given many hours of reliable service and generated power for lights, navigation equipment, radio, auto pilot and depth sounder, so it was a central energy source of the vessel. I knew of large sailing boats which sailed without an engine anywhere on the boat, but to do so was a decision arrived at through a strongly held belief in ones ability to sail out of any situation. Or, more to the point, a belief one would never sail into a situation and then be unable to sail away from it. To my mind it was dangerous to be at anchor without a power source to get away from the shore if there was either too much wind or more likely no wind to sail at all.

January 31 2003. I was stuck, at least for a few more weeks, having enrolled a professional diesel mechanic to sort the Volvo engine out. As was often the case after prevaricating over engine servicing due to fear of the cost, on dismantling the cylinder head the condition of the engine was close to a serious breakdown. The valves needed replacing, the head gasket had been breached and the piston appeared to have too much play in the cylinder. After the firm were unable to obtain a head gasket set I found a British company who stocked them. When Volvo ended the production of MD1 parts due to the age of the engine, Keyparts purchased the machine tools which were then used to create a stock of parts until the tools were worn out and scrapped. Thus there were a finite number of head gaskets left and I did not know how many, however, at £45 a set I had not invested in a spare. I wondered how many gaskets would be the ideal number to keep for the duration of my use of this engine. It depended on many other factors, for instance if I was offered a substantial advance on publishing the Voyage of Storm Petrel it would be possible to buy a new engine. A couple of spare gasket sets would probably be most useful but that £90 was money I needed to spend on the current repair work rather than future spares. I fell back on the usual faith in things working out.

A devilish wind ripped at the harbour waters, splashing so many waves against the stern of the boat next door that a smothering of salt over SP's cockpit area had accumulated. It was this particular wind direction which brought the splashing and salt was bothersome because everything remained damp. On warm days everything felt nice and dry, until in the evening when moisture content in the air increased and salt ridden materials absorbed it to become severely damp. Despite lovely warm sunshine a beastly north-east wind screamed in the rigging of the boats and folded back the ears of sandy coloured Peniche free dogs.

The 'Cascais line' was a term for the affluence which existed on a geographical line from Cascais to Lisbon. For example Estoril was a resort where sumptuous hotels retained the luxury and style of the nineteen thirties. I also knew the Cascais Line would lack the simple Peniche services of honest, reasonably priced engineers and suppliers.

I went into a fairly small café with stark, thin, furniture which scraped and echoed on the plain tiled floor. The ceiling was freshly painted deep white, embedded with numerous circular light fittings and a spiral flecked motif was vaguely reminiscent of revolving ceiling fans, which were in fact displaced by 'Sony' extractor fans. A substantial, rectangular, stepped section ceiling moulding followed the line of the counter which had a long bar and a prominent ninety degree curve led to a short confectionery display cabinet. The digital till rested upon the turn of the bar, next to a walk-through. Sixty or seventy spirit bottles on staggered glass shelves were cleanly set against a mirror wall. The overall style was brittle and sharp lined. At first I thought it was an immaculately preserved nineteen forties bar, but I soon realized it was all modern, maybe less than two years old. What had me fooled was the absence of the nostalgic clutter which theme bars have, such as posters with black and white prints of the Empire State building or perhaps the Titanic. So the absence of pretence had me thinking it might be genuine. A second bar at the rear of the café was dark and unused, with a jug of red flowers placed mid counter and giving the message, *'CLOSED'*. A white upvc door stood shut and I imagined a curly brown dog and a senior family member sleeping somewhere beyond it. At the front of the café a black television on a wall bracket occupied the corner near the entrance doorway. Underneath the television was a cigarette machine. Next to this an ice cream freezer, topped by a board advertising brand ices using the same names I knew from the UK - Magnum, Bolero, Cornetto. The board was askew and upside down for winter.

February 2 2003. The town square was busy with Sunday leisure seekers, the sun strong so that inside an enclosed glass sided café terrace I was overheating, but enjoying the warm feeling. A bunch of youths posed on mountain bikes, one was wearing a peculiar looking hip-hop uniform, with baby blue shorts and matching baseball cap. He performed jumps on a macho highly sprung mountain bike and whistled at friends in passing cars. The youths were moody looking, with bottom lips drooping in the sunshine, like a row of wilting leaks.

I found out the new hand-held gps, Garmin Gecko II, had a game on it, called 'Locate the gecko'. Marketing would never come more fairly and squarely aimed at the jaw of the consumer than the Garmin Gecko did to myself at the time. Despite this I did not buy a Garmin Gecko because it lacked what I needed to go sailing with.

A small shop tucked away in the criss-cross streets of Peniche was called Bizarre Bazaar and sold essential oils, deliciously coloured clothing and accessories with pretty designs, incense, silver lizard earrings and many other small things. I found a couple of shoulder bags for my nieces, Becky and Camilla. I liked to have essential oils on the boat to scent the furnishings and sweeten any damp corners, usually lavender. I found burning incense aggravating to my throat, whereas a drop of oil on a sun warmed wooden floor plank made a pure aroma and I often dabbed a drop of lavender oil onto the tip of the tail on my backpack. I was attracted back to the shop again to look at a pair of silver lizard earrings with long tails curling at the tips. When I bought them for myself I learned the word for lizard in Portuguese was 'legato', not 'serao' as I had imagined for some reason. I think one of the reasons there were so few lizards occupying the sunny walls of Peniche was the number of cats relentlessly stalking the gardens and borders between houses. Maybe in the summer heat the lizards would be energized enough to escape the sun lazy cats. I expected to see many more lizards in the coming months.

I began to tidy the fore-peak, a horribly cramped space under the foredeck, which was meant to be a double berth but with a height of twenty inches was really only practical for use as storage. I untied the restraining ropes of two items which had been unused since leaving Bristol - the varnished folding cabin table and a red, fretless bass guitar. I set the table up between the mast support pillars and went about cleaning and lubricating the bass guitar. Later I connected the bass to my laptop and played along with the radio, which was great fun. I wanted a bass amplifier and proper speakers but there were limits in an eight metre sailing boat. Perhaps I could cram in a tiny practice amplifier although a sturdy pair of BBC monitor headphones sounded fine. I constructed an abstract impressionist sound-scape depicting Peniche harbour in winter which could be described as something like the sound of a shipwreck caught in an undersea current dragging slowly across the ocean floor. I loved the idea of producing a CD of aural responses to the voyage.

February 8 2003. Winter was a long stretch of mostly nothing broken occasionally by the booming sound of Atlantic swells, the fire station siren broadcasting dinner time and a free dog barking at the feral cats lolling amongst the retired fishermen. The long weeks dragged and tumbled by and the time felt a little lonely. A couple on holiday from the UK quizzed me about the cruising area. They owned a seventeen metre motor vessel, which had been originally built in the Netherlands, for smuggling. To my mind seventeen metres would be as unhandy as a ship. As we talked they revealed they had sailed a Folkboat derivative, called a 'Folksong' and SP was a 'Folkdancer', also a Folkboat derivative. They had formidable experience, having taken another sailing yacht, a 'Holman and Pye' 34 footer, through the Danube river into the Black Sea, starting out in the North Sea. They told me I would not find a good attitude in southern Spanish marinas which they said were unfriendly, unhelpful and only interested in charging money to rich yachts. When I said I like the idea of spending next winter in the Canary Islands, of course there too was nothing but problems, "There is nowhere really secure to shelter in all weather throughout the whole island group," they warned and I suddenly felt like the whole Atlantic was made up of nothing but rip off marinas and unsheltered anchorages, "You'll be all right if you have a really good anchor", they reassured me in the negative. I was poised with a bowl of washing up which needed the suds rinsing off as we chatted. I was sure I had seen pictures of the couple in articles in Practical Boat Owner magazine. They were in a hurry to travel southwards to meet up with many friends on cruising boats there and so I missed an opportunity to secure my writing career by befriending published sailors.

A catamaran arrived during the night. These boats are often populated by avid men who eye a single, tall, blond, sailor through salt cracked spectacles and I felt self-conscious walking by, eating my morning banana, knowing the crew would be hoping I might be that absolute perfection of a woman sailor - perfectly sea kindly - who can rustle up a warming stew from the galley in a gale of wind at night - and be a vivacious sea going maiden, who keeps stowed in a dry locker, a pair of red high heels which are bought out during drinking sessions for exotic dancing shows. In contrast I walked past in worn out suede boots and a half eaten banana flopping around in my hand. One of the avid types was on deck wearing a strong red sailing jacket and I said through a mouthful of banana, "Bonjour!" but it was a defensive comment and the man ignored me.

I went to meet Luis Chagas, the mechanic, who told me my outboard motor was fixed. I said I would drop by his workshop on 'Segunda Feira', (the second day of the week - Monday) and he complemented me on my Portuguese. Now feeling a part of the Penichean Saturday morning flow I walked into the town centre laughing at a free dog as it chased a passing skateboarder down the street. A number of emails arrived from cruising sailors I'd met the year before, several of whom had gone transatlantic after visiting the Canary Islands. One in particular, Jean-Charles, had impressed me with the poetry of his accounts which at first I had difficulty in getting translated. Then I realized the writings consisted of short metaphorical sentences and I started to read Jean-Charles more intuitively and with it came a strong affection for this solo sailing adventurer. He wrote, after crossing the Atlantic ocean, *'Because it is not space which we cross, it is time; the sea is without place'*. About his arrival at Bridgetown, Barbados, he wrote, *'Arrival was beautiful. The island is beautiful'*. He was an architect and we'd met in Nazare and then again in Peniche. He carried on to Morocco to meet friends he had formed in architectural college.

Certain people meet who could so easily have missed each other, yet some people, met only briefly and by chance, continue to twinkle long after they are gone. The catamaran 'Peace Four' were by now in Antigua, with a very happy Ann and Nev aboard. Peace Four had arrived at Bristol Marina the previous year as a half built brand new boat. Now Ann and Nev had realized their dream of sailing across the Atlantic again. They had crossed twice before together and Ann had even sailed from New York to Ireland as a single hander. At the time of Peace Four's launch and maiden voyage I had SP half way prepared for a voyage but I was as incapable of breaking free as all the other 'I'll sail away one day' live-aboards in the marina. Ann and Nev looked at my boat and told me she could seriously be sailed across an ocean which inspired me to do most of the modifications they suggested to the boat.

Under their watchful eye I'd rebuilt the mast support structure, altered the cockpit sole to keep water out more effectively, lightened the forward and aft ends by re-stowing equipment towards the middle and made a sheet to tiller steering system. At the same time I tackled a whole list of small but crucial alterations which held stuff in place and produced a voyaging boat out of a neglected scruff. The period leading up to departure was a spiral of dreaming and audacious planning, filled with hopes and fears about sailing to Spain. I thought I knew myself well enough to know I would not have the courage to sail across the Bay of Biscay.

I had wished to go sailing to Spain for a decade and even when I'd sailed to Cornwall in 1995 it was to bring that dream closer. My previous boat, 'Juggler' was not ideal for ocean voyaging and it would be 5 years before I sailed out of Bristol harbour at the beginning of the voyage of SP. Prior to leaving it was necessary to free myself of my long term marina lifestyle and the clutter of everyday objects - a little Aladdin's shoe oil lamp, a brass dolphin and a brass unicorn had to go and it was at this point I met a new idea. This was to place objects into a plastic storage jar with a tight screw lid and bury them somewhere where I could retrieve them should I wish. I was interested in the idea as a concept, as well as a practical way to lighten the load in the boat without burdening friends and relatives. I felt a sense of fascination in hiding personal effects in public land. In a sense I would be occupying a small part of the land - making use of it in a way I had never thought possible. The lamp, dolphin and unicorn were buried in a plastic jar in a place I could go back to, but that was far away in time and distance by now.

A shop in Peniche had a muddled collection of ornaments and tableware. I was looking for a cheap stainless steel pot to use as a cap on the chimney of the wood stove when at sea. A range of paraffin burning lamps looked really delightful and one was almost identical to my buried one, a sort of ornamental lamp resurrection. The attractive lamps had practical, wide wicks. Usually decorative lamps are manufactured dumb, for use with electric bulbs, or with a candle holder inside. I was really pleased to find these fully functional and enchanting lamps so I bought one for a very reasonable 7.5 Euros. It had an interestingly shaped glass chimney with a mushroom shaped bulb narrowing into a cylindrical chimney. The base was an ink blue glass bowl with deep criss-cross mouldings. It held a pint of paraffin which would give several evenings of light. The shopkeeper took his time, padding the lamp in a modified cardboard box which he then covered with gift wrapping and whistled softly as he did so. One of the other lamps was specially charming. It was tall, slim and had a flared glass base which was painted intricately in rich colours. The slender glass chimney continued the design and colour scheme. It would look gorgeous with a flame shining through its yellow and deep green glass. However it was too tall for the boat and would not give much useful light due to the dark coloured glass. What a pleasurable business it could be to buy cheap, but authentic paraffin lamps, made in Portugal, paint them in beautiful colours and sell them in the UK. They would perhaps sell for thirty pounds on a market stall, or higher, at Portobello Road market in London.

My father used various paraffin burning devices, auxiliary paraffin heaters and hurricane lamps. Family holidays in a tent involved a malfunctioning primus stove and dad jousting with a wildly hissing pressurised paraffin stove, his shadow projected onto the walls of the tent by the flames leaping to the roof from the primus. When we all sat down again on precariously balanced little wooden fold up chairs around the primus stove which, by now, was hissing with a hot blue flame, the sound of head meeting hurricane lamp grazed everyone's nerves again. The person who had caught a blow on the hanging lamp would swear angrily at it, closely followed by dad complaining, 'Mind my lamp', to which the cursing reply would be, 'Sod the blacking lamp, what about my 'ead!'

Camping always seemed tinged with misery, beset by rain and squabbling and it was only 'other people' who were stupid enough to get swept away by flash floods or who got their cars stuck in the mud as they tried to leave the sodden field, but I began to truly enjoy camping when we went far enough south and suddenly one day there were lizards all over the place. After this point I became constantly and deeply happy. I would go crashing through whatever undergrowth and scrub I could get into, looking for geckos It was Lake Como, in Italy where I was first told there were loads of lizards all over the walls in the town. I had been swimming and playing near the tent, unaware of being surrounded by reptiles. A photograph was taken of me the moment I was told the news and dripping with water having just come out of the lake, on my wet hair a bush hat, also dripping wet and under this my face - joyous. That bush hat was to capture dozens of wall lizards, a scorpion, a strange mole cricket and flying locusts, nearly as big as sparrows. In my early teens I kept several vivariums with lizards and snakes in. One was stocked with little baby wall lizards, caught in that bush hat in Italy.

After I started keeping and breeding ferrets life became more complicated. Lizards were delicate, vulnerable to crushing injuries, viruses, unsuitable diets and temperature changes. They tended to die off. Ferrets, on the other hand, tended to increase in numbers. At the height of my ferret keeping they would flow out of the cage door, like water and be everywhere, up yer jumper, down yer trousers and in yer shoes, all at once. The smell of ferrets then was a lot worse than paraffin lamps so I suppose I was lucky to have carried the flame of paraffin lamps into the present rather than ferret keeping. The new lamp I chose had pride of place upon the varnished cabin table and I made a metal bracket to secure it at sea and support it when the table was stowed.

On a particularly warm day I sat for two hours near the slipway, just looking at the harbour, with a fresh loaf of bread. I plucked white handfuls and shared with the gulls and Princess, the thin beige free dog and wrote a long poem. Princess was being ravished by a dandy looking brown and white Dalmatian, a young male. Dogs in cars, on leads, or in yards were vicious and threatening. Those loose in the streets were friendly and harmless to people, seeming to know exactly where they stood in relation to humans. I watched a dog chasing cars and noticed how socialized it was apart from the crazy behaviour. On its way back to the taxi rank, it let one or two cars pass unhindered and was perfectly tame towards children and pedestrians on the pavement. Then I would hear it barking and the sound of its claws on the cobbled pathway as it snapped and barked alongside another passing car.

(Impressions) *Sitting in the Sun with Bread so Fresh I Bit my Thumb*
  The whispering sea. Quiet now at low tide. A rock with pigeons feeding. Enclosing the reef. Exposing the reef. Not crashing as usual. Boats all stretched out. To the horizon. None close to the launching slip. Crescent day moon leaps. Low, blue, inshore hills. A butterfly heads offshore. Car park on the mohle. A quarter empty. Boats cross the slipping water. Three swirling white gulls. Distance. Coloured in sun bleached postcards. Curled forwards. Sweeping around. A display of beach. A white line. The shallow ocean. Losing identity. Drifts inland as blue haze. Squinting in bright light. This is what I came for. Warm as toast. One swell crosses the harbour mouth. A slurping tongue of Lapis Lazuli. One this big must have come from as far away as distant friends. Only time between the eye which saw it. The storm which sent it. The beach which broke its spell. The lifeboat is resting. The crew are asleep or distracted. There are bells, pagers, buzzers, mobiles and telephones. To wake the whole lot up.
  An old salt asked for money. Sardines as eyes. Migrating eels in his shoes. Bright gulls tails. Winter survived. Cabo Carvoeiro swallowed a ship. Cleaner and better dressed as they perfect flying. Squabbling through longer days. Spring seeps and crawls from the rocks and stones. There are lizards on islands. Women in fuchsia. Cars in silver. Crabs dead in drifts. Dogs on heat. Miles of fish nets in mounds. Recoiled, spread like Nautilus himself. Hauled out of the depths and stranded in the sun. Gulls pick at particles. Left like fragments of stories. Fish tales. Lines. Shore things. Wandering courses. Divers down in wet suits. Beach combers brushing sand from mermaid hair. A digital camcorder takes time to take in the whole of the net. One pixel for every hole. One crab leg for every led wink. One trawl net piled into a hairy mammoth heap. Another spread into a great collapsed whale. Belly sliced open. Coils of floats spread out. Hawsers as long as the surf line takes to walk.
  Snags repaired again and again. A black umbrella blown out while raincoats hunch and stitch. A windy week before a windless weekend. Teak decking around the marina office in the sun. A mother photographs a father and two sons sitting on the mammoth. Not a cloud in the sky. A solitary sailor of a crescent moon will eventually reach the horizon. The Milky Way is hauled onto this quayside. Particles trawled from the depths of space by mammoth and whale. Crab Nebulae glinting. Crushed under the hooves of seahorses. Pisces turned to salt fish. Alkaid, Alioth, Dubhe. Navigational stars in The Plough constellation. Twinkles in the eyes of oysters. A grain of sand. A tear. A pearl. Dying starfish spread-eagle. Dry-spangle. Salt-crack. Polaris: the Northern Star. A submarine. A piece of driftwood. Barked orders, 'Dive!, Dive! Dive!' Thrown for Sirius. A free dog amongst fol-de-rols of netting. Pleiades cluster. Salt crystal. Fish scales. Aurora Borealis. Stinging tentacles. Trailing

all the way back to the harbour. Jellyfish dreamers blowing inland as plastic carrier bags.

February 11 2003. While visiting Cascais I was introduced to a Polish single-hander He was over eighty years old and had sailed alone from Poland down to Portugal in a very poorly maintained and equipped boat of about twenty-four feet in length. Ann of Peace Four was so concerned for his safety that she handed me a large margarine tub filled with assorted shackles, turning blocks, bolts and nuts and with a worried expression said, "Go over and sort that man's boat out, it is falling apart and he intends to go transatlantic!"

I went to the Polish boat and introduced myself to the sailor nonchalantly, trying to shield him from the near panic of those who had become so concerned. He said he had one wish - to sail across the Atlantic. I told him how seriously worried Ann was about the dreadful condition of his boat. I showed him the box of fittings, which was quite heavy, thinking to myself this was weight this little boat really could do without. When I looked over the boat I saw rigging shackles with bent pins, having bent under strain and popped half-way out of the shackle itself. There was a large split in the hull to deck join at the stern and a hole in the bow was big enough to land a tuna fish through. The result of hitting a whale in Biscay and a buoy near to Cascais. The gaps and holes were covered over (read covered not filled) with silicon mastic. He made it clear to me he thought his boat was very strong because it had not been destroyed by the impacts so far. He graphically described how, mid Biscay, when he collided with the whale, he was hurled from the main cabin, into the fore peak. It seemed the more he hit, the more he felt able to do the trip. I sensed he was someone who would be happiest doing as he wished. In fact the trip he had made already was a feat of stamina and integrity.

I also understood he was following a dream at an age at which he was entitled to be philosophically careless about dying. It was wonderful to meet the warm and sprightly fellow. He supported himself by busking with a violin, playing Vivaldi and other classical pieces with feeling. I had seen him playing in Cascais but had not connected the sailor with the busker until I saw his instrument in the cabin of his boat. He left for Madeira the following day, half way through October, 2002 and I hoped what meagre help we gave was useful. I did have the impression he would go as he was regardless of the fussing of other sailors and somehow I sensed he would be happiest left to his own devices. I thought he probably would arrive safely in the Caribbean. Looking back now I would very much like to hear how he got on. I was friendly with a dozen or so cruising boats who were planning to sail transatlantic and had kept in contact with several who had arrived and one which had just left from the island of Gomera in the Canaries (a year later I heard the Polish sailor had spent several months on Gomera and then presumably left for the Caribbean). Most were headed for different islands in the Caribbean according to the plans they had subsequent to arrival there.

Swedes seemed to favour Venezuela and Brazil. The French would go to the French ruled island of Martinique. The Netherlanders would go for the Netherlands Antilles. The Polish sailor did not use email so I lost contact with his voyage.

February 13 2003. At low tide a stinking black river was foul, but gulls continued feeding and paddling around in the mud. I looked down on the boats from the river wall, various small fishing boats, of around twenty feet in length and the viewpoint was high enough to see the hull form of each boat. Peniche boats had? had full forward sections with flared bows. The aft section either a finely constructed canoe stern, meaning it all came to a curvaceous point, or, a transom which was a wine glass shaped flat end to the vessel. Transom sterns could be raked back, which gave the boat a sort of smile. An upright transom made a boat look workmanlike and slightly boxy. A substantial athwartship (across the ship) bench was made of a single slab of wood. In the UK this would be constructed out of plywood. In Peniche plywood was expensive and not easily found.

My search for contraplacado (plywood) had been a trail of doggy, sardine cooking, washing hanging out of windows to dry, sun slanting, canaries trickling songs, scooters pup pup pupping by with carrier bags hanging from the handlebars, black shawled women scuffling along in slip-on shoes with their heels protruding over the back of the sole. Eventually I got to know where to get almost anything useful and my mind boggled at what I could now build if I wished. But now the sun was stronger, Peniche carnival was just around the corner, lizards across the land were stirring in their deep rock crevices with the knowledge of spring and I would soon be moving on to somewhere new.

Scrapped vessels lay in lines of rotting timber and rusted out ferrous steel fittings, by the stinking black river. These boats were several decades old with not a stainless bolt, screw, hatch cover or guardrail to be seen on them. In contrast, during the last decade stainless steel had become the material for almost every part of the working boats. The larger commercial fishing boats had whole superstructures in 'inox' - stainless steel. It was untreated, just briskly polished with a grinder and left bare, startlingly functional. The marine mechanic, Chagas, explained to me how it was cheaper to make everything in inox than to endlessly paint and repair steel and wood. One of the uses of inox was for large spidery anchors. They were likely an effective shape for local waters, with long curved prongs to penetrate thick kelp or hook into a rocky seabed. In the UK I found any mention of stainless steel brought an intake of breath from engineers and suppliers. It was the realm of marine hardware and considered in general to be ten times the cost of having things made in ferrous steel. This was frustrating during the preparation of SP until I found a scrap yard specialising in non-ferrous materials (Habgoods). I also found a supplier of new stainless steel in bar, rod, tube and sheet which was the turning point in my fitting out and solved a difficult problem of how to lead a wood stove chimney through the deck in a way which could also take the impact of an ocean wave on the deck.

Avon Stainless Installation Ltd in Keynsham was a bit of a trek on a push bike especially on the way home with inox threaded rods, tubing and sheeting under my arm. I just had to have stainless steel fittings - visiting yachts would turn up in Bristol Marina from far off, exotic, countries over deep lapis lazuli oceans breathing the eternal rhythm of life power through endless hot days with enchanted fish doing synchronised kissing on the water's surface. An abundance of stainless steel fabrications was a notable feature of these ocean voyagers - wind vane self-steering, made from nothing but inox and beefed up deck fittings tailor-made in pure polished stainless steel. How could such stainless riches be found, where in the world did inox, like silver scrumping apples, hang on trees? Where was it to be seen glinting on the beach like the sweaty suits of rehearsing astronauts? Was there a far distant land in which inox would run in rivers along the gutter like mercury? Fittings made of stainless steel work at sea and have immense strength while remaining almost completely unstained by corrosion. The home made and stainless steel bracketed self-steering device was the most visible innovation to have come out of my stay in Peniche. Now SP was touched by the bright evidence of self-made and creative projects which turned her from a sailing boat into a voyaging yacht and one day SP will sail into Bristol having become one of those voyagers from far away lands with her little touches of added strength and effectiveness, made in stainless steel.

I made a seat positioned under the spray hood. In the companionway three hatch boards slid into the main cabin entrance, a most protected place which allowed forward visibility while enabling access to the sink inside the cabin and the engine throttle and gear lever in the cockpit. Many hours sitting there on long night sails with the engine running gave a reassuring warmth and my head and arms rested on the sliding hatch which closed horizontally over the aperture. With the hatch slid back to my chest my body was mostly inside the warmth of the cabin, while my head was out in the fresh cold air keeping alert. The spray hood kept wind from my face and it was a most pleasant place to experience a night at sea. I had collected materials to build the seat in Bristol, but the design would not settle in my mind and I put up sitting on a folded blanket. With the availability of materials in Peniche I was able to design my own along functional lines and it came so simply and even elegantly - two stainless steel angle pieces bolted either side of the lower hatch board with the seat bolted on top - no need for hardwood knees, glued and pinned - no varnished strong backs or hidden screws to work loose with the perpetual grabbing and shoving of the sea on the boat. This was my own perception of DIY - stainless bolts and angle will not wear out or break. The strength to weight ratio was so high, I was sure my inox bolt and braces approach was lighter than traditional wood, screw and glue methods.

February 14 2003. Back in the Clube Naval de Peniche, using their workshop facilities, I finished the seat for the companionway. I also coated four spare wind vane blades with Burgess wood sealer. I did not need so many spares, but I wanted to use up some of the contraplacado (plywood) I had left over from the wind steering rudder. I made them in two sizes, for light winds and for stronger winds. I enjoyed the process of producing perfectly rounded ends using simple geometry and a compass. Then I took a little time to saw, rasp and finally, sand, the rounds into being. It was satisfying to be able to make things fairly well and I was very grateful to the Clube Naval for offering the workshop. I was as happy as a canary in the sun to be making something again.

The French boat, Karak left and I gazed out on a gecko-less sea. Those sailors were inspiring voyagers and I recalled a conversation with George on his way back from the covered market clutching a plastic bag full of rolls. He shook my hand firmly and then held up his rolls. I exclaimed, "Aha, du pain," (Aha, bread), George, eyes smiling, replied,

"Mais oui," (But yes) and feeling really competent in speaking French I plunged into the shallow pool of my knowledge and said, "Pour mangé avec du buerre et la confiture?" (To eat with butter and jam). George, his beard looking like a tide rip over the shoal of his chin said, "Certainement, est le miel," (Certainly, and honey). I began to wonder if I was delaying George and his freshly baked rolls were going cold, so I said a conclusive, "Bien," (Good) but George added, "Ou avec des oranges," (Or with oranges). I was confused by this development in our brief chat and by the idea of eating bread with oranges so I tried to resolve it by saying, "Ah oui? Du pain, avec des oranges?" (I see, bread, with oranges?). A grey moustache poured around his mouth in two curling eddies and George said, "Mais oui biensure," (But yes certainly) and failing to mix together the taste of oranges and bread in my imagination, I fell back on table manners, saying, "Bon appetit," and George held up his bag of rolls, twinkled his eyes at me and left with, "A beintot" (Seeya).

I walked on trying to imagine eating bread with oranges and slowly my mind found the concept I needed - marmalade. I realized marmalade is oranges eaten with bread. I had been away from the UK for 6 months and somehow the idea of marmalade had been forgotten.

George dressed in well worn pullovers and plain slacks whether at sea or in port. He moved energetically and lightly, with a stance I had noted in other long distance cruising folk. He looked balanced on his feet with arms slightly apart and large open hands. The fingers were permanently swollen into extra strength and his stance was one of readiness to catch hold of a swinging boom or a person in the midst of a fall. Helene was feminine with thick, well kept hair and glasses. She was a little smarter than George. There was colour in her clothing - sunset reds, storm cloud mauves, sea greens and on cold windy days they both wore fetching red bobble hats. The majority of the time they remained inside the boat with the main hatch slid closed, but also took walks along the seafront or in woods, and Helene invariably returned with posies of local flowers. They were headed for Brittany in France, where they were going to sell Karak, the boat they had had built over thirty years ago.

There they planned to retire from long distance cruising. George had expressed interest in a small wooden sailing dinghy which was out in the harbour and told me they would continue to sail small boats locally in France. So, with a whole new sailing career ahead of them they left Peniche with no 'goodbyes' or hooters hooting, they simply put to sea as they so often had. Such quiet ways had taken them around the world, several Atlantic crossings, and Japan, a rare cruising destination due to the year round occurrence of storms. When people set out on a big journey it was always slightly alarming if a conspicuous 'leaving do' was held. Confident declarations of future intentions seemed to be an omen of themselves and the most successful voyagers were somehow always the ones who slipped away unceremoniously. Peace Four had a public leaving date, but, Ann and Nev told me they were going to sail out of Bristol a couple of days prior to that.

February 17 2003. There were two types of galao, the coffee which came in a long glass with a spoon with an equally long handle resting in it. The 'direto' has a shot of espresso, filled up with milk and heated using a steam nozzle. The 'normal' often came from an insulated jug and was weaker than the direto, so making a pleasant drink for people who feel unhappy after drinking strong coffee. 'Normal' closely resembled the 'milky coffees' I was plied with as a child, by my Mum who hoped the milk would strengthen my growing bones.

The fishing port was separated from the leisure marina and public slipway by security fences and a gatehouse with a security guard. The fence had innumerable holes which had evolved, like animal paths, as a result of the flow of people into and out of the commercial harbour area. The fishing industry was labour intensive, with twenty five or thirty men aboard a medium sized trawler of twenty metres length. Auxiliary tenders with Volvo diesel engines rode piggyback, being winched up behind at a steep angle even as the main vessel accelerated away from the quay, with one or two crew still aboard. The tenders had flat bottoms, known as 'chata', with substantial bilge runners to protect the hull. Penimar was one of the main engineering works for the Peniche fishing boats. There I saw one of the auxiliary tenders being fitted with massive bilge runners made solely from stainless steel. The tenders had two functions. One, they carried crew members between the quay and the boat in correspondence with the lunchtime siren from the fire station. Two, the tender towed the end of a large net in a wide circle around a shoal of fish before it was winched aboard the trawler.

The fishing area was mostly just 4 to 5 miles from the harbour. As the net was drawn up into the fishing boat, closing like a purse bag, a cone shaped net of around two metres in length and with a circular hooped opening, a 'chalavar', was used to scoop up sardines. The tenders were called 'traineira' and a sardine like fish also had the name 'traineira'. The catch was loaded into the hold and kept alive in boxes containing seawater for three or four hours before returning. The returning trawlers kicked up a horrendous wash, rushing in to offload the catch. The noise of air-cooled single cylinder diesel engines crackled across the harbour as the cargo was disembarked.

During wintertime the boats went out once per day, leaving around 6.30pm and returning at around 9.30pm. During summertime, when the weather was calmer, they did two trips per day, adding a 4am shift which returned at around 8am. The boats were traditionally made in wood and some were still being built on the north beach. For a while boats were produced in steel but glass reinforced plastic was gradually dominating the industry.

Old fishermen were familiar with the rich taste of gull eggs gathered from the cliffs. In modern Portugal, herring gulls were protected and egg gathering prohibited, but in contrast there was an attempt by the Portuguese government to reduce the population of herring gulls. The choice of control was poisoned bread and butter sandwiches which were fairly successful on the nature reserve of Ilhas de Berlenga, where rarer species of birds, reptiles and animals were being overrun by shrieking gulls. The method of destroying gulls was questionable on environmental grounds, as the poison was bound to enter the food chain, pollute the beaches with poison-ridden gull carcasses.

The added waste of plastic bags used to collect carcasses also polluted the islands and some inevitably ended up blowing free to be swallowed by dolphins who mistook them for jellyfish and then suffocated. I was told gulls' eggs tasted delicious. It would seem to be natural and logical way to control the population by allowing people to gather eggs and eat them. There would always be inaccessible cliffs and hidden rooftops where the gulls could nest successfully. It would seem a better solution than adding poison to the equation.

The canary sings because she is happy - the canary is happy because she sings - one of the keys to happiness is living life simply. A man sat watching the centre of Peniche, his bicycle stood on its stand in front of him, a shiny new reproduction classic cycle with bright chromed fittings, a chain guard, dynamo set, and mudguards. On the back mudguard was a number plate, 1-PNI 77-99. There was a similar man in Bristol who would always greet me with an enthusiastic smile and chat. If it was raining he would shelter until it stopped, wishing never to get his bike dirty. He would often cycle long distances, sometimes before midday he would be returning from a ride of 25 miles. He knew people on several of the boats along the harbour and I would most often see him aboard a converted trawler or in the 'Buttery' tea kiosk. The Peniche cyclist looked similar in the way he joined in with the social milieu, but kept himself from slumping into the scene as many of the other retired men did. The Bristolian cyclist seemed as happy as anyone I had ever met. I think as long as he had his bike, his health and the friends spread about the routes he took every day, he would remain so.

There was much to be said for being a little single-minded to achieve contentment and I sensed it was those people who were able to gain a small niche based upon simple requirements, such as an immaculately kept bicycle and a constantly refreshed social network, were closest to real happiness. Another Bristol man, also a cyclist, seemed to possess a similar simplicity in his contentment. I would often see him sitting by the harbour with a flask of coffee, enjoying the day. He was a 'whistler' and quite proud of his particular ability in it and he told me how he whistled himself into a state of melodic happiness and how he really considered himself to be a good whistler. Apparently his neighbours were driven mad by his whistling and he had even been threatened violence. His face was interesting with the look of a pale-skinned native American, he wore his silver hair long and when he spoke about 'life' it was very intense and drawn out. One day he appeared with a small pair of binoculars he'd bought from a charity shop. He wanted to discuss them and peer at the harbour through them, for what seemed like an uncomfortably extended period of time. I placed him at arms length after he asked me to sleep with him.

I confess to being a 'whistler' too and the idea of a relationship between two whistlers would be bound to failure. In the Clube Naval de Peniche was another 'whistler' who was often busy around the workshop. As a hobby he made artistic and stylized boat pictures out of sawn woods of contrasting tones and textures. When I was engaged in a project I often had a tune on my mind which surfaced in bouts of whistling. One day he entered the workshop with a whistle at the same moment as I let fly a lilting refrain of my own. We looked at each other with a strange recognition, two canaries in the same cage and I was sure he was thinking something like, 'Gosh, the English whistle just like us Portuguese do'.

Another Peniche person always greeted me with a wide smile and a wave. He looked to be aged around seventy and would always gesture at the sky. If it was going to rain he would say, "Chuva" (rain) and point to clouds approaching from far off in the west. If it was not going to rain he would simply wave a hand at the sky and beam like a sunflower at me. He lived in a pastel yellow villa which was entirely shuttered and had smart concrete steps leading up to a balcony, from where he often called out to me in greeting. The small exchange was a daily vitamin pill which gave me an extra smile most mornings. I always walked away from this encounter with a feeling of wonder at how some people seem to have the ability to be just happy. Plenty of other men in Peniche looked tired and worn out by life, sat on public benches, old retired fishermen. The difference was a real lesson. I asked myself whether I would be diminished in my spirit in old age, or someone who sparkles warmly into the daily life of others, young and old.

As a particularly scruffy Peniche man ambled by on one of my walks in search of contraplacado, a string as a belt and a grubby old beret over a stubbly chin on a grumbling old face, I said, "Bom dia!" and his whole face mobilized into a big smile as he replied, "Bom dia!" I was pleased to have said good day to him because it brought out a most friendly expression on a growl of a face.

March 2 2003. On the first of three days of Carnival I walked into the town centre to have a look at Peniche in high spirits. A blond wigged, mini-skirted man sauntered by, the first of many transvestites. Next a black man wearing a leather mini-skirt and glossy make-up strolled by elegantly. I thought he looked very sexy. I chose a seat with a view of the street in the enclosed terrace of the pastelaria 'Oceano' and relaxed with a galao coffee and an errufada. A small girl came in with perhaps her mother, the girl wore a long red-checked skirt with a lace head-scarf and looked very sweet as the archetypal country maiden. A crowd of lads went by dressed as fishermen, with crab pots swinging from lines around their necks, flat caps and old yellow or green oil-skin Salopettes. They swigged out of beer bottles and were rowdy for 11am pushing each other about playfully and leaving beer bottles in inappropriate places. A small girl arrived in a white tressled dress draping around her to the floor, with a silver conical fairy tale princess hat with a swathe of pink material trailing from the point. A boy in a batman suit sat driving a red fun ride jeep, which had not been activated by a coin so was not moving. A little girl dressed in a milkmaid outfit with a long dress in a rural check, beckoned him and they ran away together. A small, olive-skinned boy offered me a tired looking box of Elastoplast and I understood he wanted me to buy it. I said no thank you into his sad little eyes and he skimmed around the rest of the café Oceano terrace and sold nothing. Outside the guy in blond wig and short skirt wandered about looking for his mates who had left the Pastelaria Presidente. Beer bottled men stumbled by stuffing bolos into their lipstick smeared mouths, making drunken sounds.

The blond-wigged transvestite went to the park across the road, still looking around for his crowd, looking furtively about, like a nervous hooker, under the palm trees, near the public toilets, eyeing the cover afforded by thick bushes and the thinning out of people. A float drove by pulled by a flat bed Nissan. It had a central palm tree over an umbrella terrace where several people sat on chairs taking refreshments. A band played oom-pah on the rear, with silver plated brass instruments rather similar to my own Ramponi silver plate C-melody soprano saxophone.

The sun had broken through a four day cloud bank and I felt excited that the month of March had begun. A sky blue luxury coach piled high with people, had rear view mirrors which are set like the feelers of ants. It was a Wednesday and the final carnival procession had ended the previous afternoon. The sun had shone strongly and the procession was really fun. There were about thirty floats accompanied by costumed dancers in themes, such as a protest against the Prestige oil hazard. The troupe wore yellow oil-skins painted with black oil marks, like black and yellow cows. The float itself was a van made up as an oil tanker. On the whole though, men were in drag, with hairy and muscular legs clearly maintaining a masculine presence beneath their costumes. The oom-pah band with silver plate instruments mimed to Latin style music. They looked very much like a real band as individuals took sparkling solos. Half of them wore a band uniform and half were in drag. The café terrace connected to the double trailer of this band was populated by male transvestites serenely sipping cocktails. One of the persons was of a great age and I found out this particular float had been going for thirty years.

After the final day of carnival I expected everything to have died down, but in the centre of Peniche was a crowd who were still drunk from the day before, obviously having stayed up all night. One of them was banging beer bottles together and he made me feel a little threatened, but they were good mannered after all. The beer bottle banger and two friends came over to me and introduced themselves. The leader of the oom-pah band float appeared in the café doorway blowing a party squeaker. His eyes were puffy from being up all night and he looked wrecked. I remembered his face clearly from the parade the day before as he walked in front of the band float with mock ceremony and importance. The crowd of friends who had said hello to me gestured at me and told the band leader to say hello to me. He chose to wobble away down the street blowing his party squeaker, obviously heading for his bed. It was eleven am.

Yesterday while crowds gathered and filled the seafront restaurants in carnival mood I did several jobs on the boat. I removed the self-steering rudder which was completely covered in long hairy marine growth. After scrubbing and hosing it clean I left it to dry in the sun. Later I gave it two coats of anti-fouling. When it was dry I re-bolted it to the stern and felt pleased to have solved the fouling problem, which in just one month had made the rudder useless. Next I took the spare anchor chain and warp (rope) from the forward bilge and cleaned it. After the diesel spill in the bilge I decided to find somewhere else to stow it. I had never had to use it so far, but if I ever did it would need to be accessible and not coated in sick making diesel. I found an interesting stowage space for it next to the oven by drilling a hole in a blank face of plywood to see what was behind. This revealed a tall thin space about two feet, by two feet by five inches wide and dry, unlike the damp sludgy bilge.

March 9 2003. Tourists began to appear in the pastelarias. After the quiet of January and February they stood out, doing strange things like buying ice creams. They jumped out of my way with exaggerated politeness saying, "Pardon, oh pardon, pardonnez!" as they walked away licking at the ices before they melted in the hot sun. I heard myself ordering in Portuguese and realized I had spoken quite competently, if only to ask for a coffee, but casually and decisively. Tourists usually spoke Portuguese so hesitantly the sentence would be like this, "Uh, hello, I mean, oh, erm, por favor. Oh dear that's Spanish, is it faz favor? Urm, faz favor une caffee with, avec, con MILK, and, um, you want sugar don't you, yes, ci, um, two, deux, dos, coffees, with , one with et one without, yes, coffee, yes, milk, urm sugar, sucre?"

I had on my painting clothes - sleeves rolled up with little flecks of white paint all over my arms, my face spotted with paint and I smelt of turpentine. The holiday makers were spotlessly clean and had no smell to their light pastel coloured clothes - wishy washy yellows, baby blues and innocent whites - a uniform of leisure, a coat to protect against foreign things. The over-politeness of tourists appeared condescending and they cleared away from the pastelaria as if to say we'll just get out of your way, we only want ice creams, we will soon be far away. Some Portuguese people think the British are delightfully polite and imagine one day they too will wear pastel, clean pressed clothes, buy ice creams and smile a lot.

Some cruising yacht people seem to be almost the same as regular tourists. Instead of daring to relax and disappoint a few local expectations they put up a ridiculous shield of pleasantry. A sort of universal non stick personality which keeps the foreigners at arm's length.

March 10 2003. Two UK boats turned up, one on delivery to somewhere distant, the other a completely blond haired family who had spent the winter in the Canary Islands. I asked them about moorings in the Canary Islands and got depressing news that they had spent £120 a week in a marina. This was an extortionate amount considering SP costs £10 per week in Peniche. They complained about the lack of culture there too, saying it was just a tourist region but adding that there were some nice beaches. The told me I could save money by finding a protected bay to anchor in but this would require four heavy anchors and readiness to clear out if the wind started to blow onshore. In my mind's eye I saw a picture of a winter Atlantic storm at night and having to leave an anchorage to put out to sea with a heavy wind forecast. If the engine failed the boat would be blown far out into the open ocean before the storm passed. The British family had cruised in the Azores group of islands the previous summer and said it was beautiful and as cheap to moor as Peniche. There were nine islands and people were really friendly.

Ocean currents at the seabed can run in opposition to the flow at the surface. The Coriolis effect inclines the movement of water to the right in the Northern Hemisphere, and, to the left in the Southern Hemisphere and the effect on a current is a change in direction as it gets deeper and eventually the deeper current can flow entirely opposite to that at the surface. Azorians may unconsciously live in fear of their possible geographic fate and the Azorian friendliness may be a counter current at the surface, running in opposition to the fear of volcanic catastrophe flowing in the depths.

In Portugal I sometimes bought butter made in the Azores. It was a little too creamy for my taste and it was this feature which was marketed with pictures of smiling cows grazing green pastures on the lid. Butter in a plastic box, like a margarine tub, was better because otherwise it melted out of the packet and into the bilge. Before I left the UK my plans were encapsulated by the phrase - Sail south 'til the butter melts - and now the butter was melting. A glitter of ocean lay blue and silver at my feet below the café terrace - Cascais - or Lisbon by the sea.

March 22 2003. A friend visited for a relaxed week with me aboard SP. After five months in Peniche I sailed with Neil to Cascais. The engine was weak and sickly but an easterly breeze came off the beach and so we went well in a calm sea. Peniche was another world compared to Cascais, which reminded me of the Mediterranean, with beach front bars and tourists lounging with mobile phones and speaking English and American. The warm sun had already put swimmers on the beach and they played tennis in bathing costumes. Various pretty young girls sat around with long hair scraped back into tight ponytails and scowls on their faces. One waited for a boyfriend who worked in the café where I sat. He wore an apron and a white T-shirt, he was black, attractive and looked Brazilian. A canary twizzled out a song somewhere near. SP was in Cascais marina at last, but it cost much more than I had anticipated. I had thought it would cost twice as much as Peniche, which would still be within my budget for a while until the high season prices in May, but I had read the charging table wrongly. I was now paying as much for a week as Peniche had cost for a month and in the high season the price would be doubled again.

I wondered about finding work in Cascais. A job would give me more money to pay for engine repairs and I could even stay in Cascais for a longer period, living in the posh marina. I was in a good position to seek work, with the boat as a base. I could also go out to the anchorage for free when the weather was fine.

Neil and I visited the Museo Maritimo in Lisboa. The maritime museum had dozens of Portuguese traditional boats of many strange shapes, some quite small, others very large. Neil was very impressed by the Nazare rowing boats which were rowed by a single person, often a woman, while the men were out fishing further afield. They looked very heavily built and not an efficient shape to travel through the water. The boxy hull rose up forward, reaching a sharp vertical point about two metres high. Neil and I could not decide exactly what the function of this design was. It may have been a symbolic form which reached upwards away from the sea, like a church spire, to the heavens. Or, perhaps it evolved out of the need to beach the boats, which were then hauled above the surf line by teams of oxen. Nazare beach was particularly steep due to the canyon of Nazare, an incursion of the Atlantic depths right into the bay of Nazare. I'd seen the waves plunging violently onto the steep sand and erupting skywards on a most dangerous beach to land a boat. Perhaps the high prow helped to deflect a heavy sea around the boat rather than swamping it and prevent a pitch-pole onto the beach. Maybe the vertical bow would help to right the boat if it was turned over by the surf.

In Lisbon a man offered us sunglasses as he hissed, "Hashish?" The Portuguese government had a lenient policy towards soft drugs and in an open square near the river there were men holding out lumps of hash for sale. They trailed behind us hissing over and over, "Sunglasses, hashish, sunglasses, you want hashish, sunglashish, sunglashish". When one of them stared at me perversely I became annoyed, which at least gave me the determination to shun them.

People walked past in bathing costumes looking pale and graceless, taking the sun on their skin as a tonic. I too looked at the sun as a healing, life giving force to touch my hair with gold and my skin with bronze although in reality the sun's harsh beams generally have an ageing effect on the body.

Fishing boats around nine meters in length were moored in Cascais bay and fifteen or twenty small open boats, some of which were painted vivid blue, green or red and were of a specifically local design. Out to sea cargo ships made protracted progress towards and away from Lisbon. By 11am I had heard more English spoken than in 4 months in Peniche. I left the Duche Bar and went to look for a job.

March 24 2003. I noticed an irrevocably English couple, the man with a face like a frog which would look very respectable in a dinner suit at a yacht club annual dinner and the woman conventional in holiday pastels and stylish sunglasses. I pictured her in denim jeans, a floral print head scarf and faded cotton smock, looking sprightly, young, excitedly handing out mugs of tea aboard a sailing boat. They paused at a news stand, she selected a postcard and wondered aloud how much it would cost. On realizing the postcards were 45 Cents she replaced the card and said to the frog-faced man, "NO, it's too much!"

I went for a wander past endless cafés and restaurants. The beach front felt merely exploitative and the only locals I detected were those refitting redundant café terraces. I felt depressed about life. Despite being ideally situated in a luxury marina and having entered the official geographical region of the 'osga' (Portuguese name for gecko) population I felt a little homesick. After being with my friend Neil for a week I found myself very much alone after he left, for by now I had been away from the UK for over seven months. The thought of going out to anchor, instead of being within the convenient luxury of the marina seemed daunting, but I scanned the beach and the seafront looking for a place to leave the tender if the boat was anchored and I wished to come ashore, but there was nowhere secure and I wondered how I would cope being out at anchor, disconnected and lonely. The marina only allowed tenders to be moored for an hour per day. The idea of anchoring was like moving out of the house into the garden. The marina price increased dramatically after April, to one hundred and seventy Euros per week, of course this was out of the question.

People like myself had to consider the traditional impecunious sailors technique of 'early bird discount' - going into a marina after dark and then leaving before the office staff arrived in the morning and snatching the odd shower during quiet times or grabbing a few litres of free water while visiting rich friends who could afford the marina rates. The previous autumn, while I was in Spain, I never considered anything other than laying at anchor and I was very happy about it. But the storms and rain of the past four months had shown me the Portuguese coast could be far from a postcard scene.

March 25 2003. Several times I drank hard liquor with two Swedish sailors. The younger, Matt, produced Agua Dente which tasted like methylated spirits. He also prepared a Scandinavian dish of salmon marinated for two or three days in dill, salt, sugar and white pepper, which was delicious. The fish was eaten on toast, spread with a paste made of one teaspoon of mustard, one tablespoon of French mustard, two tablespoons of vinegar, one hundred ml of oil and lots of dill cut into small pieces. We talked into the early hours and I had the sense to stop drinking well before it would have made me ill although I stupidly mixed whisky, Aguadente and brandy, but surprisingly I felt healthy enough when I awoke the next morning. It was a warm day, ideal for doing some hand washing. I met a Welsh couple who offered me some phone numbers to do with finding valves for the engine.

They had their engine rebuilt over a four month period and when it was finally ready the gearbox failed. There were several well known sailors who went to the most fearful and remote areas of the world without any engine at all. It would certainly make a consummate sailor out of you, but an engine was necessary for safety. I was getting worried if the weather was unsuitable to go elsewhere by the time the marina prices went up for summer I'd have to move out of the marina without a healthy engine. The Swedes were planning on locating a cheap, safe mooring to the south of Lisbon, where a long finger of land jutted out into the ocean, called Cabo Espichel. Beyond the headland a long section of coastline led all the way to the Algarve, 90 miles further south. The Algarve would be very warm in the summer and I heard many warnings about it being soulless, exploitative and overrun by English, German and Dutch seekers of sunshine and exotic scenery. The Algarve was a highly attractive coastline from what I had seen in photographs and I was sure there would be interesting niches to discover, festooned with geckos. The job idea receded in the face of fifty percent unemployment rate in Portugal. The language barrier meant I could really only work in an 'English pub' and I had never liked such places. It would be pointless to bind myself to the discomfort of working amongst a constant stream of whingeing Brits. I could pull out my saxophone and see how Cascais responded to chaotic renditions of *'The Pink Panther'* and *'Take Five'*. Alternatively I could look for an English language teaching job, but without a certificate of competency in teaching English as a foreign language, a TEFL, it would be unlikely I would gain work, despite my liking the idea of doing conversational teaching.

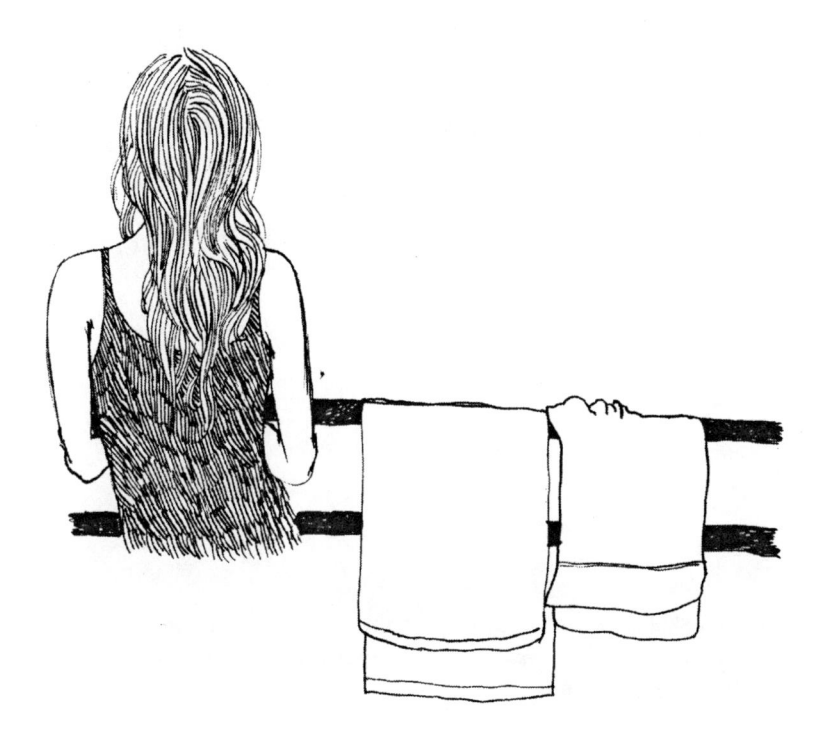

The warm sun had already put swimmers on the beach and they played tennis in bathing costumes. Various pretty young girls sat around with long hair scraped back into tight ponytails and scowls on their faces. One waited for a boyfriend who worked in the café where I sat.

They paused at a news stand, she selected a postcard and wondered aloud how much it would cost. On realizing the postcards were 45 cents she replaced the card and said to the frog faced man, "NO, it's too much".

Several times I drank hard liquor with two Swedish sailors. The younger, Matt, produced Agua Dente which tasted like methylated spirits. He also prepared a Scandinavian dish of salmon marinated for two or three days in dill, salt, sugar and white pepper, which was delicious.

Cascais, City of Gold

March 26 2003. Wealth was all around but plenty of people were not part of it. I looked out over the rooftops from the top floor of the Cascais Villa shopping centre. A large house stood behind high palm trees, it was painted pastel orange and had a pagoda style roof, painted shining gold. Beyond the golden roof top was ocean, grey and scuffled, like radio interference, holding several anchored ships in miniature over the rooftops. High ragged silver clouds made me squint and frown. When I arrived at Cascais marina I paid a month's mooring up front because it was cheaper like that., but I felt stifled by the rich atmosphere in the complex of shops, bars and luxury yacht agents which made up the marina complex. Cascais itself was equally stuffed with boutiques, lingerie shops, ornaments, gift shops and expensive cars. A most beautiful park existed nearby, where peacocks screeched, songbirds squeaked and chattered high up in eucalyptus groves, oblivious cats lazed on tree stumps as ducks fussed around them. Dozens of picnic benches made of heavy planks looked like sacrificial altars, in the shade of thick foliage. Palms, ferns and vanilla trees rustled and clattered dryly against each other. The damp loam under the trees smelt of lizards. My eyes darted around following the unfamiliar fauna, which reminded me of the illustrations depicting habitats of reptiles in the pages of the reference books I cherished as a child. The spiky shadows of palm trees looked like lizards feet; gum tree leaves and vanilla pods, like tails and lobes. A patch of prickly pears and yucca plants with light grey stones, the shape and size of ostrich eggs on the pebbled ground. I could imagine fat cobras and monitor lizards, camouflaged by cacti shadows, flicking black tongues. Many happy hours passed in the park as loneliness turned to solitude and I came to see it as a paradise.

Red-bodied damsel flies, darted like water nymphs and terrapins piled on top of each other to sunbathe on stone islets. Cool, intoxicating smells filled the spaces between Corsica pines and huge eucalyptus trees. A crow lived in a high domed cage in the mini zoo where rabbits, guinea pigs, peacocks and bantams hopped, strutted, and scratched. A stone mound, a large folly, a pile of bubbling rock as big as a house, had a spiral path to the top. Small grottos and stone seats lurked amid trestles of vines and roses. Wooden benches offered rest by pools of ducks with minute ducklings, honking geese, a small red-beaked black swan and more silly terrapins. All this was capped by a modestly priced café in a circular wooden hut next to a large pond with a nesting pair of mute swans. Peacocks paced by the tables and cats brushed the table legs and licking their lips, asking for scraps. Paths wended everywhere, people sunbathed on tidy lawns. A patch of banana trees had huge rubbery purple flowers drooping towards the ground on thick green stems. In the park were geckos, too, but I had not seen them yet, but I grew much more contented when I found a few places where I could sit and read or write, without interference or tension.

The Cascais Villa shopping centre was ideal in this respect, despite the relentless spectacle of consumerism. The top floor was a food hall with all sorts of outlets. It was spacious, bright with natural light through huge windows with views of the sea and Cabo Espichel, 167m tall, jutting out 20 miles to the south-east. A huge selection of food and drinks was available in the outlets surrounding the seating area and because there was such competition the prices were fairly low. From the Chinese stall I could have a plate of fried rice with a spring roll for two and a half Euros The French patisserie did a chocolate croissant and a galao for 1.9 Euros, although it came with a plastic spoon in a conventional coffee cup. A proper galao must have a tall glass with a long handled spoon.

Plenty of lowly pastelarias existed in the criss-cross of older Cascais streets between the park and the shopping centre, although these old streets were not populated by free dogs as in Peniche. The locals in Cascais seemed less receptive than the robust and lovely Penichenses, none called, 'Bom deeeeeyya' and some local people appeared belittled by the pervasive tourist industry. Cascais had embedded a small fishing industry in the middle of the tourist milieu. A building with a balcony surrounding the upper floor functioned as a work store for nets, pots and lines. Fairly recently a medium sized pier had been built with a crane at the end. Two fishermen loaded a string of a hundred crab pots into a rowing boat stacking them in the middle of the growing pile. Eventually the single boatman climbed around to where the oars waved about in the slop of the sea and rowed away in the blue painted boat which was about four and a half metres in length with heavy wooden oars. Almost all of the traditional Portuguese boats were flat bottomed which enabled them to be beached and then dragged through the surf line. The larger (10-20m in length) working boats were incredible shapes, with high curving stems (the front) and sterns (the back), like Viking longboats and with very apparent influences of ancient Phoenician trading ships. Some of them I could imagine carrying Osiris along the River Nile. The wonderful crescent moon shape of many of these vessels went way beyond utility. The root of the designs appeared to have much to do with representing various locales by distinctly shaped boats. The specific purpose of a boat was broadcast by the hull form and the way it was painted. For example the 'Lancha Da Sardinha' was used for fishing sardines and was found in Peniche. A 'Valboeiro' was used for ferrying people across the river Douro at Oporto, with a small decorated cabin where the passengers could shelter. There were variations according to who was normally carried, the 'Barcos das padeiras' took bakers. The 'Barcos das toucinheiros' took bacon sellers.

It can be seen by these different ways of classifying vessels and uses how there exists a distinctly Portuguese eye for detail in social order. The typically Portuguese bureaucratic mentality was in these boats. They were arranged in quite specific colour schemes, forms and functions. The 'Bote Do Pinho' (trans - Pine boat) was used almost exclusively for the transport of pine branches from the southern side of the River Tagus across to numerous bakers' ovens in Lisbon. The 'Varino' also from the River Tagus was a beautiful freighter from the 1880s, richly decorated with its mast severely raked back and a high prow and the bow strongly toothed which made it look as if it would fair very well in a conflict with another vessel. I did not know what they were for but they gave the boat a strangely fascinating visual impact. Some of the boats with smaller crews had a 'water dog' aboard who would guard the vessel when the crew were away. One of the modern fishing boats of Peniche had a dog aboard which barked without pause, whether the boat was under way, or alongside. The crew ignored the racket. I could have been driven barking mad by the noise, but instead, it just made me laugh.

All these vessels were highly distinctive and startlingly attractive. The Museo Maritimo in Lisboa has a number of actual boats, including a 'Rabelo' with its absurdly long manoeuvring oar pivoted on the stern castle. These were used for transporting up to a hundred casks of Port wine along the Douro around Oporto. They had a large square sail and were 19-23m long, being crewed by six or seven men. Viewing this fantastic boat while standing at the tip of the oar, I was struck by how unmanageable that gigantic sweep would be in a tricky current. The side force on an oar attached to a moving boat is tremendous and I was left agape at the seemingly crazy design.

Some passenger and cargo vessels of the River Minho were not built by shipwrights in boatyards, but in the shed of a farm near the river, by farmers who had skills in carpentry. A newly built boat would have its prow festively garlanded with flowers and an ox-cart would draw it down to the river. A book I spent time browsing in the library in Cascais was full of paintings of the various types. It would appear to a casual observer like a picture book of fantasy ships built to carry enchanted princesses over magical seas in fairy tales. The sails and rigging were often constructed in the most extreme fashion which looked as fantastic and unrestrained as the make believe ships of children's colouring books.

Most of the Portuguese boats had a form of lateen sail, a triangle shape, attached by lashings on the longest side, to a diagonal spar supported by a short mast, often set at a bizarre angle, either forward or backwards from the vertical. The Wharram catamaran, Peace Four, had similarly angled masts, one at a lesser angle than the other. In Bristol I thought it looked unconventional, rakish and askew. In Portugal Peace Four was a piece of living water-borne culture. In the set of her masts was an absolute link with local traditional boats. Now I understood the significance of this type of mast configuration. James Wharram was a well known designer of the 'Wharram cats', a breed of catamarans influenced by the sailing rafts which carried the ancient Polynesians across large areas of the Pacific Ocean. In the late 1950s James Wharram sailed, with two enthusiastic crew members, to Spain and Portugal in one of his earliest designs.

The 'Saveiro Meia-Lua' from the Costa do Caparica, looked like the sultan of Arabia's slipper. Despite being 15-18m in length, it was without a keel and was rudderless, being propelled and guided by three or four long oars on either side. The picture in the book I read showed the vessels dramatically upward curved bow and stern posts. A stylized eye decorated the bow. Another with a very 'Near Eastern' shape was the 'Boliceiro', from the northern port of Aveiro, with a bow rising up into a curve which ending up pointing at the top of the short mast. Vivid and colourful designs decorated the bow and stern and despite the elaborate form and decoration it was given, the Moliceiro was designed for a robust and filthy job - gathering and carrying seaweed throughout the lagoons of the Aveiro estuary. I was deeply impressed by the art in these boats. The expression of diverse and extreme forms was largely eradicated from our over-rational and technologically dominated lives. One type of sardine fishing and seaweed gathering vessel from the region of Ilhavo was black with no decoration whatsoever, a curious contradiction.

(Reference: Telmo Gomes (1997), *Embarcacoes Portuguesas. Embarcacoes Regionais Da Tradicao Portuguesa: Portuguese Boats, Regional Boats in the Portuguese Tradition.* Edicoes Inapa).

I smiled to myself when I saw a rudder which closely resembled the one I'd recently constructed for the wind vane self-steering. The Traineira had a longish rudder swept slightly forward and with a square end. My own Peniche rudder grew out of a combination of available materials and simply not knowing how to make anything more elaborate, or elegant. It appears I was unknowingly influenced by the traditional Penichian rudder form of the traineira. I had not seen the older rudder form which mine resembled because all the local traineiras (auxiliary work-boats connected to the fishing boats) rudders were no more than slabs of stainless steel welded to stainless steel shafts. I had unknowingly arrived at a uniquely local type of rudder design by chance. I like to think I was helped by a steering muse.

Some days later on a visit to Peniche I walked to the north beach and came upon a tall statue of a woman holding a crowned baby. She was 'Nossa Senhora de Boa Viagem' - Our Lady of the Good Voyage. A dozen vases of fresh flowers stood at her feet and I was moved to place a one Euro coin there. I knew somebody would see it and have it, but it did not matter, good luck to them. I would always be more than a little proud of my distinctly Penichian rudder design and on the 45 miles between Peniche and Cascais the 'wind rudder' self-steering was completely successful.

March 30 2003. A day of rain had patches of sun when my wet suede boots began to dry, but again and again, heavy rain swept in. A Swedish sailor, Toiva, and I took a two and a half hour journey to Seixal, opposite Lisbon on the southern side of the River Tagus. Armed with umbrellas we set off to Cascais railway station and caught a train immediately. Toiva said about the trains, "They never stop, they are always on time. In Sweden they stopped all the local trains, yes, they were costing too much and they simply took them all away". The Lisbon suburbs flickered by to the left and we stared out of the right hand windows at the estuary as the train followed it inwards. The scene looked like the Bristol Channel on a typical grey day and low cloud, heavy with showers, blotted out the opposite bank, 2 miles to the south. An age old, cheerless chop of waves bit and swallowed at the shoreline. Near to Oeiras, Toiva pointed out an old building, the Forte de Sao Bruno, one level was built below the tide line and prisoners used to be locked in to be drowned as the tide flooded.

I asked, "In Salazar's time?" Toiva said, "No, a long time back, well yes maybe in Salazar's time too."

In Lisbon we took a five minute walk through grimy puddles and beggars hunching in the spray of rain soaked roads. After a fifteen minute ferry ride across the river Tagus we arrived at Seixal and plodded towards town over marble cobblestones, sand drifts and puddles. Seixal once had a successful cork industry but when plastics were developed it closed down. Global demand for cork remains strong but Seixal no longer has a part in it and has contracted back to a small fishing village. Spread along a wide shallow back-water of the river Tagus, Seixal was quaint with largely empty streets and houses possessing plain lines. Small brightly painted boats, with the day's rain in their bilges, floated at moorings just off the sea wall. A strong orange coloured sand and the spaciousness made the scene appear like a water-colour painting. After knocking several times we waited across the street from Toiva's friend, an engineer who was helping fix his engine. Nesting swallows flew in and out of a pair of open patio doors on the upper floor of an abandoned house next door. The sun broke through and my suede boots steamed with evaporating moisture. The hosts were late. Heavy rain soaked my boots again and so we went to visit the P.C.P. (Partida Comunista Portuguesa) - the Communist Party of Portugal. Inside there were anti-war slogans at one side of a large hall with a bar opposite which offered a daily menu - Saturday was fried fish with rice. We sat picking through a putrid smelling mess of fish, rice and bones. The fish on my plate lay with gaping mouths and hollow, fried eyes as I forked through the flesh looking for a decent boneless mouthful. The taste was slightly repulsive tinged with something wholesome. New upholstery and wall paint repeated the unconquerable choice of previous redecorations in the party's eighty years in existence - red again - we laughed. Toiva told me how the Communist party had run a large headquarters in the centre of Lisboa but when, post Salazar, the new democracy was established the P.C.P. were moved to the south side of the river, a much less conspicuous position, further away from Lisbon city centre. The headquarters had a substantial and high mast, topping it a prominent hammer and sickle. We could not pick it out from the ferry amongst the heavy residential and industrial development on the south banks just to the north of Seixal.

Our hosts eventually arrived and led us through a passage into the back garden, where we talked about engines and mechanics. Above us were vines strung with fat silver raindrops and shrivelled bunches of grapes. A fig tree looked happy near the house and numerous plants from around the globe grew verdantly. I seized the opportunity to ask whether there were geckos in the garden. Lynn pointed to a water butt filled with leaves and said there were two that lived there. They came out in the warmer weather. Gourds nestled amongst masses of passion flowers which partly concealed a ram's skull attached to the wall. I exclaimed, "Gosh, it's very elegant, with the horns sweeping back out of the skull and the way they spiral to fine points," Lynn explained, "Oh it was my brother, he went hiking in the hills and he just found it and bought it back as a souvenir". Lynn's partner Tony was Portuguese. With a friendly face and a chuckle, he asked me, "So, are you praying to Odin to get your engine fixed?" I said, "I think I need to pray to Volvo Penta".

On the way back to the Lisbon ferry we stopped in a bar for a beer and a galao. On brackets in each corner of the room were three televisions, all switched on at high volume. Mercifully, a fourth remained switched off. Later we sped back along the southern shore of the river Tagus aboard the fast catamaran ferry, propelled by water-jets. Peering through the rain spattered windows, we tried to spot the hammer and sickle tower of the P.C.P., but failed. Back into puddle laden Lisboa, to walk along the north bank to Cais de Sodre, the train station for the Cascais line. At the ticket machine a begging man hovered so close to Toiva as he purchased his ticket that he ended up buying it for an intermediate station named Caxias, rather than Cascais. I got the correct ticket for myself. When we reached Caxias, about half way to Cascais, I noticed the ticket inspector approaching and checking all passengers had tickets. The train pulled out of Caxias as the inspector took Toiva's ticket. I saw him do a double take, but managed to distract him by thrusting my own correct ticket at him. He handed back Toiva's and took mine and then moved away. Toiva said, "He cannot even read!"

The next day I went to the top floor of the Cascais Villa shopping centre, in the food hall. I noticed a sailing yacht out at sea as it sailed over the top of the golden roofed pagoda style building visible from there. The weather was in stark contrast to the previous day's rain, warm and bright with a shift in the wind to the north. The yacht tacked in towards Cascais and watching it made me acutely aware of how privileged I was to have come here on a sailing boat. Palm trees waved in the breeze and the ocean was divided by a line, one side was lapis lazuli, the other was amethyst. Cabo Espichel was just visible through a milk blue haze. A cargo ship lay at anchor like a model in a toy shop window. The sailing boat quickly reached the near shore and made the marina entrance on the same tack. I was a little excited about who could be on the boat as I had met several really pleasant people in Cascais Marina who had given me advice about my engine and local contacts.

I met two journalists - one a Swedish war correspondent who had recently returned from Iraq and usually covered all conflicts in the African continent. The other was a timid Englishman. Timid because he came to stare at my boat out of surprise at a small UK yacht reaching this far and he found difficulty stepping aboard. He said, "You've sailed all the way from England and I can't even get aboard," as he peered into the interior of SP and admitted it was suited to one person living in. Still slightly exasperated at how small she was, he asked, "But what do you find to do all the time?" Toiva, his son Mat and I began listing the things to do on a boat, *"Listen to the radio, read, write, cook, repair things, tidy up, fix leaks, explore long unopened cupboards and lockers, look for items forgotten about, find things which have been lost for months, clear out accumulated rubbish, drink, sleep, wash clothes, plan the next part of the journey, play guitar"*. We all agreed there was plenty to do. Then out of pride I added, "Designing and building self-steering wind vane systems". The war-zone journalist's son was suddenly interested and he asked in Swedish, "What's that?" I waved the plywood flap back and forth to demonstrate the interaction between the wind vane and the self-steering rudder and the contraption was admired by all.

There followed a slightly depressing discussion about Cascais marina, which was struggling to operate in the current economic climate of Portugal, which, someone claimed, had 50% unemployment. Opened in 1998, it was expected to attract hundreds of local and foreign boats as well as a thriving bar and restaurant trade in the dozens of food and drink outlets. Many of the original, nearby, Cascais bars and restaurants were 'encouraged', to relocate and close so the marina could become the sole leisure centre of Cascais. This was all pushed through by various local officials, several of whom were apparently subsequently scandalized in corrupt dealings. Meanwhile the marina complex continued to charge high prices to visiting yachts.

Cascais had a distinct rich and poor social structure. Whole families occupied the pavement near to the Jumbo supermarket and begged for coins from retirees with villas who strutted by with hardened hearts. Tourists with leather wallets bulging in their bum pockets frowned disdainfully at women clutching babies who weaved amongst the traffic queues with outstretched hands. Many of the cars were new being purchased on credit. Meanwhile in the marina more than half of the trade outlets remained empty. Most businesses which opened made the mistake of aiming at the upper tier of consumers by trying to sell gift-wrapped luxury chocolates, bourgeois perfumes, absurd household ornaments in sea themes (black and white minstrel sailors cavorting around cheap decorative clocks with anchor motives). Most new businesses failed within a year. The price of a visitors berth was almost unbearably high during the low season and in May I would be excluded absolutely by a doubling of the mooring rates for the high season. If the rates were aimed at the middle sector of cruising yachts there would be many more berths filled and for longer periods. The micro-economy of the marina would be freed up and more of the bars and eating places would survive. Long term cruising yachts do not spend much money at one sitting, however, each week they buy food, equipment and repairs and visit the bars to meet and socialize. But most cruising sailors used the protection of the marina for only a brief respite from the sea and then sailed on to look for less ostentatious moorings.

The Day of the Gecko

March 31 2003. Warm sunshine set me into a dreamy, careless mind as I walked out of the marina towards the town, or the beach, but not the park today, I decided. My laptop computer had failed with some missing file in the registry, as well as the floppy disc drive door being somehow broken. I was ready to give up on the whole personal computing world, apart from my trusty hand-held Psion series 5. A friend phoned me and talked tediously and at length about his affairs. I then wanted the solitude of a café, or ruined castle, away from chit-chat. The only thing I needed a laptop for was to store my photographs. I was sure there was another method of taking them off the camera and keeping them safe. I walked out of the marina, away from the boat thinking over my situation. The engine was a big concern and this problem butted itself onto thoughts of the previous evening's very enjoyable curry, using black-eye beans, chick peas, mushrooms, green peas and fried spices. I felt organized, self-sufficient and satisfied to be eating for around three Euros and the added advantage was my next meal was already cooked and would taste even better. The curry led to a lost saucepan lid, the previous morning I'd dropped the lid of my favourite stainless steel saucepan into the water. It receded as it sank, tilting silver like a Dover sole. The lid came to rest about three and a half metres down on a clear sand seabed. I could just see it still, but I was not confident enough to dive to such an ear-splitting depth. Furthermore the presence of the boat and marina pontoons made me feel less inclined to dive in. I really liked the lost lid because with it I could make perfect rice and it enabled me to leave cooked food until the next day without flies or germs getting into it. The lid remained tantalizingly close to me on the boat and I knew I would find a solution. A particular friend in the UK would dive down to such a modest depth in the flick of a mermaid's green eye, but first I would have to persuade her to visit me. One of my main concerns was I had not come across a single gecko from the late summer sweat of Gallicia to the early spring heat of Peniche.

My route away from the marina took me past a run down house, or villa. It had a garden thick with palm trees and ivy grew on a massive wall which met the iron railings along the path I walked.

There it was, about 70mm long, its feet fanned out as it held itself flat and still against the smooth concrete wall. It was in shadow, at the edge of the sunlight, next to a dense growth of ivy. Its body was brown with a lighter stripe down the centre of the back which continued along a thin tail. The look of the gecko was quite different to the wall lizards. It was absolutely motionless and the head, body and tail were wider, flatter in shape. It had an expression of a little frog-eyed all terrain vehicle, or one of those new Volkswagen Beetle cars. It was alien, special, intimate, self-absorbed, secret, quiet, delicate, gentle, magical. Suddenly it moved, in an absolutely straight line, at a diagonal to the vertical, across the smooth surface and disappeared into the ivy. I walked on feeling light headed, grinning to myself, with restored buoyancy in the voyage. A new phase was coming in. I had reached the gecko line.

Sunglashish, Ponderous Plaques and Honking Saxes

April 1 2003. The first day of April was warm and hazy. I went to the Parco Marechal Carmona to visit a pleasant café set in an octagonal shaped, wooden building with a terrace surrounded by privet hedges. The people there seemed to be workers having a break with no beach types at all. Close by was a pond with a fountain giving the sound of splashing water and cooling the ambience of the terrace. Peacocks howled from the trees and prowled around the tables making strange honking sounds. There was an albino peacock. Masses of eucalyptus trees stretched upwards into the sun, one had a plaque,

'Eucalyptus Globulus. Family - myrtaceae. Originally from the south-east and south coast of Tasmania, now grows throughout the world'.

Long shreds of bark hung from the slender, smooth trunks twisting up to the dazzling light green and sky silver canopy. These slender giants were streaked with colours of hazelnut brown, ash grey and polished aluminium, flowing up the trunks around complex knotted patches, like rapids in a stream. Shards of cinnamon coloured bark clattered dryly to the ground in gusts. Eucalyptus leaves were scattered everywhere, like rusty scythes, in shades of dark clay, silver-green, raspberry and crimson, shoe leather brown and banana black. When broken the dead leaves smelled of expensive bath oils and chest medicine. I picked a fresh leaf crushing it found a heady, sensual smell of woodland nettles, avocados, spicy tea, lemon, thyme, sweet pea and caraway seed bread mashed and sun warmed. I sat down and sniffed the leaf with too many impressions to capture as a single memory.

A constant raking, weeding, planting, tying and watering was carried out by a band of workers wearing baseball caps and short-sleeve shirts, looking like overgrown cub-scouts. One of them fled past the café, closely followed by another wielding a springy rake and a moment later I heard a twanging and bouncing noise as the rake pronged the ground behind its foe. Next a security guard huffed by, keys a-jingle, radio hissing, in a brown uniform with yellow trim, but the park workers cleverly disguised themselves as colleagues and the security man had pursued nothing but the scowl on his face.

A folly in the form of a dome built from boulders, like a cairn, as high as a house had a spiral path rising to the top. In one side a cave diminished to a point in the centre of the structure. The stone was in convoluted, tortured shapes, like spent coals, and heavy - a Portuguese fisherman could just about lift one. Next to the folly were clean loos, probably put there to take advantage of the water supply laid to the folly which no longer had a fountain. Nearby a large wire netting enclosure housed a mini zoo with guinea pigs, rabbits, chickens and guinea fowl fussing over a sea of cabbage leaves and sweetcorn. From perches and suspended roosts, pigeons, bantams and white fantail doves rained lice, turds and more cabbage and sweetcorn down onto the floor. In separate whitewashed brick cages were chinchillas, large white, lazy rabbits and chickens with yellow Easter chicks. Two large circular cages with domed roofs housed three birds. In one a sweet crow and a terrified Jay with no tail. In the other a large bird, part falcon and part fowl may have been a *Caracara* bird which I remembered reading about in Gerald Durrell's *'Drunken Forest'* - a friendly, characterful and tame bird with big sad eyes. I'd met this bird in the previous winter when visiting Cascais. Then it had looked bedraggled, wet, almost featherless, with a worn out, doomed expression. Now it looked at me through a big shiny black eye under a speckled crest of feathers, with a strong beak and healthy feet and a long straight tail with white lateral markings, making it look hawk-like. With round tipped wings and a friendly expression, like a fat falcon, it watched the park scene and I wondered if it was a phoenix which had re-birthed itself. During my previous visit to Cascais I had gone to see the Harry Potter film - *The Phoenix*, with friends Nadine and Dan. On a stroll with them though the park I had chased a cat from the back of a pigeon. The cat shot to the top of one of the rabbit enclosures and glared down on me like an enraged witch. I wandered out of the glare of the cat-witch to the cage containing the fat falcon bird which stood on the concrete floor in a puddle, looking emaciated and largely featherless, it's sad eyes gazing out at the wintry park.

The scene of the cat and the pigeon had been played out in those dark pupils. Now though, the bird was reborn, phoenix like and spring had also brought about a transformation in every single aspect of the park. The gecko observation of the day before left me feeling satisfied and contented that I had reached my destination. The weather was improving relentlessly and I hoped April would be a turning point from the wet south-westerly to dry northerly weather. The gecko population seemed to have a tacit sense of ideal climate and my not sighting a single gecko in the region above Cascais should have driven me further southwards earlier. The Narnia voyage was a search for a region blessed with warm, dry winters and exciting summer heat to bring out sinuous reptiles onto sensuously baking patches of earth, splattered with hordes of succulent aloe vera surrounded by rubbery pastures of ice plants.

In a Narnian climate the wood stove, so integral to SPs cabin, would be redundant and it would pass, perhaps painfully like a kidney stone, out of the boat. The silvered bronze chimney would remain standing like a monument to the cold land where the voyage began. I did not pass by the particular wall where I saw the first gecko the previous day, because knowing they were there was enough. I was living where geckos lived.

Back in the park I enjoyed the sight of a shoal of green-brown fish travelling at speed around the pond. A single goldfish moved with them, within the main shoal, but struggled to keep up when they accelerated and turned as one. Laboriously flapping fins and tail the goldfish was constantly overtaken and left to one side or behind the swiftly moving shoal as it altered shape and direction. A portion of the shoal became a long chain a couple of fish wide. Like a hundred motorcycles passing a solitary cyclist the shoal streamed past the goldfish as it swam, all fins and effort.

A heap of turtles, or terrapins - tartarugas in Portuguese - had climbed into a precarious pile on top of a rock in the middle of the pond. Ten or eleven of them occupied the islet and more paddled around the base, clawing at the lower edges, looking to add themselves to the pile. Those on top triumphantly held their heads out in the sun. A minute later the whole lot collapsed in a floundering, splashing, shell-shock of re-entry. They hung around aimlessly suspended in the water. Sometimes they made across the pool, bright red-cheeked heads straining upwards, clawed paddles flinching back and forwards, feathering their webbed feet on the forward move.

A man squared up to a male swan, meddling with the galleon proud white bird which aggressively matched his pace along the edge of the pond. The man poked his foot towards the swan which responded with heavy pecking and undoing the man's shoelace. Reserving it's huge white, bony wings the swans beak inflicted a number of strikes on the man's ankle, who finally withdrew his foot and grinned at onlookers and after retying his shoelace, he walked off with a smarting ankle and a spring in his step.

April 3 2003. After the Lisboa Museu Maritimo a couple of weeks before I was not expecting much in the local Cascais sea museum. It cost 1.54 Euros for some reason. Inside was a cool and soothing, modern space with low lighting. The night before I had been with my two

Swedish friends. Aboard 'Alice', their 9m sailing boat, a 'Great Dane 28', we'd drunk much too heavily and stayed up far beyond the midnight hour, amusing ourselves with a board game which had come free with a bottle of gin, a harmonica and a saucepan banged with a wooden spatula. At four am I managed to resist the suggestion of going to get my guitar and instead went to bed after drinking two mugs of water as an antidote to alcohol poisoning. The atmosphere in the sea museum was a perfect cure for a hangover - softly lit and quiet. There were only two other visitors.

A display of sea creatures was made up of models and stuffed specimens of dolphins, sharks, whales and most of the fish found in the region. A large sunfish was absurd, as if two fins had been attached, top and bottom, to a huge, flattened, blubbery head, two metres high. Toiva and Mat, the Swedes, had seen dozens of Sunfishes in the Bay of Biscay, but I saw none, despite being in the same area at a similar part of the year. There were fractured bronze cannons and spherical stone missiles, trawled from the nearby seabed. Baleen whale mouth parts looked like industrial filters.

Colossal nautilus shells were spiral sheets of curved glimmering pearl. There were clothes and attire of Cascais fishing folk. Photographs of working boats being hauled onto sandy beaches were juxtaposed by scale models of the boats in the pictures, appealing as new toys.

April 4 2003. The Cascais arrufada (locally evolving phonetic spelling of *errufada*) seemed to have two states. The normal day to day arrufada had less of the coconut topping and was less sweet. As such it was a satisfying snack, half way between a bread roll and a doughnut. At festivals, such as Christmas, New Year and carnival extra topping was added and the bakers put a few extra measures of sugar into the mix. Furthermore, the bready body of the arrufada was much more yellow in colour. On a normal day in a normal week I expected a normal variety of arrufada, but it was over-sweet and a strong yellow colour, turgid with sugar and coconut topping. The garishly flavoured festival variety was due to the shopping mall where there existed no such thing as 'everyday' and instead was hyped into the best, the sweetest, the most beautiful of all. The mall promised almost everything, but simple contentment is a cleverly concealed secret. It was not until I returned to SP that I realized how glorious the world outside the mall was. I started up the engine to study the soot from the exhaust pipe, perhaps dislodged while I was climbing around the exhaust to work on the fuel lines. The diesel gave such a reassuring note out at sea as SP left a certain wake behind, whereas sailing without an engine was often more like the meandering wanderings of a drunken sailor. Some seek only the romantic inspiration of quivering sails and the blowing of dolphins, but I liked to see the coastline sliding by and the dolphins busy leaping in a sturdy bow wave as SP motored onwards under power.

April 5 2003. Aggressively spending, pleasure seeking, faux bourgeois marina visitors in sports saloons, drinking and having too much fun until 3am made me feel uncomfortable and after a couple of weeks when the marina fees went sky high I would have to go out to anchor in the bay. Meanwhile Toiva, Mat and myself, blotted out the surrounding inequalities by drinking hard liquor into the early hours. It was fun playing the guitar and singing Pink Floyd songs, but a part of me craved sobriety and solitude. My quiet voice whispered about ecstatic morning strolls along gecko clad walls, the shady or sun drenched hours of daylight wandering - gecko hunting. Cascais was a stew pot full of tourists, sailors, retirees, bar owners and locals. My mobile phone had taken to ringing often and visitors arrived at the boat with invites to visit this or that beach, or bar. I started bumping into people on café terraces or in the street who would then come up with good ideas about where we could go to have fun. The gecko hunter must have solitude and a delicate process of organization and problem solving went on in my thoughts whenever I strolled alone. I rarely solved problems while walking around with other people. The winding ways of my gecko hunting and sailing were a carefully trodden path, a solitary fairy path of balance between letting go of and holding on to the world. *Selfish?- completely. Content? - deeply.*

A yacht swept through the marina aisle with two women and two men swaggering in the cockpit, sunglasses glinting. A mobile phone was pressed to the ear of one whose eyes darted to meet mine as if checking the audience was attentive to their leisure business - silly humans.

April 7 2003. To my delight I found the habitat of the first gecko was actually inside the park Carmina Marechal. Where a wall joined a hedge alongside the path next to a road, I'd spotted the gecko. I padded slowly and quietly towards the corner of the park, where was the gecko wall. A closed municipal building had an adjoining seed nursery and gardening implements propped around, away from the wholly public area. In a corner where a tall stone wall joined a privet hedge were some banana plants with giant fan-like leaves spreading reptilian shadows and a monstrous flower drooped almost to the ground, dropping great waxy plum coloured petals, and flies buzzed over them as if they were the scalps of gecko hunters gone before me. There were three geckos - a pair and an individual - all practically identical, small, no more than 100 mm long, a light mottled brown - the colour of the stone and concrete wall. They had distinct faces which seemed to smile with speckled gold eyes and darker, cat like pupils.

When I returned home a boat I had met in Peniche was in the marina. Roger was an engineer and he offered to help with my engine. In optimistic sunshine I rowed to their boat with a bowl of exhaust outlet water. The water was black and so I was pessimistic, but Roger observed it was not actually oily and he told me it was almost certainly soot from the exhaust pipe. He suggested the lack of power could be a throttle cable problem and this jolted my memory about a faded notebook which had come with SP when I purchased her. In it was a note about not pushing the throttle all the way forwards because beyond a certain point the cable just kinked. The engine problem seemed to have been solved in a single conversation. When I tried to start it up, it refused to fire in the 'start' position which was completely forward, however as I eased back the throttle to a fast tick-over position the engine fired into life. I had a reasonably healthy engine and now I could concentrate on getting the sacrificial strip put onto the large fore sail. I felt ready to go cruising again. Roger and Sandra told me they were going to explore the River Gaudiana during the summer months, when coastal marinas would be very expensive. The river had 40 miles of navigable and sheltered waters with free moorings at dozens of small villages. The Gaudiana was on the border between Portugal and Spain. Another exciting idea was to travel up the River Gaudalquiver, also in southern Spain, stretching inland for 50 miles up to Seville - a flaming hot city, rich in culture where, I was told by a visitor, geckos clad the city centre walls by night, hunting insects drawn to the street lamps.

April 8 2003. I found a workman-like pastelaria with a functional, cool shady atmosphere. Scratchy, thin legged chairs and smooth round tables filled the floor and older, cross looking women masticated over bowls of caldo verde soup - 'Green Soup' was a simple vegetable soup which cost one Euro. Older, angry faced men digested over newspapers and I felt sure I would illicit a smile by greeting them in a Peniche accent, Bom deeeyyya! I stayed away from the shimmering aisles of Cascais Villa shopping mall because however diverse the snacks and drinks on offer are it was not a comfortable place. Despite the bright daylight ambience and splendid views over the sea, something miserable was there. When I ordered a galao and arrufada with butter in Portuguese a temporary but tangible trust formed between myself and the peach shirted waiters and waitresses at the counter. I used the language familiarly, even forcefully and I was determined to avoid apologizing for my limited ability to speak it. It was possible my accent sounded completely absurd to the locals, but perhaps I spoke like I had lived in Portugal for half a year, as I now had. Even though the hard tiled floor and walls of the pastelaria rebounded every sharp clink of spoon on glass cup, or pile of plates being replaced, it had a social feeling and I did not feel stared at, talked about, watched by security men or monitored by video surveillance, as in the mall.

One afternoon I took tea with a poet who had six books of poems published and was writing *Two in a Boat: The True Story of a Marital Rite of Passage*. Gwyneth Lewis wore a floppy cotton sun hat and I told her she looked like the classic English lady writer abroad. She sharply replied, "English? I'm not English boyo! I'm Welsh, you see". We laughed at the inappropriate stereotype. Gwyneth and her husband had been on their yacht in Milford Haven marina the same week as SP. However, they had not the sailing experience that I did and had met with many obstacles when trying to leave the UK. We talked about the truth of sailing, agreeing it was mostly quite unpleasant aboard a small boat at sea with so much movement and the difficulty of doing something as simple as having a wee or pouring a kettle into a mug to make tea. We agreed the biggest mistake would be to expect a long term sailing trip to be wonderful once a warm climate was reached and we laughed at the way everyone seemed to believe there was a distinct change in the climate once south of Cabo Finisterre. They had wintered in Leixois and with all the rain, wind, and cold had been within a signature of selling the bl***y boat, divorcing and going home.

I told Gwyneth they would make ideal cruising sailors having got to know the reality but managing to stay friends. Her book about the voyage was published a couple of years afterwards. It was about the breakdown of their relationship under the strains of voyaging. Gwyneth had written another book she described as a happy approach to depression and she was interested in how I appeared to remain so cheerful while voyaging and living alone. I explained it was solitude itself which I found to be so enlivening and how I tend to avoid crowds of people and their motions. I prefer my own company and simply enjoy being selfish. After three hours we came to a wise conclusion - sailing away in search of paradise will not make one happy and content, if one is not already happy and content.

Another day I walked along the beach in hot sunshine observing the beach population. It looked sweaty, swarthy, hairy, overly fit and overexposed and felt like a fish out of water. From several miles out to sea a crowded beach appears as smudges of colour where crowds are no more distinct than flowers in a meadow viewed from a passing train. I prefer the distant view and I felt intimidated by the strong codes of dress and conduct at the beach. In places where people undress together social codes become palpable. The beach was a place of rigid behaviour codes rather than the enhanced freedom and carelessness promised in the travel brochures. I escaped to the Duche Bar and took a seat overlooking the sun and sand from a safe height. A kilometre to the south west a boat passed through the marina entrance under sail and the sight of it reminded and reassured me of all those acute tensions and anxieties which existed 'out there'. The all enveloping anxiety brought on by sailing actually offers a sanctuary from other people.

A group of people entered the Duche Bar. A tall woman wore denim dungarees with a red long sleeved top underneath. She was really casual and relaxed without the showy 'cool' of the beach. The group she was with were completely non-threatening in looks and body language. They had children and I decided they were probably passionate about interesting things and I felt good seeing this type of people whom I somehow aspired to be like. Another group entered, this time hairy, beach types who smelled of bottled beer, sweat and testosterone. One wore a baseball hat turned backwards and none had much on in the way of clothes. The differences between the two groups were fascinating. The attractive and serious types of the first group never made eye contact with me and wore flexible and complex expressions. Their faces seemed to show success as well as difficulties undergone and they looked approachable.

The second group scanned the bar constantly. Their eyes were like summer flies, briefly settling on mine and others faces, soliciting, tasting, assessing. Their faces were suspended in mid-coital arrogance - eyes smiling and twinkling, mouths mouthy, lippy. Far away across the waves a growing bank of cloud spoke to me of coming rain while sunbathers turned brown and drank more beer.

April 10 2003. Some traditional Portuguese dishes used very simple ingredients. I supped a plate of caldo verde - green soup made of finely chopped kale - known as Portuguese cabbage. The soup was cooked with mashed potatoes, onions and olive oil. It tasted satisfying, healthy, plain. There was an even simpler sounding 'Soup with a Stone' - sopa de pedra - originally made by a wandering monk who would ask his hosts whether they knew how to make soup from a stone. He would boil water and, adding the stone, ask if his hosts had any other ingredients to add. It would be vastly improved by the addition of potatoes, beans, meat, onions, olive oil, salt, pepper, herbs and other spices. On a good day the monk may have achieved a rich soup of ham, coriander, olive oil, pepper, bacon and sausage. On a bad day just the nostalgia for flavour embodied by the stone. Sweets and biscuits available in small grocery stores were made of varying mixes of eggs, almonds, sugar and butter, some bright egg yolk yellow with the consistency of very soft boiled eggs - quite disgusting as it made me feel like a feeding snake. I tried wafers which contained a white, creamy filling. They were sold by weight out of plain cardboard boxes, stacked in clear plastic. They tasted like cake mix, just sugar and butter mixed and placed between two thin wafers. When I told the shopkeeper I liked them she said they were nice when really fresh, but after I found a short, curly hair in one I was sadly put off for life.

My favourite dish was 'Frango no Churrasco' - charcoal grilled chicken with chips and I enjoyed this when I went to Lisbon with Toiva, the Swedish sailor, in search of a sail maker. On the train into Lisbon a carrier bag, from an expensive shop had the words, 'La beaute est un langage?' written on it. I thought, surely beauty is an attribute, not a language. We eventually found Velamar and arranged for a ultra-violet protection strip to be added to my foresail which had pulled SP all the way from the UK to Spain, a friend indeed. After leaving the cheerful woman at Velamar we walked over one of the seven hills of Lisbon, to arrive at a busy area near a huge bridge across the River Tagus. Previously known as Salazar's Bridge, now it was known as, 'Pont de 25 Abril, 1975', in commemoration of Portugal's liberation. A cheap restaurant offered a street terrace and we leapt into tourist mode by ordering Frango no Churrasco. This was a whole chicken, opened lengthways, flattened and grilled over charcoal, basted in olive oil, chopped garlic and hot pepper. Served with a mound of chips liberally seasoned with sea salt, it was scrumptious along with a cold white beer served in a tall thin glass. It cost 4 Euros each. Eventually we arrived back satisfied after with our day in Lisbon.

Another time I enjoyed Frango no Churrasco was in Cascais after Roger had examined the exhaust water sample and after he reassured me it was not oil or diesel coming out of the exhaust pipe but soot and the heartening news had me agreeing to go for Frango no Churrasco with Roger and Sandra. They were sceptical about other tourists and the industry which greeted them, but we agreed it would be a real treat to eat something out. The evening was warm, the restaurant terrace almost deserted, we ate the meal mostly with our fingers and it was delicious. In Peniche I had eaten out only once (not counting 140 errufadas) when a UK friend, Neil, came to stay and we tried the definitive Penichian fisherman's hot pot - Caldeirada a Pescador. An earthenware casserole arrived onto the white tablecloth, containing, eels, mullet, skate, prawns, squid, shark, with layers of onion, potato slices, tomato, garlic, bay leaf, olive oil and parsley. If a little too salty, it was very filling and a memorable experience, partly because Neil had treated me, saying how he was getting a cheap holiday staying on SP. I had prepared a sufficiently long berth for Neil's six feet plus height by removing the wood stove and this enabled me to clean the area and paint the wood stove with stove black. I had not yet refitted the wood stove because the two studs which clamped the flue pipe to the chimney, sheered on removal and needed welding work.

My mother phoned from the UK and I was very surprised to hear of temperatures there sinking to -3C overnight and rising to just 6-7C during daylight. Conversely, the temperatures around Lisbon were occasionally very warm and winter was almost forgotten. Weather reports showed snow and sleet on high ground - os terras altas - in central and northern Portugal. When Toiva and I had gone to Lisbon it was sweltering under a windless 24C and Toiva had remarked at how unbearable the capital would be in August. When we had arrived back in Cascais the chilly air was scintillating and my tired, aching back and legs were instantly cured. The Lisbon we had seen was torrid, bustling with tourists and sellers of sunglasses and hashish, amongst other rubbish. We had visited a really touristy area called the Rua Augusta, which was filled with clothes shops and cafés with street terraces. Near to the Cais de Sodre - the train terminal for the Cascais line - we walked along a street with endless shops selling all manner of machinery, piping, tubing, valves, shackles, fishing gear, chandlery, welding equipment, chainsaws, plastic storage barrels, coils of ship's rope, sheet and strips of industrial rubber, piston rings and generators etc. It was in utter contrast to the consumer shopping streets we had been in earlier when I had been eye shopping for a bikini. The price of those tiny scraps of coloured material which would hardly cover a crotchet let alone a quaver, were extortionate, around fifty to a hundred Euros

I had forgotten the pricing structure of bikinis - the less material the higher the price. I told myself I was not a sixteen year old beach babe and so, instead, we went off to ponder the more practical side of sailing around hot countries, in the street of endless machinery and mechanics shops.

In a Cascais book store I found an English copy of '*The Chronicles of Narnia*', by C. S. Lewis and bought it as an inspiration in the voyage of SP. 'The Lion, The Witch and the Wardrobe' had enchanted me into noticing how the street lamps around Cascais marina were almost identical to the one at the entrance to Narnia in the book.

April 17 2003. At no cost I hired a cycle from Cascais town council. There were two points where attendants in small sheds took passport details, telephone number and residence address. The cycles were a distinctive red and silver with metal panels attached to the rear wheel declaring ownership by the Cascais municipality. These bikes were to be seen everywhere, in the town, and up to a dozen miles out. Tourists seemed to treat the region as a large cycle park, as they rattled along the white cobbled pedestrian pathways, but the roads were hectic and crowded, not at all suitable for bicycles. I cycled up to the Jumbo supermarket to exchange a Calor Gaz bottle. It was right through town and was a tricky ride amongst waves of traffic moving at breakneck speeds and so I too rode on the pavement for safety. Pedestrians were annoyed at yet another pavement hogging cyclist and they gave me lopsided frowns as they licked at ice cream cones.

In Cascais there was hardly anywhere to cycle that was not dominated by rushing traffic, however a Roman built road followed the cliffs out to Cabo Rasa and beyond, to the major surfing beach of Guincha. This was a wide cycle path alongside an equally broad footpath. Here there was still conflict as ambling pedestrians occupied both the cycle path and the footpath and the problem was made worse when the smooth red tarmac of the cycle path switched sides at several points and was labelled now as a cycleway and then as a pedestrian way. Some seriously dressed racing cyclists ploughed along at 20mph, twisting and winding past unheeding pedestrians. A mile out of Cascais was a market and café, at a place called Boca de Inferno - the mouth of hell. When two or three coach loads of wobbly tourists disembarked at the same time the cycleway became the sight of a massacre as red hire bikes and speeding racing cyclists ploughed through travel weary passengers as they disembarked onto the pathway. The Boca de Inferno was a cleft in the cliff with a blow hole created by the Atlantic waves and during gales the Boca de Inferno sends columns of spray high above the cliff tops. Alistair Crowley was one of the proponents of modern witchcraft and he was said to have faked his own suicide in the Boca de Inferno where there was now a commemorative plaque. If I were to be infamous, I would prefer to be known for disappearing somewhere in The Parco Marechal Carmona - my idea of paradise and my plaque would say:

'One spring morning she dissolved into a bright leafy hedgerow, near a wall where a small colony of geckos lived. It is said that on warm sun filled days her image can be seen reflected in the golden eyes of basking geckos, as she creeps around them grinning with happiness'.

I did not find the Alistair Crowley plaque because the place was riddled with other tourists and those places were nearly always tainted by human excrement.

I walked on feeling light headed, grinning to myself, with restored buoyancy in the voyage. A new phase was coming in. I had reached the gecko line.

(Impressions)
The Year 1966
I am 5 years of age, at Pixies Hill Primary School in Hemel Hempstead, Hertfordshire. I am learning to write by copying the shapes of letters from a blackboard. Distracted from the voice of the teacher by the sight of swirling flight of gulls outside, my mood is lazy and staring out of the window over a wide green playing field, my heart jolts minutely as I focus on two grey, slender primary feathers stuck into the ground next to one another, like a pair of windsurfers. I had planted them there during lunch time - to see how long it was before somebody trod on them. Now I could see them quivering slightly in the afternoon breeze and my experiment had shown me delicate things can remain so, despite the turmoil which threatened to crush them, but the experiment was neither scientific, nor artistic - I was merely twiddling with the threads of the weave of life around me. The two feathers turned to pink and brilliant green and the playing field reversed from flat green grass into sapphire blue and like a sliding theatrical backdrop, Cabo Espichel rolled out to fill half the horizon. I too transformed, my hair lengthened, my breasts grew and my body climbed though the years upwards to a lanky 1.8m until I was looking out over the sea from the top of the Cascais Villa shopping centre. Two windsurfer's sails looked like two feathers set into the blue sea and I was learning to write as I juggled with ideas, metaphors, similes and new words to find resonant descriptions. 37 years ago shopping centres and wind surfers had not yet existed. Two feathers set into a field like parallel windsurfers. Three geckos clinging to a wall like a tab in the ocean. Things to grasp hold of like nectar to collect.

April 2003. A sign board alongside the cycle path described the area, this was written on it:
Sintra-Cascais Natural Park. Enclosed by the northern limit of the Sintra council area of jurisdiction, along the mouth of the Falcao River, and the Cascais Citadel at the other extreme, the Natural Park enjoys a tremendous variety of landscape arising from three underlying structural blocks: the eruptive massif which makes up the Sintra Mountain ridge or Serra and is the predominant feature of the area, mainly rural in character, to the north of the Colares River; and finally, forming the interface between these and the ocean itself, we have the seashore region, an appealing succession of limestone rock faces, low cliffs, dunes and beaches culminating in Cape Roca.
Despite all that, I had not seen geckos again. Something had to be done.
Pedro was a diver and a fisherman - he was tall, huge, with dark hair growing from his arms, chest, chin and nape, less so on his head. He wore a black woollen cap which, he said, "Keeps my brain warm, so I

can think". Pedro had a booming tenor voice which spread out from his chest in gusty, garrulous streams, like lava from a volcano. He was Brutus out of the Popeye cartoons. The two Swedish sailors, Matt and Toiva, Pedro and I, went to a newly opened restaurant in Guia, 2 miles west of Cascais. Pedro was also a saxophone player and we had been invited along by the Swedish restaurateur to entertain the clientèle at the opening of the new restaurant. Pedro was hoping to secure regular work there. However, in contrast, I was already looking forward to being out at sea and alone again. I loved playing my saxophone, but I could not exist on free beer and pizzas - the pay being offered - not now, but, next time, of course. This time was merely a try out and we were billed for our drinks and snacks. I felt a little angry when I got back to SP, even though no one had done anything to annoy me - I was reminded of the musician's lot. There were so many players who jumped at the chance to play in a restaurant because they thought this was success in itself, but it was not the case, a musician must arrange to be paid well before giving a performance. I felt out of sorts because I had stepped back into the shallow world of bars, beers and bombast. I was the sort of player who did it for sheer pleasure, as the bar owner observed, but this did not mean I did not need money. The treasure of my passion for saxophone playing was, in the end, rewarded by little more than a few compliments. Pedro talked about the possible fee for playing in the future, forty Euros was agreed by the bar owner, but this was soon diminished, by the musician's innate fear of cash, combined with a lack of self worth, to free beer and pizza. I was ready to leave Cascais and I had fitted the newly repaired foresail back onto the fore-stay The repair and fitting of a new ultraviolet protection band to the aft edge of the sail was very expensive, costing 198 Euros, a similar amount to what I would have spent in the UK. Sails are a boat's engines and they are a very economical means of propulsion, but not free of cost. I tried to tell the sail maker I was going to pay for the sail by playing my saxophone to him as he stitched, but he would only give me my sail in exchange for cash. When I got it aboard I was frustrated to find out the new uv protection strip was stitched beautifully in place along the leech, the trailing edge of the sail, but not along the bottom. The triangular sail rolled up along its longest side, the hypotenuse of the triangle and when fully rolled up one edge spiralled upwards from the lower end while the other spiralled downwards from the top. At the point where they met the sheets were attached. The sheets were two ropes leading back to a pair of winches in the cockpit. The sheets were used to control the fore sail. As the uv strip was only stitched to the aft edge, the lower section remained unprotected and I would have expected a sail maker to know this but only the work I had asked for was done. Toiva said, pragmatically, "So, you wait until the bottom goes rotten and then you get the same done to that part".

Then Mat passed and as I explained my woes we became ensconced in a complex assessment of just how annoying this oversight was. I said, "I'm really pleased with the part of the sail which has been done, but, you know, it feels like the job is incomplete". Mat understood, saying, "Yes it's a good job, but then it is only half the job, so, it's half as good". We stood contemplating the sail and I knew I would go sailing with it soon.

An alteration in my hrt (hormone replacement therapy) had peculiar effects. I walked towards Cascais from the marina in a hormonal dream time, with rose-scented thoughts and my ideas had after images, of fluffy yellow Easter chicks and silver hares, an oddness bought on by variation of my hormonal levels. In this mood I chose a small pastelaria offering a selection of small sweet tarts, empadas, cakes, as well as savouries; dainty little chicken pies, delicate lamb samosas and quiches.

The savouries and sweets were displayed on pretty paper lace and had tiny flags pinned into them with the names written in light green felt pen in a round feminine script. I was studying the pastry collection with deep pleasure and wearing an inane grin, like some Barbie doll. The yellow painted pastelaria had attracted other customers who were sensitized to the feminine realm that day. A couple, who sat nearby, talked in Spanish. They were female and I knew they were lovers too by the way they exchanged small stroking caresses.

A Red Letter Day, a White Wolf, his Goan Master and his Request for my Green Fleece

April 24 2003. A melodious whistling caught my ears and I was drawn to it until I got talking to Cosmi. He was from Goa, India and accompanied by three white dogs. One of the dogs was a wolfhound, with startling green eyes. He had Irish blood mixed with pure wolf. The second largest dog was a husky with head held high and he panted like he had just pulled a sledge. The third dog was small, with feathery ears and light hazel streaked coat. He defended himself vehemently against the largest which had new teeth and liked to place objects between them, including the feathery eared one with the light hazel streaked coat. Cosmi said, "Today the shops are shut. It is in memory of the liberation of Portugal from Salazar on 25 April, 1975," he told me, "Portugal was a feudal monarchy for 1,900 years, a fascist dictatorship for 75 years, and a so-called democracy for just 25 years". Cosmi spoke English, Swedish, French, and Portuguese, he had also lived in Sweden. He was a professor of 'economic and biological tropical medicine' and sent seeds of various unusual flora back to Goa for his mother to plant in the garden of his home. He said, "Everything grows there!"

He slept rough in a ruined house and spent most of his time on the beach with his dogs. He said, "I cannot get a job because they want me to cut off my beard, I went for a job driving a van and they told me I could have it but only if I shave my beard off". The melody he had been whistling was an old song, Grandola Villa Moreira, written by Jose Alphonse, celebrating freedom, equality and fraternity. Banned under Salazar, when Portugal's day of liberation arrived it was played on many radio stations. Cosmi told me the petit bourgeois of Cascais did not like the song and that is why he whistled it. He told me one of the reasons he kept three white dogs despite sleeping rough was to remind Portuguese people they were not as white as they would like to think. Gesturing at the dogs he said, "Look, THEY are white, Portuguese people are not white like them, they are brown," and laughed. Silently, I wondered what a psychoanalyst would make of Cosmi, his three white wolves and the political and cultural assumptions he was making against the Portuguese. Young Portuguese people identified more with Brazil, 3000 miles to the south-west, than they did with Europe. The Spanish were not like this about South America. Brazil was the country Portugal would become - if the weather was warmer - the rich were richer - the girls were sexier - and the lizards were bigger.

Cosmi asked me to give away my green fleece jumper, saying how he liked wearing green because it was the colour of life. He told me blue would suit me better because I often wore jeans and offered his own blue fleece in exchange for my green one. In a 25 Abril, 1975 moment, I agreed to let him have my favourite green fleece jumper. Later, I thought how Cosmi had actually given me the gift - the chance to provide somebody else with exactly what they wanted. I was wearing another, red, fleece when we met so we arranged to meet at four pm To exchange. I decided not to take his old one because it would smell of wolves and beard and the zip did not open all the way down which was less handy. When we met at four he seemed happy enough to hold onto his own fleece as well as accept mine. I had two other zip front fleeces on the boat, they were easily available in the UK charity shops, in dozens of colours and often of super quality.

It was a good day for consumers too. I had taken a purchase back to the Jumbo supermarket to gain a refund and had been given my money back without question. A mosquito repelling device which emitted high frequency sound and claimed to be the same as the noise made by male mosquitoes who had already mated, to repel fecund females, went on to explain how fertile females were the only ones which fed by biting mammals. I had thought, for 9 Euros, it may be a real wonder gadget. Toiva and Mat were sceptical and coming from Stockholm they had special knowledge of mosquitoes, but I disregarded this fact at the time. I slept with the battery powered device next to my head for two weeks while mosquitoes came at me with that little high pitched buzzing noise and I lost hours of sleep while I regularly smacked myself in the ear trying to whack the biters. Switching on the lights did no good at all because I could see only fleeting glimpses of them. They were clever enough not to land anywhere where I could swat them. On the packaging of the device it claimed to clear an area within 1.5m It simply had not not worked. La famille Auchan, French owners of Jumbo, had their priorities right and I walked away from the counter with my nine Euros and integrity intact.

Of course I had actually provided valuable field trials of the device for free and my efforts in bothering to bring it back and complain might have been rewarded with a free mosquito net or something. But no, I had only the purchase price and a thick ear from the previous two weeks of manual repellent action.

April 25 2003. I went to Peniche on the coach to pick up my laptop which had been repaired. I chose to go all the way to Peniche to use the company who had fitted the hard drive the previous autumn. 'Trilogica' were friendly and helpful as well as very reasonably priced. I had enquired at a service shop in Cascais, where they charged 98 Euros per half hour. They told me, as I gasped at the high price, "We are very quick," but I said, "I can't afford to be THAT quick". The fact was to replace the operating system and do a backup of my files would easily take an hour. Therefore I could foresee a bill of nearly 200 Euros. Trilogica, on the other hand, charged me one hour of assistance at 28 Euros Even with the coach, train and bus fares of two round trips to Peniche from Cascais I was still way ahead of the super quick rip-off service shop in Cascais.

A most pleasant outcome of this second trip back to Peniche was meeting a friend on the coach. Sandra worked in an office on the quay in Peniche, selling day trips to the Ilhas Berlengas. She had a most attractive voice which I had always thought very sensuous, like the smooth orange sand banks of the warm shallow southern side of the Tagus estuary, where she was born. She told me about her pet tartaruga - turtle - how it began very small, the size of a matchbox, but grew as big as a hardback book and that she dare not handle it any more. The day progressed through a walk to the station in Cascais - a train into Lisbon - a bus to the coach station - a coach to Peniche - and finally, a walk to Trilogica. The whole day flowed along - despite my getting up mid-morning and almost deciding it was too late to go to Peniche - buses and trains were all awaiting my arrival and left within minutes of me boarding. Meeting Sandra was all part of this serendipity.

April 26 2003. After feasting on a birthday curry, made with chillies from the garden of Lynne and Tony in Seixal, I went for a stroll in the Cascais evening. I was very tempted to buy a Times World Atlas from a marquee where books were for sale. I chose to let it stew for a while and walked back towards the boat. A voice boomed along the central Cascais street, "Clarissa!" It was Pedro and he had his saxophone with him, so we had a beer together and when I mentioned it was my birthday he insisted we play our saxophones together on the beach. "Come on! Clarissa! Don't be a lonely eskimo," he urged. So we went to get my 'horn' and stopped off for a beer in Skippers Bar in the marina.

Next we stopped in a local bar for a maceira - Portuguese brandy - drunk standing at the bar and as quick as I dared. There were several of these pit stops. We played together on the beach, until a Japanese doctor asked us to move further away from the houses because he had to work in the morning. We then moved to another spot, where the fishermen stowed their gear. Passers-by looked down from the harbour wall above and clapped our performances. Some English holiday makers dropped a twenty Euro note down for us and at this point Pedro decided we must go and play in a bar. We ended up in a crowded bar looking over the beach, and playing to applause, somewhat drunkenly, while downing more maceiras. The twenty Euros was spent, the saxophones made it safely home and I spent the following day in a dizzy haze, sitting in the park, stroking the feral cats and recovering from a memorable birthday.

April 30 2003. When I could no longer see the massive Cascais Villa shopping centre which had visually dominated the town with its blue glass frontage and wave shaped roof, the Cascais line had mulched down into the distance. The previous five weeks, sprawled along the receding coast and the Serra do Sintra mountains reared up like a great wave of limestone about to break over Cascais. I was 10 miles offshore and had just thrown up. Perhaps the drinking had weakened my stomach, but I felt out of sorts as the boat lurched about under me, but at least the wind vane steering worked well. This gave me time to boot up the laptop and copy the route details down on paper in order to use them to get around Cabo Espichel to Sesimbra. Cabo Espichel was crowned with a lighthouse and another building which had also been invisible from the Cascais Villa shopping centre from where I had often gazed out, over the 20 miles of sea, at the headland.

Nearing Espichel I saw a reddish cliff face with dramatic strata running at forty degrees from the horizontal. The red colour was perhaps the same iron rich land which I had remarked on in Seixal, where there was a picturesque orange sand. As Cabo Espichel came abeam, there was a different look to the cliffs which seemed to be a lighter rock smudged by green plant growth as the brighter light hit the south facing side. At the foot of the cliffs slow motion waves burst into white fans. No sound reached me. The rocks were full of holes and sockets - caves eroded by the sea over thousands of years - I felt utterly alone under this spectacular cape pointing to me like a finger at a thunder-fly. Once Cabo Espichel was rounded the cliffs led in an easterly direction. I chuckled to myself as I thought how the cape looked like a basking gecko, but I did not photograph it because it was only my own obsession which formed this impression. As I sailed towards Sesimbra, the waves grew less and the evening eased in under an attractive blue sky. Lately the daylight had lasted until 8.30pm. I chugged around the harbour wall at 7pm to arrive in a peaceful little marina surrounded by colourfully painted fishing boats. Vivid symbols graced the boats, some with five pointed stars, others with eyes the shape of squid. Cliffs rose high above the port and it reminded me of Barry harbour in south Wales, only with palm trees and prickly pear cacti.

After tidying up the boat and paying 6.10 Euros for a nights berthing I took a walk into Sesimbra, a mile to the east of the marina. I thought it was like a combination of Nazare, Peniche, Cascais and Barry Harbour. The latter because the cliffs rearing up steeply over the port were similar to Barry, as well as for the quiet. Nazare came to me for the sweeping arc of beach with the town spread around it. Also there were tiny charcoal cookers plonked right in the middle of back roads, scenting the air with pine smoke and forcing cars to gingerly steer around One was electric powered and scented the air with nothing. Sesimbra reminded me of Cascais because there were loads of ugly residential developments jutting out of the green clad hills behind the town, the result of being a dormitory town of Lisbon. By the look of the cars and some houses there was certainly money around, but it was a calm and unhurried town. It reminded me of Peniche because there were dogs everywhere. One in particular was quite mad because it ambled down the centre of the road and at the approach of a car it rushed headlong at the vehicle, turned in a scratching of paws and yapping. Cars slowed a little from 50mph as the dog ran headlong at them and this enabled the dog to run alongside, barking fiercely up at the drivers window for a few hundred metres.

May 1 2003. The next day I awoke with the exciting feeling of being in a new port and having an unseen town to explore. A gecko of quite a substantial size paused briefly on a rock and, like a word on the tip of the tongue, slipped from sight and remained present but invisible. The landscape was gecko perfect - thick foliage and slabs of rock and sun beaten rough ground. Sesimbra faced south and the beach looked and sounded idyllic - the backs of small receding waves nuzzled the sand with the sound of short in-breaths and the town behind was mindful of the the prevailing north wind which so often brought clear weather to the sheltered shoreline. 8 miles further east was the entrance to the River Sado and after this the coast turned southwards down to Cabo Sao Vicente, where the coast turned sharp eastwards along the famous Algarve. A single port existed between Sesimbra and the Algarve - Sines.

After a single day exploring Sesimbra, which made me glad to be away from Cascais, I set out for Sines and the Alentejo coast.

3 May 3 2003. On a Saturday I sailed to Sines on a fresh northerly breeze. It took eight hours, but I was not sailing slowly, SP was in her favourite mode - wind from the aft quarter, not quite completely from behind - the same aspect as when I crossed Biscay - we moved fast with white waves curling away from the bow, slipping past with a seething noise and falling away behind. The self-steering gear held a better course than I could and I moved into a new mode of cruising - not being bound to the tiller I relaxed more on the boat - I sat at the cabin table to eat lunch, played guitar with dolphins diving and slicing dorsal fins through the motion around as if they could hear the music of the guitar. Fifteen minutes sleep using the kitchen timer to wake me felt relaxing and soothing as the tensions of being at sea, the lurching, the strain of working the boat alone, became self-governing.

Finally I did what I had so far been unable to at sea - I listened to cds with headphones - singing along at the top of my voice, I knew not a soul in the world could hear me, apart from the dolphins and they seemed to celebrate any expression as if movement and sound was joy - and it was. All the doubts and efforts and sceptical remarks from other sailors when I was building the wind vane steering were resolved. The device was to change a cruise into a voyage by freeing up the hours I previously spent hand steering. I listened to Cesaria Evora, a singer from Cabo Verde Islands, as the sand coloured, heat-hazed Alentejo coastline drew closer towards Sines.

When I arrived at Sines harbour the wind was blowing hard and the marina lay downwind. SP hardly had any reverse power because the propeller was designed mostly for forward motion. I lashed the main sail, readied bow and stern ropes and positioned fenders on the port side. The wind hit the water making cat's paws and everything was in motion as I entered the confined space amongst the pontoons anxious about hitting something, but I'd seen an empty berth where the boat would be facing into the wind and so would come to a calm and controlled halt. I arrived at the berth well prepared and where the boat came to rest gently against the pontoon, three men stood beckoning, waving their arms as if they wanted to catch the boat. One was customs - Brigada Fiscal, one the marina manager and one to grab wet lines. I think I surprised them all by calmly handing a prepared line as the boat nestled obediently into the pontoon. Usually arrivals in strong winds were just havoc with people throwing ropes which then got caught in a gust and ended up around the propeller and maybe, as the arriving boat got stuck broadside on to the stern of another, a slow grinding scrape and a twanging as tangled fittings wrenched apart. As a rule the incompetence was multiplied by the number of 'helpers' present.

Sines had the peace and naturalness of Peniche, with the tranquillity of Sesimbra. The people seemed unconcerned about the rest of the world, which existed way to the east, for Europe and, thousands of miles west, for America. Another flow here was something of Africa which was just beginning, like a barely detectable sub-tone, for I was conscious of the African continent becoming an increasingly viable option to sail to and I had already been playing with that fascinating idea for a week. I had sailed 60 miles south of Cascais which now seemed a boring mash of consumerism and failing bars. Now I could no longer understand what I'd seen in it. I suppose it was merely the first really southern feeling place I had sailed to. The feeling of being in the south was met on arrival in La Coruna, which felt wildly south of Milford Haven. Then on arrival at the Cascais shores it too felt really southern. Now though I was clear of the Lisbon dormitory towns of Cascais and Sesimbra and I'd reached the region of Alentejo. I found it rural, full of palm trees, yuccas with great deadly spikes and banks of prickly pear cacti. Really southern. A cool wind blew from the north still and this had a completely restorative effect on the mind and body. It may have been the extra relaxed sail under the wind vane self-steering which had taken so much less of a toll on me. It may have been the little spring trickling out of the base of the cliff with a tiled surround, picturing a saint, with the words, '*Santa Luzia. Agua Santa. Para tratemente dos olhas*'. Water trickled from the base of a cliff at the top of which stood a medieval castle. In the keep of this castle, Vasco de Gama may have been born in 1595. The water, it said, was good for the eyes. I applied a little to my eyelids and said a prayer. Other thoughts were of the urban sprawl above the water-table which supplied the spring, of broken drains and leaking sewers leaching downwards through the cliff. It was now time to be less enthusiastic about geckos, to just let them come which they would now I was well into gecko lands.

Two windsurfer's sails looked like two feathers set into the blue sea.

Pedro would say, 'Life, lasts only 2 days, but don't worry, because carnival lasts 3 days'.

They were female and I knew they were lovers too by the way they exchanged small stroking caresses.

The self-steering gear held a better course than I could and I moved into a new mode of cruising - not being bound to the tiller ... played guitar with dolphins diving and slicing dorsal fins through the motion around as if they could hear the music of the guitar.

Chapter 4

On Not Being an Omen

Again I decided my black furry bag with a tail seemed too potent among people who held old superstitions. It would be unfair to catalyse someone else's delusions. Let them do it to themselves without entangling me in their dreams. A person with a tail, or the appearance of a tail was as strange to some people as a talking animal. I mostly saw superstition as delusion, such as flaunting the old sea dog's rule about never going to sea on a Friday - I sailed to Sines on Friday because the weather was suitable. Omens were nothing but fragments of hopes and fears resonating in the world around, but like beauty, they are in the eye of the beholder. There was nevertheless a need to respect people's views and the cages they make for themselves out of beliefs they willingly bind themselves to. Like stories, myths involve scenes linked into chains of dramatic events. Amongst these story boards of the imagination we vicariously sense our own circumstances, intentions and desires. The ubiquitous form: Beginning; Middle; End. Everyday time tends to be within that schema. First there was a princess, then she was captured, and then she was rescued by a gallant knight. Before rescuing her the knight encounters potent symbols such as a dragon, or scrying witches. Meanwhile the princess was offered an eternity in never never land by a faerie prince. Figures and events are set into the imaginary framework of beginning, middle and end. Faeries move in-between, they are depicted at borders, hedgerows, the edges of woods and streams, neither one thing nor another and at crossroads as well as upheavals and life changes. Any appearance of faeries can be viewed as the mark of a turning point, an omen of change. Faeries are blamed by the superstitious and thanked by those who are less fearful of life, or gods, or God, or fate, luck, goodwill, a black furry tail, etc. Personally I thank the geckos and keep my ironic tail to myself.

Adega De Sines was an eatery with marble tables, tiled floor and walls. Small wooden stools at the tables, a heavily moulded ceiling from which three large white glass globes hung and grubby lamp shades, as was the whole place. I ordered a meal with a tumbler of wine and felt I'd found the best place this side of Lisbon. Next to the door a charcoal grill smoked liberally and the wine perfect for early afternoon. Two small dogs lay in the doorway - in the UK dogs would be forbidden by some health law - the very grubbiness of the place gave such flavour. A plate of chips with three grilled pork steaks arrived under my nose and smelt glorious. An open jar of oil with garlic and strong chilli, with a dipper applicator and a virtually empty salt cellar was to my left, the wine to my right and in the centre a rectangle of paper with the name of the eatery printed in blue, the telephone number and a picture of a cooked chicken. This was the region of Portugal known mostly for its food, the Alentejo - they did rustic and delicious cooking. With the still red table wine (the only one) the meal was delicious, exactly what I wanted. The morning had been challenging in minute but enervating ways. I felt it to be a test which I had succeeded in passing and the the grilled pork and chips was my reward to myself. Initially it rained just as I set out with a list of tasks in my pocket. When I finally made it up the cliff road to the town I was already chilly and damp and slightly put out by another UK Sailor, who had been tediously boring, in a, 'When I was last down the royal Dorset (yacht club), blah, blah', way. The annoying character had offered me a lift to the library, but I thought it absurd to waste the crucial bit of exercise of walking a mile uphill. Then in the post office I had tried out the internet kiosk but it was a frustrating mash of instructions and demands for a charged credit card to be inserted. I looked for help at the counter but another customer ticked me off for not pulling a numbered ticket from a post at the door. Eventually, swallowing my pride I took a ticket, but then I was behind three others in a queue. The Portuguese post offices had all been so slow as each person walked across the space between the queue and the counter until I simply lost patience and discarded my numbered ticket in the bin by the door and left in a huff. I had apologized to the ticket holder next to me for trying to claim I was ahead of her when I had wanted to ask for assistance while trying to access the web. Next I failed to find a TMN shop, TMN was the mobile phone company I used in Portugal. Various directions pointed to a general area, but I was actually walking around lost. I peered into a bikini shop and, being on the lookout for one, went inside to ask directions. The shop was occupied by a young girl who looked so bored it was as if the place had not sold a thing for over a week. I nearly freed myself of this feeling of being stuck by walking away, but I went inside and was surprised to be greeted by the counter assistant with a really bright, cheerful smile followed by assured set of directions to the TMN shop.

My obstacle ridden morning felt brighter as I continued to the TMN shop. Just as I was being asked how I could be helped a telephone rang and the counter assistant swerved attention from me to answer it. I was fuming because I had already waited while another customer chatted endlessly at the same time as propping the door open as if to leave at any second. This was a feature of Portuguese shops. One may wait long minutes while a conversation at the till deepened and boomed in front of you and then the chances were someone else would dive into the shop and ask for change just before the long awaited, 'Bom dia senhora', and usually a conversation was implanted into the precious attention span between oneself and the counter assistant which was maddening. After I was promised the 25 Euros credit would appear as a text message on my phone, "In half an hour", I had carelessly left with no receipt. After an hour nothing had happened. After eating at the delicious charcoal grill restaurant and supping the ruddy wine I felt better. I noted to myself about how I mostly wander around quite hungry. A banana does not make a meal with wine. The credit still had not appeared and so I walked back to the TMN shop, but of course it was closed for two and a half hours. I wondered if the man had run off with my twenty five Euros and chided myself for not getting a receipt.

The Biblioteca Municipal De Sines, the public library, offered free internet use. I was able to look at some of the 125 emails which had arrived since I was in Cascais five days ago. It was almost impossible to reply to anyone because the keyboard was faulty and the PC was so slow. Most of the email was junk and spam, but it was taking two minutes to delete each one, so after nearly an hour I politely asked if a newly arrived person reading a newspaper behind me if they wanted to use the PC and she did and so I left. For each frustration there was an associated satisfaction for this mixed day. I reckoned I had not left anyone annoyed because I had been actively considerate and this made me feel pleased. The temptation had been to get angry with the slow computer, start tut-tutting at the tedious post office queuing system and nattering shop keepers, but I managed to choose not to. In the afternoon I sat in a pleasant sun speckled terrace of a bar called the 'Ponto De Encontro', the Point of Encounter. It was trendy and cool but unpretentious, with just a few young people talking in German, English and Portuguese and the terrace was sheltered and sensuously dappled by a wide spreading tree with bright green leaves creating? the shimmering sound of wind and high branches moving. I sat down to write, with a galao and when the TMN credit came through felt everything slotting into place.

May 6 2003. The Intermarche supermarket was set outside Sines. Access was given to cars, from a large intersection over a motorway. Pedestrians were completely neglected in the planning and building. I persevered around the edge of a huge roundabout, so big it had wide gravel spattered areas which were quite safe to walk along. Already I had seen three tigers, a pair of Llamas and a micro herd of Bison. A circus was encamped on the outskirts of Sines and I watched the tan and black striped tigers pacing to and fro as a man worked at the bars of their cage, propping open the shutters with a long pole.

After passing over the roundabout, I went down an embankment towards the back of the Intermarche. The ground was thick with ice plants, pine cones, dry sticks and a weave of roots and leaves, a very snaky terrain, but I saw nothing apart from a black dog rolling and kicking its legs in the air on a patch of sand. I climbed across a V shaped water-channel, almost dry and so easy to cross. The dog leapt up and scampered off as I approached. The rear car park of the Intermarche was just a few more steps and I found the front entrance to an accompaniment of, 'I believe I can fly', through external loudspeakers. The absurdity of out of town shopping made me laugh.

Once inside I sat in the café with a galao and a croissant. A strong gusty wind blew outside and I savoured the relative shelter of the interior of Intermarche while looking forward to some shopping after the awkward walk to the supermarket over snaking roads, through crowded foliage, past a herd of bison, a trio of tigers and a pair of llamas, then finally over a moat to confront a mangy dog.

On the way back another cage had been revealed which contained three green-eyed lionesses, consorts of Aslan. The night before I had been treated to a meal out by Roger and Sandra, the UK couple I met in Peniche and Cascais who reached Sines a few weeks before me. They took me to the same eatery I had been in before to ravish Frango No Churrasco with a glass jug of red wine drunk out of tumblers. And there was the same jar of garlic and chilli soaked oil with a dip stick applicator. They painted a dramatic word picture of a crypt in a town called Evora, where five thousand skeletons were stored in an underground room. I would, they said, come out of there with an altered perception of mortality and even cocky youths would come out with a mortified expression on their, usually rubbery, faces. We went on to talk about how short life was, how it was already May, the fifth month of the year and the fact it would soon be Christmas. We agreed it was of utmost importance to enjoy the few precious moments of possibility in each day.

'... *an hour here or there when our lives seem, against all odds and expectations, to burst open and give us everything we've ever imagined'*.
From a review of Michael Cunningham's book, *The Hours'*.

After the meal we took a galao on a café terrace and before I knew it I was sitting back aboard SP, the wind howling outside, thinking to myself - another day gone! I got an early night and felt a little melancholy.

May 9 2003. On the terrace of the pastelaria several tables were filled. One had four tall northern Europeans who talked in a way which made them look like they had lived in Portugal for some time - theirs was not the amused, curiosity of tourists, rather they talked with level expressions as if the subject was the serious matter of retired life in southern Portugal. They touched their faces and hair much during conversation, showing a slight nervousness, the self-consciousness of foreigners. They wore casual, but tasteful, cotton/nylon mix slacks and shirts in delicate pastel colours. They wore small ladies watches and dainty neck chains. A striking feature of these women, were their short haircuts. In all four cases the style was straight, clean, subtly highlighted with colourings to hide any greyness and clear of the neck, ending in a continental shelf, where the hair mass dropped steeply into the nape. The tallest got up to pay, walking past another table where four Portuguese women chatted.

The tall northerner stooped down and picked up a paper napkin which had blown off the Portuguese women's table, then lifting one of their empty plates she slipped the napkin underneath and with a little smile she walked away. A message implicit in the action of the northern woman was the need to pick up 'our' litter and create a cleaner, better, society and this small moral ticking-off, of course for the Portuguese women, was an insult. The Portuguese would never put something which had been on the pavement onto the table.

A cylindrical plastic vending machine, coloured primary red, yellow and blue with a see-through middle which was filled with plastic balls, each containing a toy. The words *'Mix! - 1 Euro - Bouly'* and a gremlin cartoon figure offered fun to children. When children managed to persuade their parents to buy one the parents invariably snatched the new, fascinating, transparent sphere as it dropped into the trough, before the child had a chance to savour the novelty. The parent then hurled the perfect globe at the floor to crack it open and free the toy it contained. The child would be left with nothing but a disappointing toy and the broken pieces of the globe. The child would be so bewildered by the smashing of the object of desire, the globe, they would fall quiet rather than being engaged by a fascinating new thing. As they walked away the child would throw backward glances at the machine containing those spheres filled with coloured objects and at the pieces of the broken sphere. Desire had been broken, rather than granted.

An English couple sat in overly strong, direct, sunshine. The rest of the terrace occupants having chosen shade. An arrufada was noted as, 'Very nice, mmm'. The coffee was criticized as a bit cool, but the man said, 'I don't like mine too hot'.

A group of Portuguese men talked with strong voices, newspapers and cigarettes. Their tiny coffees all finished, they laughed and greeted friends as they passed, with beaming smiles and handshakes. A glasses case rested on the table in front of one of the older men and a mobile phone on a wallet lay on the table in front of a younger man. An attractive woman, passed, talking briefly - forcefully - with the mobile phone man. The group fell quiet for a few moments until the wife walked away with whatever they discussed set to her satisfaction and then the men depleted any tension with quick comments between themselves, soon returning to vigorous humour and conversation again.

The group was a container of their shared experience and the hermetic seal was re-formed as they joked and laughed with each other. In contrast, an English woman smiled as people passed by, entering her zone of comfort, the smile was a tight lipped mask of agreement to let others go by. It said, 'I am nice and you passing close by will not change that. Despite you being a strange foreign type'.

Portuguese people were more likely to frown when someone entered their zone of comfort. And they would comment if the trespass was too great. However there were no spiky defences to avoid. In contrast the English, *'I am nice'* smile gave off the message *'Your passing close to me is all I am thinking about, so don't try anything, ok!'*

Apparently, in the Mediterranean sea there were comparatively few

UK and US yachts that year, due to the perceived level of global terrorism with the proximity to Palestine, Israel, Libya, Syria and Algeria. A large motor cruiser from the UK stowed the red ensign when in port to reduce the risk of being chosen as a target of terrorists. Despite these fears, many of the UK sailors making southwards down the Portuguese coast had mentioned Morocco as a destination. The U.S. boats tended to be on their way around the world, although entirely avoiding Africa. Sailing routes were mostly followed as recommended in mainstream navigation manuals, utilizing the trade winds across the Atlantic in seasonal patterns. With the widespread use of gps navigation thousands of boats used almost identical paths across the Atlantic as they went first to one position and then the next, in accordance with a few highly trusted books on the subject. The accuracy of gps navigation meant two boats using the same co-ordinates as a turning point could sail a 1000 miles and arrive at a point within a couple of metres of each other.

May 12 2003. I observed a young gecko hanging, from two outstretched left limbs, in a little crescent form, resting body weight on the two folded right legs. The tail curved around to a delicate 'S' shape and its eyes glinted bronze. In a delicate, croaky voice the gecko spoke, 'Je lezarder,' and taken aback at the idea of a Portuguese gecko talking French, I asked, 'Lezarder? Qu'est ce que c'est?' The gecko replied, 'You'll have to ask a Frenchman', and without another word disappeared into a gap in the wall.

The next French sailor I met was Michel. He explained the meaning of the word, lezarder - enjoying the warmth of the sun and lazing around doing exactly what felt best, being relaxed, self absorbed and sexual. The French 'lezarder' sounded like, 'Lizard day' and for me meant just that - a sensual day, spent like a lizard. Michel was a video editor for French national television. He had recently worked in Baghdad, having no close family ties, he was often employed in war zones. Many years ago Michel had attended lectures given by the post-Freudian psychoanalyst, Jacques Lacan. Michel told me he never understood Lacan's theoretical statements, yet he heard the lectures as if it were a song. He said, "I could not understand the words, but I liked the melody".

One day on a walk through fields I saw a snake. It moved blindingly fast, a black 'S' written across the grassy path at my feet. All snakes in Portugal, of which there are numerous species, are called 'Cobras'. I had wanted to walk into the rural, arable land of the Alentejo and I spent a long day exploring the hinterland of Sines, picking an agricultural track out past a wind farm, a eucalyptus grove, a pine grove, smallholdings with donkeys and dogs and a traditional windmill no longer with sails. The route turned back towards Sines after I reached a view of the sea and turned into a quarry, deep, and on a Sunday, deserted. It had grey rock cliffs and water standing at the lowest level. Gulls peppered the grey water as if it was an estuary from which the tide had ebbed. Eventually I emerged through a broken wire fence on to the coast road. Further along the road in the direction of Sines I found the Clube Nautique De Sines where I sat on the terrace with a drink of water, a coffee and a maceira - Portuguese brandy. Two tugs worked around a tanker as it headed out of the harbour.

Families took Sunday refreshments and I noticed the difference between these people and the ones I watched on the terraces in the town centre. These were much more easy going and less conscious of how they looked, although they all looked well dressed. The boat club people were more easy going and comfortable with themselves than the townies. From the bar came a sensual, swirling melody which attracted me back just as I was leaving. I sat at a stool and noticed a framed caricature behind the bar and recognized it as the woman who was serving. Over a hugely plunging cleavage she explained how she downloaded music compilations from the web. The one playing was made up of Moroccan music, but she had no titles. Next to me two men spoke in slurred broken sentences. They were the chief engineer and his mate from a ship which had put into Sines with engine problems.

The Indonesian mate was not so drunk, but the Danish chief engineer kept saying, "No, no more beer, I have to go and fix my computer". This went on as the mate vied for more alcohol and the engineer resisted although they were both already well drunk.

'Saudade' was a quintessentially Portuguese word expressing the feeling of love with the sadness of loss. It was the message of Portuguese *fado* - songs, played on a twelve string guitar and sung with absolute melancholy. Saudade means - *this is the sound of my soul* - and saudade is the blues. Fado was learned by ear and by feeling the fingers pressing down the strings. Each player brought a personal interpretation to fado and so it was the people's music, like the blues in the Mississippi Delta. On her website, fado singer Cristina Branco described this quintessentially Portuguese word: 'Saudade was too, the word used by the Portuguese sailors as they left the quay for seas never explored before.'

One day I visited a pharmacy and asked about malaria prophylactics.

The pharmacist spoke good English and became very interested in the idea of sailing to the Gambia. I'd said I wanted malaria protection for Senegal and Gambia although those west African countries seemed a very long way in distance and culture and I began to open myself up to the reality of the possibility of sailing there. Of course having found out I could buy malaria prophylactics at a low cost over the counter I found myself buying them and then walking home to SP clutching the unlikely potential in the small plastic chemist's bag with my imagination taking flight across seas never explored before.

The idea of going to Africa had been absolutely absent before I left the UK, although I had been deeply impressed by articles written by those elite voyagers who had sailed there, with pictures of their boats surrounded by mangroves and portraits of the most friendly looking people I had ever set eyes upon. Stories about how interesting and safe Morocco was had largely erased my fears about hustlers, bribes and thieves. The idea of going even further, all the way to Gambia, really, really, excited me. And really scared me too.

On the terrace of the Pastelaria Vela d'Ouro I noticed a local woman:
1. *She was tall.*
2. *Her hair reached the small of her back.*
3. *She worked in the library.*
4. *She was as attractive as a Paris artist's model.*
5. *She wore a denim jacket and jeans.*
6. *She ate soup.*
7. *She read a massive volume of the writing of Gabriel Garcia Marquez.*
8. *She had a leather handbag.*
9. *The wind swept the table clean of sugar wrappers.*
10. *She wore an ornately scrolled silver ring.*
11. *She wore silver earrings with tiny azure beads strung in them.*
12. *She wore a plastic fashion watch.*
13. *She sensed she was living in a book somewhere.*

I rose from bed late having been disturbed at 3am by mosquitoes. During the morning three separate visitors came to the boat as I was washing, brushing my teeth and eating breakfast. The marina pontoons were a little too social for the morning at least, when I liked to have time to myself. Eventually I left the marina to walk up the steep road into the town to use the internet PC in the library or at the cultural centre. They both offered free internet use but I could only do printing in the first, or use a floppy disc drive in the second. The weather had been the same since I arrived in Sines. It blew from the north-west, gently in the morning increasing to a stiff breeze in the early afternoon, remaining until after midnight. I found out there was a free world music festival held inside Sines castle each year. The castle keep was where Vasco De Gama was believed to have been born. A statue of him stood looking out at the western horizon. He discovered the sea route from Europe to India via South Africa, in the days before the Suez canal was built to connect the Mediterranean with the Red Sea and thus the Indian ocean. The Sines 'world music festival' had an interesting range of musicians; reggae band, Black Uhuru, an interesting looking folk roots band from Finland, Cristina Branco - fado singer from Portugal, a blues player and an exciting looking African band.

The festival was on the last weekend of July each year, but I expected to be under the throbbing heat of the Algarve by then, on my way to the River Guadiana. The castle occupied the centre of Sines with its high walls dominating my favourite terrace, the Pastelaria Vela D'Ouro - the Golden Sail. On stepping through the small doorway to enter the castle I was surprised to emerge into a virtually empty space with flat grass and sparrows chirruping. On my first visit the only movement was to my left, a tiger coloured tom cat growling at the door of the tourist information office, which was shut for lunch. The only other features were several derelict buildings, open-roofed and grass-floored, where locals liked to take a pee. My grudge about ancient ruins continued.

One day many people were in Sines - cars queueing around narrow bends and groups of smart Portuguese or Sineenses standing around. A May wedding, I wondered, when bouquets of flowers were carried towards the church next to the castle.

Near to the active church was a chapel where an exhibition of photographs by Jose Melo was showing. He left Portugal aged eighteen, to escape the repression under Salazar, living in France and then Amsterdam. His images were an intensely rendered account of the people and scenes of Portugal. The perspective of an ex-patriot showed a tangible sense of loss and saudade. A series of images had been taken in Sines when a cargo ship had exploded in the harbour, killing two local dock workers. The photographs showed locals looking over the wall towards the docks, a kilometre to the north west, where a plume of black smoke continued to emerge from the stricken ship. The smoke was carried away to the south by the same north wind which continued today. The caps worn by the men and the lined faces of women or pretty girls all looked like the towns people of today too. Aida was the voluntary exhibition attendant and had been in conversation with a local woman. I asked when the photograph of the ship had been taken but she did not know and together we three wondered when it could have been. The chatty local woman, Inezia Rafael, said she thought the ship exploded in about 1979.

Other images were taken in the far north of Portugal in a mountainous region known as Tras-os-Montes. The black and white images showed people, houses and dogs leading a rapidly disappearing way of life. My favourite single image was of a portrait photographer of Lisbon. In it a fairly old man was looking straight at the camera of Jose Melo. Eye contact was strengthened by the effect of heavy glasses which slightly magnified the subjects eyes. He leant on a large plate camera which looked to have been his tool for decades and had become scruffy with repairs in the bellows made in stitched leather and in the wooden case and stand, in brass strips fastened with screws. He wore a flat cap. The eyes of the photographer of Lisbon could only look at potential subjects for his own lens. In this old photographer's gaze the lens of Jose Melo was viewed as a subject's pupils. In turn the viewer of the print could connect with those habitual eyes as they surveyed their subject. The face of the Lisbon photographer was serene, almost beautiful, with an affable expression, but his eyes looked out from a deeper point than his face. While his smile was a little tight-lipped and fixed, his eyes were deeply engaging.

Out on the street a crowd of people had gathered along the road. The event which had brought bouquets and formal attire was not a wedding but a funeral. A shiny clean vehicle carried the coffin past. This was followed by hundreds of mourners. The majority of mourners were not dressed in black, but wore everyday casual clothes. I learned it was a local father who had been killed by his son.

The Jose Melo photographs had made a strong impression on me, especially the images of the locals in shock, watching the ship on fire after it had exploded. I had paced slowly around enjoying the photographs in silence apart from little groans of appreciation, but at a certain moment music was broadcast, the fado singer Cristina Branco, who was a regular subject of Jose Melo. Some of the magic in the silent photographs was lost in the intensity of the fado music. The exhibition hall was in the chapel Misericordia. An altar was in place but the walls and floor had been cleared for exhibition use. At the left side of the altar was a marble panel with veins and bunches of intertwining connections in the structure. A tap with the knuckles gave a soundless response of solid marble, perhaps part of the base of the altar. It looked like an image of a nebula, an accidental, or perhaps not, visual representation of a part of the cosmos in an old chapel.

On a Friday I met Reinhardt, a German, who worked as a 'life coach'. We got on well and so the rest of the day was spent touring the coast to the south of Sines in the car he had hired for his stay. I had been using the internet PC in the Centro Cultural de Sines and Reinhardt strolled into the room as he browsed a painting exhibition. We talked briefly and immediately found much to talk about and a common approach to the problem of life. Reinhardt explained how he had just returned from working with a theatre group in Times Square. He told me how he gave clients the opportunity to learn about being playful as a dynamic and effective life strategy. I was very interested in hearing about these ideas while Reinhardt was just as keen to hear of my voyage.

After carefully assessing his motives I agreed to us going to see the coast to the south. We went to Porto Covo, a small fishing village set amongst scenic cliffs. Next we drove to Mira de Milfontes, a tranquil river estuary meeting the sea where a small town had grown. I was particularly interested in visiting there because it was possible to enter the estuary by yacht, but only in very limited weather and sea conditions. I would be passing this point sometime and I wanted to have a look at the conditions at the mouth of the estuary. There were white breaking waves right across the river bar and I judged it as treacherous in all but perfect conditions. Slightly further back, upstream, the wide, softly flowing river made a most attractive scene. It ran through a green clad valley and we found a fish restaurant at the water's edge, looking out on a small pier where one or two persons came and messed about in boats, or just sat watching the warm evening. The meal was very pleasant, but expensive. On reflection I judged the flavour of the salmonetta, a red sea fish, as well as the tranquil atmosphere of the setting as well worth the expense, as a one off. We drove the 30 miles back to Sines via the inland road, which took us through mountains and a small town called Cercal. In the large centre square it was easy to imagine large markets being held there where cheeses, vegetables, meats and fish would be sold from the rich lands of the Alentejo. It was just as easy to picture Roman merchants, in togas, strolling around the old town square.

Reinhardt said how he had flown back after working in New York, stopping at Portugal for 4 days as a way to rest before returning to Munich. He said it helped to reduce the effect of jet-lag. I felt he had not completely countered the stress of working in New York and flying to Europe, because he drove a little too fast through the mountains on the way back. I find cars terrifying because I am accustomed to travelling along at 4mph an hour in SP. To approach a bend at 60mph felt reckless to me. Reinhardt said he was 'playing' in his driving, which was probably a very healthy thing to do. He asked me, "Do you like being driven fast?" I replied, "Nnn, oo, not really," by which I meant, 'not at all and slow down will you.' He did slow down and admitted too, that he should not 'play' all the time, especially if it was with another's life. We parted, having shared some very interesting ideas, splendid views of the seashore and rural Portugal and a special meal. There was a hint of coolness between us, which I put down to Reinhardt not having relaxed after New York and jetting across the Atlantic into another time.

What Reinhardt felt about our encounter I did not quite know. I wondered if the life of a gecko hunter set in the Alentejo fields, bursting with purple heather and masses of colourful wild flowers and the deep azure sea sprawling bright white amongst the rocky shores all in a perfect springtime warmth, had not in some way rubbed Reinhardt up the wrong way. Perhaps Reinhardt liked to be the one to reveal the power of play to others in need of his insights. Just maybe he saw in me a person who had gone even further than he in exploring my own 'Narnia'.

Jet-lag can be a funny thing, but so could too many hours spent out in the midday sun looking for geckos.

·1. She was tall.
2. Her hair reached the small of her back.
3. She worked in the library

May 15 2003. The *End of the World.* was extremely windy. My first really strong wind sailing that year. Cabo Sao Vicente was 55 miles south of Sines with no shelter along the way. I had set off from Sines at 3am to sail to Sagres, aiming to arrive in the evening. Cape Sao Vicente was known in ancient times as the Promontorium Sacrum and 'Sagres' also had 'sacred' as its Latin root. The ancient Portuguese navigators would anchor at Sagres to wait for favourable conditions for setting out on long voyages. The crews would row ashore and climb the cliffs to perform rituals and offer prayers, seeking safe passage as they left the known world. So, yet another 'finis terre' and by then I had become quite accustomed to messing about in boats just beyond the end of the world, first Land's End, then Finisterre, the furthest point west in Europe and then the most south-westerly tip of Europe.

I had been warned by other sailors about the possibility of waves swamping the cockpit, particularly around Cabo Sao Vicente. They said I must keep the washboards securely fixed in place. Washboards are slide-in plywood boards which seal the main cabin off from the cockpit. They warned me that after the first wave fills the cockpit the boat is very vulnerable. The cockpit of SP holds about one ton of water. The sailors had put the fear of god in me by describing how the second wave is invited in because the boat has become sluggish and low in the water with the weight of the sea which has come aboard and you must keep the second wave from entering the cabin on top of the first. So I reduced the water-holding capacity of the cockpit by lashing two diesel cans down in the aft end, thus preventing forty gallons of sea-water from entering.

Around Cabo Sao Vicente things were dramatic, the wind was right from behind and I sailed fast, reaching 7 knots at times. The waves got steeper and more threatening as I came within 5 miles of Cabo Sao Vicente. I thought, 'This is it, Cabo Sao Vicente is gonna get me'. But it did not and I think SP had very good sea keeping qualities, despite her decks being just 20 inches above the water. She lifted easily to the waves and I had water running around the decks, but not over the coamings and into the cockpit. Often as steep waves rose up and approached fast from behind I would think, 'This one is definitely going to crash aboard.' But no.

After I had rounded the cape the wind suddenly blew much harder. Another UK yacht had reached the same point as me and we headed together across the 5 miles to where the anchorage of Baleeira lay. The wind blew the tops of the waves off in fans of spray and I grinned as SP kept pace with the other, bigger boat. I put on my oil-skins for the first time since crossing Biscay the previous year. Heavy spray hit the cabin and spray hood and I cowered there, willing SP towards the shelter under the distant cliffs, now dead upwind. I was enjoying the sensation of violent motion and surging forward at speed, but I knew it may be necessary to stay out at sea until the wind lessened. The anchorage lay a couple of miles upwind and I did not know whether the engine would push against the wind and waves. Also, I worried about turning in behind a harbour wall, into an unfamiliar bay with moored fishing boats and quays, in those conditions. I opted for a decisive run into shelter and so I unlashed the anchor at the bows and freed up the chain in order to be ready to stop and hold the boat in an instant. The engine banged away inaudibly in that wind and slowly to my left the harbour mohle slipped past. The waves boiled around huge blocks of concrete and over to the right a line of rocky islands jutted out from the cliffs. It was most picturesque but seen through the blur of salt spray and wind I thought how different my expectations of the Algarve had been.

I thanked myself for altering the anchoring equipment to suit my experience when I was fitting out the boat. The chain came readily to hand and the anchor bit hard into the bottom when I dropped it in 10m depth. The boat lay suddenly much quieter with forty metres of 8 mm chain tethering her against the ripping gusts of wind. I took several bearings on buildings so I could see whether the anchor was holding. Then I rested, cooked supper, and tried to shake out the tensions of a long day with a challenging finish at the *End of The World.*

May 19 2003. The village connected to the fishing harbour of Baleeira was Sagres. It was windswept and had a dreamy atmosphere as if everyone was half asleep. There were some tourists but they seemed punch drunk under a combination of strong sun and wind. Another single-hander turned up to anchor and later I met Ralph, a German. We quickly made friends and over the next few days we explored the End of The World in company. We went to the Fortaleza, an old military fort occupying a bluff next to Cabo Sao Vicente. The fierce wind continued and we agreed there was a unique tranquillity to this region of wind blown capes. It felt enchanted, primal, empty. Much of the architecture was strangely domed and painted white. I noticed peculiar tapered chimneys on the roofs with decorative slots and oval openings. There were basking geckos, screeching swifts, ephemeral egrets, eyeing gulls, traversing ravens and, perhaps, a red kite swinging over the cliffs.

In the Fortaleza De Sagres I overheard a couple from the UK as they asked an assistant, "What is the wind rose?" The wind rose was an ancient circular design made of rough hewn stones set into the inner ground of the fort. It measured 84m in diameter, with 42 sections emanating from the centre. It was destroyed in the great earthquake of 1755, at the same time as the annihilation of Lisbon. In answer to the UK tourists question the attendant said emphatically, "It is a wind rose". The two white-legged holidaymakers walked away smirking and saying to one another, "But what is a wind rose?" Actually not much was known as to the purpose of the wind rose, a creation of Henry the Navigator, salty voyager of the fifteenth century who ran a school for seafarers in the forteleza. The wind rose was highly evocative of those old navigational maps showing bearings and routes, like bicycle spokes, at various known points. However the wind rose was not made up of 36 ten degree sectors which would match the 360 degrees used in navigation and maths. There was a deep mythological aspect to Cabo Sao Vicente and numerous palaeolithic and megalithic remains in the form of menhirs and burial mounds in the area. I found the atmosphere perfectly relaxing after my eventful passage from the Alentejo coast. The anchorage was free, and fairly well protected. An assortment of cruising vessels arrived most days and so I did not feel too isolated from the known world. One surprising arrival was 'Havsula', with Jim and April aboard, who had left Bristol a couple of months before myself. Then another yacht anchored with someone aboard who I had met in Bristol. It seemed the End of The World was a popular destination.

May 23 2003. Where a wave meets a sandy beach, a tumbling tunnel of sea-water mixed with sand forms. I found myself right there, being twirled around like some character in a fairy tale who was passing between two separate worlds. I was fully clothed and had on my back a rucksack containing my digital camera, my Psion computer and other valuables, such as passport and money. I scrambled upright as the receding surf rushed past my feet in a dizzying white sparkle. The dinghy then came tumbling towards me on the next wave and I grabbed it and hauled it up the beach, picking up my desert boot minus one sock as I escaped the turmoil. It was not dangerous, the waves were only half a meter high, but the power and force of them had caught me unawares as I approached the beach to land. In the last couple of days a southerly swell had been making life aboard most uncomfortable, as SP rocked from side to side relentlessly and occasionally violently. I learned to view the beach upon which I was to land a dinghy with much more scrutiny and to pick the best point at which to get ashore. Timing was crucial. One must wait for several big waves to pass and then row like mad towards the beach, leaping out with no hesitation once the breakers are reached. The dinghy could then be hauled clear of the next wave, before it was thrown against ones legs, or swamped. When I went to sleep that night I had sand in my hair, eyes, nose, ears and everywhere else. The lucky thing was I had carefully and consistently been wrapping my computer and digital camera in two layers of sealing freezer bags and they kept dry. I did have to dry my passport which had been in a bum bag. I did so by placing tissue paper between each page. Several postage stamps became unusable. The next day I felt a lot cleaner after I'd washed my hair in the fisherman's sink on the quay. The days now became very warm, around thirty degrees Celsius, it felt wonderful to walk in the heat with water in my hair evaporating and cooling my head. My desert boots were still wet but this too felt nothing but pleasant in the heat. I had to buy a straw sun hat, to protect my head from the heat.

The following day, after sewing a pretty green string onto my new hat to save it from the wind I rowed ashore. I wore a new pair of sandals which I had purchased at a 1970s price in a funny old shop. The sandals were in a box with other out of fashion styles and had a thick covering of fluff and dust. The shop keeper hummed constantly to herself. To one side there were a couple of chairs and a thick rug with an embroidery needle piercing it, it was her way to pass the long days before the three months of tourism swept the Algarve during June, July and August. The land was coated in flowers of purple, yellow and violet. Stands of cane, four meters tall, were everywhere between the houses. The wind swished through these dense growths and numerous paths led into the cane growths. I explored several of them and inside the cane growths the path wended past monstrous agaves and orange flowering prickly pear cacti. Usually there would be a derelict smallholding amongst the canes and occasionally a tiny cottage with fishing pots and nets draped along the fences. Dogs barked from behind lean-to's made of scrap wood and bound together by gravity and creeping vines flowering in white trumpets.

I visited Havsula, out of Bristol Marina and despite being anchored close to one another for several days now, we had only greeted one another two or three times. It was best to let other people remain undisturbed and when we did meet up it was mutually pleasant to drink some wine and chat about our journeys to Baleeira. Jim and April told me the luscious green foliage all turned brown and dry in the heat of July and August. They also informed me about a ten degree increase in temperature during the same period compared to May. The heat had got quite hot enough for my liking but Sagres was made bearable by the cool north wind and I was reluctant to go far along the Algarve coast where I would lose the refreshing breeze.

Sunday 25 May 2003. The day before I'd circumnavigated Sagres on foot, over mostly scrubby ground, beach, road and occasionally thick bush. The sun was hot but a strong north wind made it feel cool. Nevertheless I had too much sun. A couple of hours before I got back, I became aware I was becoming disoriented. I began to count on my fingers each time I felt odd. When it reached five instances I resolved to sit down in the shade, then find some water to drink and then head directly for SP. Occasionally I would notice myself somewhat blindly crashing forward through scrub and it was this which alerted me to possible sun stroke. My finger count reached five instances of floppiness and so I ate an orange, but there was no shade, unless I laid down under a bush, so I headed towards the south-east, where the dinghy was tied up on the beach.

The wind was strong and rowing the 200m to SP was as much as I could manage, as spray soaked me. I was only just able to reach the boat and as I passed Havsula, Jim and April were looking concerned. They suggested I take a rest by hanging onto their boat before I made the last fifty metres, but I just wanted to get aboard SP. I was a strong rower, having learned as a child while my parents and sister went dinghy sailing I would spend hours playing in a little polypropylene boat, called a Sportyak. The Sportyak was made by French company Bic, who also made biro pens. The Sportyak was an excellent little tender, but too small for most people. The problem was that waves tended to splosh over the low sides and soak the crew and cargo, but they were unsinkable because they were double-skinned. My faith in Sportyaks stems from about 1969, when my father, my sister and myself crossed the River Colne, from Mersea Island to Brightlingsea, with a bucket full of cockles aboard. The thousand meter crossing was a real struggle and the boat was almost full of water. We got back brimming with salty experience. I hated sailing then and my sister loved it. I would rather be captain, or have nothing to do with it. And so back to Sagres. When I got aboard SP I was soaked, tired and sun blasted. Half an hour later the cabin was shut against the howling wind and two paraffin lamps warmed both the evening temperature and the atmosphere. On the radio I heard an absorbing program on BBC World Service, the story of Alladin and his lamp, with backing music by DJ Pete Tong. For several hours I had a pain in my stomach. Perhaps I ate too heavily after a sun-drenched day. The previous day I had made a Portuguese dish called 'cataplana' which turned out to be one of my finest ever, I thought at least. Cataplana was more a method of cooking than a recipe. Any ingredients to hand were added uncooked to a pot and cooked for twenty-five minutes.

The traditional cataplana pot was made of copper or aluminium in a shallow dome shape, the upper and lower halves of which separate. cataplana was simply food cooked in its own steam inside a sealed pot, so a form of pressure cooker, and I used mine. The wind remained in the northerly quadrant, but was only strong in gusts, rather than constantly as it had been lately.

I sat in the pastelaria Conchinha, in the Placa de Republica, central Sagres. Sagres was spread out and sparsely built with large areas of scrub land and cane about and between the urban parts. The wind wrenched at palms and the hissing noise alerted me to thoughts about SP at anchor, although she had not dragged in 11 days.

The previous day's long exploration of the locality struck me for the absence of wildlife. The single notable species was a gracious white egret which flapped around over an ornamental pond in the garden of some desolate, wind blown villa. I saw no geckos and only one or two wall lizards while the rest of the fauna was made up of herring gulls snails and sparrows. The latter were a constant presence, which thrived amongst the protection of palm fronds and kept up a robust, happy, chirrupchirrup in daylight hours. The pastelaria Conchinha had a parrot in a cage which amused itself by stretching down from the perch to pick sunflower seeds from a bowl below. It was a very quiet bird, with hardly a whimper. Earlier in the week I had sat outside on the terrace and on hearing various chuckles, giggles and kissing noises I thought there must be some monstrous and strange baby on someone's lap nearby. Being polite I did not look to see where the sound was coming from. Out of the corner of my eye I sensed there was a baby in a white shawl breast feeding on a young woman's chest. Occasionally the girl would make a loud kissing noise which would be followed by an absurd cackling, like a gleeful baby fresh off the nipple, only strangely amplified with an unreal tone. Up to the point when I left my mind had concocted a bizarre picture of a baby possessing an over-developed voice box. Then as I got up to go I unselfconsciously glanced at the group with the baby, to see a large white cockatoo, not a baby, treading deliberately about the girl's chest.

Monday 26 May 2003. I saw more wildlife inside the pastelaria than on my circumnavigation of Sagres. A girl and her mum were laying broad green leaves into a couple of shoe boxes which were filled with dozens of caterpillars. Around the edge of the box were yellow fuzzy cocoons enmeshed in a hairy mass of web. Several caterpillars lay inside half spun cocoons, their heads working to and fro with strings of hair as they encased themselves for transformation. The mother and daughter gently laid leaves and caterpillars in layers. She spoke good English and told me the caterpillars would soon all go into cocoons. When they emerged in mid-summer as butterflies they would mate, lay eggs and die very quickly afterwards. I was glad I did not ask whether they were food, but it would be an easy question to ask because most creatures which can be found in any numbers were eaten by the Portuguese. Among the wild flowers, scrub and herbs growing on every piece of vacant land, rustic figures stooped with buckets to hand, collecting snails. The edible snails were not large and had attractive spiral stripes of light brown and cream. There were thousands and thousands of them on every wall and in every bush and agave. I did not know the exact method of cooking and my understanding of snail eating ended about ten years previously after my father had placed a half eaten bag of whelks into his coat pocket and forgotten about it. Several weeks later he wore the coat again, but it took my mother and father most of the day to work out where the awful smell was coming from. In the past I had enjoyed whelks with pepper sprinkled on them, bought from a seaside stall, but on the whole English seafood was tasteless, rubbery and the only flavour was salt-water and bits of green weed. The actual animal has almost no flavour, but lots of texture - English seafood was all in the chew, but mind the grains of sand, or whatever it is which gave a sudden, estuarine, 'Je ne'ce quoi.' Seafood lovers are made or broken on this novel grittiness - mostly broken.

On a menu outside a restaurant in Sagres I was surprised by the range of animals on offer. There was fried quail, fried rabbit, fried ostrich steaks and fried swordfish steaks. 'Turkey-Cock Broach' sounded somewhat delicate. 'Fried Little Cuttlefish' sounded sweet. 'Fried Clamps' sounded gripping. There was 'Octopus Rice', poor things; apparently octopi are highly intelligent. A local speciality which was highly expensive due to the method of gathering it, was 'percebes', barnacles. Around Villa de Bispo, close to Cabo Sao Vicente, intrepid harvesters wear full wet suits and use mountaineering gear to abseil down the cliffs to the rocks at sea level. Barnacles grow quite large, they are not just the tiny volcano shaped shells which cluster on seaside piers. They hang out of these shells like rubber pot plants and it is this body which was eaten. I would not try this dish, apart from it being expensive, I believed people would cook and sell anything if it could be found in abundance. To me barnacles were merely a problem because they covered the hull of SP and reduced her speed. The day I saw 'Osga' - gecko - on the menu would be the day I would fall out with Portugal, but they were clever enough as a species not to have become abundant enough to be harvested. Nonetheless, geckos were very popular as pets in many parts of the world. Why not fried swift? They were always screaming overhead, but I had been told some Portuguese eat small birds and so the joke ends there.

The Lands Beyond *The End of The World*

Thursday 29 May 2003. When I tried to pull up the anchor to leave Baleeira it was stuck. I had been warned about the bay being full of obstructions. I eventually freed it using the winch and motoring ahead to untangle the chain. I sensed the chain had become wrapped under a rock. It was with relief I motored out into the open sea, for a fouled anchor could be costly if a diver was needed and a lost anchor would cost 200 Euros to replace. When I motored away I was dismayed to find I could only make two knots. Even a journey of less than twenty miles would take all day at that rate. Gradually I left Sagres behind and drew closer to the Ponte De Piedade on the horizon, 15 miles away. Within 2 miles of the shore were more fishing pot markers than I had ever seen. At one point yellow 'special mark' buoys (a yellow buoy with a yellow X on top) guarded an area of about a mile square. These appeared to be linked to more yellow floats by ropes around the whole area. Small open boats worked amongst the crowds of fishing pot markers, of which I counted 120.

Further along the coast the tourist trade had overwhelmed the fishing industry and the shore became speckled with ugly residential developments. The enchantment of windy Sagres had gone, but the sea rippled with ribbons of sunlight making halos around my shadow and that of the boat. Cliffs changed from robust limestone bluffs, to tortured folds, riddled with caves, arches and golden beaches. I was being re-enchanted by another spell - the Algarve I had seen in pictures was forming in front of my eyes. It began at Cabo Piedade, the calm sea and hot sun persuaded me to close to within fifty metres of the cliffs. Five metres below the boat I could see rocks and sand rising and falling under the ribbons and halos of sunlight. It reminded me of the *Voyage of the Dawntreader* when the 'sea people' appeared on the sea bottom as the voyage progressed in a shallower sea nearer to Aslan's country. A turtle, no longer than my little finger, paddled away as I passed.

Simultaneously I was disenchanted by the tourist developments, which instead of being wild and lonely the cliffs had become capped by little figures, wearing swimming costumes and baseball caps. At Ponta De Piedade dozens of trip boats milled about amongst the 'grutas' - caves, some disappearing while others emerged from arched caverns. A slow, deep, gentle, swell, like a giant breathing, alternately raised and lowered the cave roofs. Two large passenger boats were anchored within thirty metres of the cliffs. On the upper deck I saw crowds of people slumped in the shadeless heat of the day, while a charcoal grill sent a plume of hot, grey smoke up over the cliffs. I chugged past wearing my usual mess of safety gear - harness and life jacket. This safety concern was even more a requirement now because most of the time SP was steered by the wind rudder and if I fell overboard she would continue sailing endlessly away. I heard, in English, the words, "Look that boats come from England," and smiling faces peered out from under white cotton sun hats to wave at me. A mile further along this exotic, red, cliffy, shoreline was the port of Lagos (pronounced, Lah-gosh). Soon I entered between the harbour walls to see a colourful tourist town, with a large modern marina. I needed to charge batteries and do some laundry. Although Lagos was bigger than Sagres it was not much more than a big expensive marina and a tourist town filled with English, German and Dutch holidaymakers.

Friday 30 May 2003. 'Cervecerias' were cafés selling beer and coffee with only one or two pastries on sale. 'Dragao' attracted me by its simplicity and by the name - Dragon. Inside it was fairly cool and a relief after the tourist traps of Lagos. I watched a Portuguese baby take more of her very first steps, held by the arms of an elegant young mother. At another table a man spoke in a strong voice, as if he was going through the terms of a newly imposed by-law and the barman sat at the same table staring at the floor, nodding in futile agreement. The speaking man drank a brandy and smoked cigarettes. The path from where I'd left the dinghy after rowing ashore had led through bristling trees, shimmering shrubs, tiny purple anemones in crevices and small ruins standing amongst high beige grasses where a blackbird sang. Alvor was a promise of a welcome rest, zero marina charges and a very attractive, sheltered anchorage. To reach the anchorage it was necessary to pass between two harbour walls, one with a red striped light structure on the end, the other with the same in green. After this the channel passed into a wide expanse of calm waters, protected from the sea by sand dunes and beach.

Terns shrieked and flapped daintily by in creasing crescents, more wing than bird, buoyant as model gliders, turning sideways and plunge diving in an instant. A mile to my right lay a smudge of buildings and between me and there were low banks of creamy orange sand. I had a detailed route planned on the gps with eight points to reach and turn at in order to follow the best water through the lagoon to Alvor. Five hundred meters after passing safely through the entrance SP ran aground and an incoming tide swirled about pushing her harder on. It was not a problem because there were three more hours of rising tide to provide another metre and a half of depth. I pulled out the spare anchor rope from its long term storage place in case I would need to use it and unlashed the fishermans anchor from the stern deck for the same reason. I thought it was a good time to exercise my running aground routine, seeing as I had just run aground, but this was in safe, tranquil waters. It is usually wise to immediately lay an anchor out into deeper water to prevent waves from washing the boat into shallower water. The anchor was attached to a rope for this because it would be impossible to row away from the boat with a chain falling in a bight. After an hour the boat swung around indicating she was beginning to float free and eventually I found the channel and tentatively carried on to Alvor. In the north was a rustic scene of a tree dotted hill crowned with a ruined nineteen twenties villa. A rock cliff jutted down to the water leaving a tiny strip of beach with purple flowering creepers garlanding the shore.

Alvor was a small fishing community with a low level of tourism, just several fish restaurants with terraces and the anchorage was busy with long distance cruising yachts. On the quay side was a disused fish auction building where retired fishermen sat in the shade wearing amused but sympathetic smiles as tourists struggled to maximise the pleasure amongst grilling sardines, sun-burning swimmers and swinging sun hats for sale in the gift shops lining the street leading up a hill towards the main shopping street. The contrast with Lagos was stark and I had begun to dislike Lagos, the last slave market in Europe, for its overbearing tourism and crass cosmopolitanism.

In Lagos I had enjoyed Dutch style chips with mayonnaise served by a typical Netherlander, whose shop sported a large Netherlands tricolour. For 3 Euros an hour I was able to use a fast internet computer, in a tourist bar and after being anchored at Baleeira for two weeks I'd enjoyed staring at the mass of tourists and the white painted people pretending to be statues for money. However, after two days I'd had enough. On the whole I'd disliked the atmosphere of Lagos marina, surrounded by the usual bars and restaurants offering English breakfasts and English newspapers to English people. I had nothing against my fellow nationals but I found people on holiday a bit wearing because all they wanted was to see and do as much as possible during their allotted fortnight and this compression of time caused them to stare at everything in an effort to gather as many memories as possible before it all became just a memory just two weeks later.

Sunday 1 June 2003. In the Alvor Catholic Church, a sign written in English declared, *'Mass held in English on Saturdays at 6pm'*. The terrace of the Yacht Club café Bar on the shore at Alvor looked out towards SP at anchor. It was free to stay as long as I wished, although I had to pay 12 Euros for 'light dues', as a contribution to upkeep of the harbour entrance. I could eat three meals a day for 4 Euros, as long as I ate aboard SP. It was perfect weather, brimming hot sunshine every day and a cooling sea breeze strong enough to whip off my straw sun hat. But I wished to sail further.

Monday 2 June 2003. I thought the bus from Alvor to Lagos was expensive at 2.50 Euros. The road went inland to pass over the river which formed the lagoon at Alvor. I saw a signpost giving, 'Lagos 10 miles', whereas from the Alvor entrance to Lagos harbour mouth was just 4 miles. It seemed usual to not sell return tickets on Portuguese buses. I felt the return journey Alvor - Lagos - Alvor, at 5 Euros, was too much. This would have been a thousand Escudos before the Euro currency was brought in just three years previously. I remembered once paying 1000 Escudos for a night in a Pension, for three persons, but it was twenty years since I last visited Portugal.

In Lagos I needed to find a replacement sail slide, a small plastic lug which linked the sail to the track on the mast. Neither the sail maker in Lagos marina or the chandlery in Sopramar, a large boatyard nearby, had the right type of slide. Sopramar let me have a different type to try out. I said the boat was in Alvor and I may not be coming back to Lagos but the man said, "I'll trust you." At 1.50 Euros I almost bought the slide but thought better of spending money on the wrong thing in the vague hope it may work. I bought a sail repair needle for 2.25 Euros. I also bought six crimp-on electrical ring connectors for 3 Euros The next place I looked was a fishing boat supplies store, but they did not have any sail slides although I bought two anti-chafe guards for 3.20 Euros - plastic tubes to slip over the wire rigging helping to prevent the mainsail wearing against it.

The bus fare and the other small items came to 13.45 Euros. Luckily it cost nothing to remain at anchor in Alvor. Meals were cheap as I made a large pot of stew in a pressure cooker and ate it over two days. My favourite lunch was fresh bread, butter, one large green tomato, mayonnaise and sea salt. A boiled egg eaten with crunchy bursts of sea salt was delicious too. I would then have an orange and a cup of tea. Lunch cost less than 1.50 Euros. Breakfast was home-made muesli. I kept a store of porridge oats, sultanas, desiccated coconut, wheat germ and dried banana chips. To some people eating muesli with just water added - not milk, was strange, but oats have such a creamy taste when mixed with a little water I found it a pleasant breakfast and tremendously healthy. Every day I ate an apple, a banana and an orange. Fruit and vegetables in Portugal were usually grown locally and were good quality. The fruit could be delicious, although the best bananas were those imported from the West Indies. Bananas from the Canary Islands were poor quality but very cheap. To eat out cost at least 4.5 Euros which was too much although I often had a Tosta Mista, a toasted sandwich made with cheese and ham because it cost only 1.6 Euros.

While I was in Lagos I thought I would visit the museum to see a kitten with two heads preserved in a jar. In his, *Travels to Portugal*' Jose Saramago went to the museum of Lagos. An attendant stood behind him at each exhibit and suggested, 'The People', as the universal meaning of each museum piece.

Tuesday 3 June 2003. The day I went to Lagos museum it was closed, as were many public buildings on Segunda Ferias - Mondays. The People would have to wait, or maybe The People needed a day off. In the centre of Alvor a small square with café terraces had not changed much since Alvor was only an occasional tourist destination. One was more of a restaurant and the other a cervejaria, for beers and coffees. A pizza menu would obviously be drawn from a freezer and microwaved into a flabby trade-off. I sat with a galao outside on a grey but hot day. Some crab coloured tourists emerged from a doorway of a small church set between the two cafés, the Igreja Da Misericordia. Next to it was a building as thin as one door with a plaque stating, 'Museu Etnografico', the Ethnographic Museum.

The church was attractive in its simple architecture. An entrance doorway surrounded by slender rectangles of light, hard stone, left unpainted. The front of the building was painted white and a stained glass window, the same shape as the doorway, but smaller, was sited above the doorway. A stone bell housing in the form of an arch curtseyed down to pyramidal cornices marking the ends of the sloping roof. A black steel, or bronze, cross was mounted above the belfry. A neon tube surrounded the cross, to add pizazz to ferias, or festivals and a rope tied to the bell clanger fell away sideways to a haphazard knot tied to the railings on a balcony of the Museu Etnografia. The church was mostly modern. It may have been one of the hundreds all over Portugal which were destroyed in the 1755 earthquake during Sunday morning mass. The catastrophic earth tremors were considered by most of those left alive to think it to be the angry will of God. Many Portuguese liked the term, 'oxal', meaning, 'God willing' and stemming from the Moorish words for 'the will of Allah', so an almost wholly Catholic people called on the name of Allah and this seemed country wide, not focussed in the Algarve. The word 'Algarve' had Arabic origins, meaning, 'over the sea'. During the Moorish occupation the Algarves were the people from Morocco - over the sea. There were many local names and words using, 'al', such as the villages 'Alcalar' and 'Alcoutim'. Alvor was derived from words for 'where the light comes from.' After bad weather the Portimau people would look for clearing sky in the west, over Alvor. Alvor was a bright, perfect, anchorage surrounded by radiant, apricot coloured sand. Cattle egrets and the ironically larger, little egrets flopped overhead and landed like para-gliders among the cows behind the grassy seawall or, at the tide-line like herons. After their wings were folded they stood there looking bigger than they really were, magnified by their whiteness.

After a tosta mista, deliciously dripping with butter, I had the strength to go exploring and first I peered inside the church. Five women sat in the pews in a small huddle. A mass of flowers was set in between them and the altar. Inside this raft of colour was a corpse. Rather than being embarrassed I quietly glanced around the inside of the church where the mourners were simply sitting for a duration with the deceased. The inside of the church looked modern, with saintly but stylised stained glass in frames, instead of windows. It felt like a living church at least and I noticed there was no air of false reverence or grandeur, rather the atmosphere was respectful, simple and practical towards the business of death and life. The day before I'd looked up from a bus at a derelict chimney to see a mass of sticks and the long sharp beaks and heads of a pair of nesting storks sitting there.

Near the Alvor quay was a shop selling African goods. I made friends with 'Zita', who worked there. She had once lived in Mozambique and also South Africa and her relatives lived in the Peniche region. Zita told me the African goods shop was soon to close because the tourist figures were down that year. I commented on the far wider choice of holiday destinations offered to the modern tourist, such as Thailand, Florida, Kenya and Zita added, "Yes, nowadays people are flying over to the Caribbean for a two week package holiday, they've got so much more money".

Zita made jewellery with silver and gem stones - little trees laden with gems like leaves, or fruit - and she had a stall near the beach called La Rocha, near Portimau. Zita said she would like to travel the world and I struggled to find the words to describe what I thought pleasurable travel was about - a reason, or an interest, almost a quest, but more a speciality. Certainly a purpose and some form of challenge. Pleasurable travel needed more than travel itself. Otherwise, travel was largely pointless because no matter where one went, there one was - so if one was unhappy in one place there was little reason for one to be happy anywhere else. However obvious this may appear it was an easy mistake to think moving 900 miles away from home would somehow bring about a transformation in personal happiness. Zita mentioned some UK pensioners who had come to Portimau during the winter, for a twelve week break. The total cost of the package, including flights, accommodation and a main meal every day, came to 6 Euros per day. This package economy meant it was cheaper to come to Portugal for six weeks than to keep the central heating running back in the UK. Another type of traveller I met was a couple who lived in a truck and had purchased a small area of land, back towards the Serra Da Monchique, a mountain range 20 miles inland. They made a living by busking together in Lagos, he on the guitar and her on the flute and they seemed happy travellers, or settlers.

Wednesday 4 June 2003. I was seeing plenty of exotic zoology - on the bus to Lagos there were camels in a field where a circus was encamped - I felt as if I'd passed into northern Africa. On a walk eastwards out of Alvor to see what animals lived there I saw nothing until I settled in the pastelaria 'Loureiro', on the Portimau road. The terrace had four cages containing parakeets, love-birds, parrots, zebra finches and cockatiels. The noise was as much as the human ear could take and squeaks, shrieks, squawks and other avarian utterances had the amplitude and sharpness of piezo horns being tested to destruction. On a complex of perches sat a white cockatoo, with a lemon yellow crest and black eyes. This bird was not enclosed, instead it was chained by one ankle, to the bottom rung of a wooden ladder running centrally up the perch structure. The pastelaria owner - it was doubtless 'his place' - slid open a window next to the cockatoo and offered a piece of orange. The lemon crest of the bird erected into six plumes. The piece of fruit was picked up in one claw and relished by the beak and tongue of the bird, deliberately and with pauses and glances at me.

I had been ignoring the fact that geckos are mainly nocturnal feeders. The ones I had managed to spot were just taking a bit of sun and on the whole there were very few creatures about during the daytime. The terrain of the coastal strip where I tended to stay was very disturbed by mankind, even the rough scrub, though covered in heather-like plants and wild flowers and surrounding places such as at Sagres, had been disturbed greatly in the last few decades. For several miles around Sagres roads were laid and plots of land, marked by wooden posts, were complete with electricity, water supplies and drainage services. The whole countryside was a mass of telegraph poles and electricity pylons and it was all for sale. Once in a while a plot had been purchased and a villa plonked there. The land was then fenced and laid with smooth grass, palm trees, agaves and swimming pools. The effect was somewhere between a golf course and a tropical island. There were always masses of flowers erupting from the ground, creeping along walls and bursting from lawns, vibrant and wonderful but not at all indigenous and even the ubiquitous palm trees had been planted. I saw nurseries with hundreds of mature palm trees for sale in large pots. These properties had extensive irrigation systems which seemed to flow permanently and consisted of networks of black plastic tubing, laying on the ground, with small holes emitting a mist of water to keeps the lawns green and the flowers blooming. These residencies were invariably silent, cheerless places, with roller shutters covering the windows and no cars in the driveway. The owners were perhaps foreigners off earning money somewhere. Somehow I failed to imagine these villas as ever containing any joy or even providing any relaxed, leisurely, times to the owners. The Alvor anchorage was in a nature reserve and the egrets were wonderful, but Portugal was a country in a process of upheaval and development. Even since I visited twenty years ago there had been vast alterations with hotels, golf courses and residential complexes having sprung up along the coastal plains to mar the scenery with ugly concrete. Twenty years previously there had not been a motorway to the Algarve, just local stone strewn roads. The whole coast of Iberia had been developed and at every port and anchorage I had been in other sailors, who had visited before, pointed out groups of new houses and hotels which were not there before.

Thursday 5 June 2003. On my walk to Portimau I had plunged into an old olive grove which had become thick with oats, or some type of tall grass. The seeds were perfectly adept at penetrating socks and after a while my shoes felt so uncomfortable I had to take them off and pick out hundreds of long, sharp seeds with stiff hairs spreading out backwards. Even in the fingers those seeds penetrated into the palm and began climbing the sleeve, like insects and just as creepy. I saw what I took to be a gecko move fast down an olive trunk and disappear into a black split in the old wizened tree. Many of the trees were stumps and those standing were coated in a pale green lichen. The grove had been abandoned years ago and on each side was building work where the ground had been torn into plots and mounds of sandy subsoil by heavy machinery. I thought how this lovely old olive grove would soon meet the same fate. In various derelict plots of land along the road to Portimau were ruins of homesteads and agricultural buildings where the owners had long since been tempted to sell up and move into one of the new blocks of flats to live miserably ever after, or they had died and their heirs were far away in the cities earning a living. I was certain anyone holding ownership of even a tiny piece of the Algarve would be aware of its value to developers. On the other hand there were so many derelict buildings and neglected plots of land in Portugal, there must have been great inertia and the cost of clearing and developing land was not available to the traditional smallholder who must wait for a golf course or hotel developer to come along and make them an offer. Often a building was half completed and then left for years without further works being carried out, with tangles of iron reinforcing rods protruding from concrete walls, awaiting the next floor, which would probably never be added. On these forgotten projects was daubed, 'SE VENDE' - For sale - in white paint. The quality of building works was often at the point of collapsing before completion. Back in Sesimbra a multi-story block overlooking the sea had fallen in at one end during the building. Looking along the remaining two thirds of the structure one could see the whole edifice was cranky, the lines bowing out and wavering up and down.

On a second trip on the bus to Lagos to pick up the sail slides I caught the museum open. Inside the museum was an impressive church with walls crowded with gold painted scroll work, ornate groups of pillars, painted biblical scenes and all manner of edging, framework and capping, painted gold. Dozens and dozens of pink fleshed cherubs strained out of this inferno of religious décor. The ceiling was painted in sky blue and gold, with pillars painted in a perspective that carried them far beyond the roof. When I approached the museum a woman was holding an excited conversation outside the police station opposite. After I had entered the museum by paying 2 Euros, a vague tension existed there too, as if a person had recently been ejected and was now complaining outside the police station across the street from the museum. Dead salamanders, dead ermine, dead crabs, dead black cobras, dead flying fish and a kid goat with eight legs, which was also dead, drew me on past fishing artefacts, models of local fishing boats, nets and tools.

The Algarvian chimneys section interested me because I had been wondering what the strange objects were on all the houses, essentially a ceramic pot, painted white with slots and holes around the mid section. The top was either round, pointed or minaret shaped and various embellishments made them attractive, looking like oversized pepper pots. Most were not chimney pots any more, which was why they stayed white. They were merely the Algarvian style.

They made a living by busking together in Lagos, he on the guitar and her on the flute and they seemed happy travellers, or settlers.

Monday 8 June 2003. On a Saturday I moved SP to a part of the lagoon where she would be high and dry at low tide. The place I had chosen was just two hundred metres away, near a couple of Wharram catamarans that dried out on a wide, smooth sandbank. Catamarans do not lean over because they rest on the ground like a sledge, whereas SP laid at an angle of 50 degrees and that was what I wanted. After 900 miles of sailing I needed to look at the hull, the rudder, the propeller and stern gland where the propeller shaft passed through the hull. Various sea cocks and sensors, such as the sink drain, the engine cooling water intake, the cockpit drains and the echo sounder, needed checking. Barnacles, green weed and brown growth had recently slowed SP to half her usual speed. Several days before I went to the sand bank at low-water to choose a suitable spot with a slight slope so the boat was not laying quite flat to ensure that as the tide came up again the water did not reach the inside of the boat before she began to lift upright again. The spot needed to be free of boulders and old anchors, or anything which could damage the hull side.

When the tide was in there was nothing but a wide featureless expanse of water, so at low tide I carefully noted down a number of objects which were in line at the exact position where I wanted the boat to rest. There was a dark green bush on the sea wall which stood in front of a white water tower some miles behind it. There was a sloping road with some conspicuous buildings below it which could just be seen around the small headland where a rock cliff stuck out prominently. There were several blocks of flats a couple of thousand metres to the east and light could be just seen between the second and third block. If I moved ten metres to the north, the slit of light between the flats disappeared. If I moved ten to the west the dark green bush went out of alignment with the white water tower. If I moved ten to the south then the conspicuous buildings below the sloping road disappeared behind the small headland with the prominent rock. Therefore I had established a circle with a diameter of 10m within which I could place my boat without being able to see the sandbank. When I motored over to the spot and searched for the objects which would line up, the bush had been trampled flat during the night by a herd of rampaging cattle. The conspicuous white buildings beneath the sloping road had actually been camper vans parked on the shore and had driven away early that morning and a new block of flats had sprung up in front of the two I needed to see.

While I was chewing my lip and thinking about what to do next the boat ran aground and that was where she stayed. After some work with anchors and winches I had the boat twisted around to face the right way so she laid down on the bank like a head on a pillow, not too flat. Actually the transits had not disappeared, but they all looked completely different from the cockpit, 3m higher up than from where I had spotted them walking on the sandbank. All went well over the next four hours as SP gradually fell sideways and came to rest like a stranded whale. The day continued with hard scraping and sponging under the blazing sun. A number of people came to visit whom I had not met before as careening attracted attention with the boat laying at such a dramatic angle. The real draw was being able to see the underneath of the boat which all cruising folk spend months aboard, crossing oceans and trusting their worlds to the unseen part of the boat, the hull and below it the curvaceous keel.

An expensive delicacy of the Cabo Sao Vicente area was percebes - barnacles. People collected percebes in wet suits, abseiling down high cliffs to the rocks below at low tide. Several of the percebes on SP were fat and juicy and when touched they contracted, spurting out a jet of water. They were all swiftly removed with a paint scraper. I could only do one side on one tide and then wait for the tide the next day, so it took me two days to clean the whole hull. The second day I had no bread and knew I would be shaking with hunger by lunch time, so, as SP began her inexorable tilt I cooked a pile of pancakes. Flipping them at a progressively harder angle as SP lay over, but I knew the cooker would be unusable within an hour or two. Moving about when the boat was heeled was difficult and to enter the cabin I had to stand in the sink and then make my way along the backrests of the bunks. It was impossible to sit down inside with everything at a crazy angle and several small items flew 'sideways' as I clambered about. The water tank in the bows became higher than the sink and the water poured from the tap into the cupboard behind. I quickly cut a bung from some rubber and stemmed the flow. I also had to make a bung for the diesel tank breather. After I had cleaned most of the hull I stood waist deep in the cool water and scoffed pancakes - tasty with butter or hazelnut and chocolate spread. The tide came back in the early evening. SP felt like a new slipper as she eagerly moved through the water without dragging a freezer of percebes along with her. In the last few days the heat had increased immensely although it was cooler out on the water especially when the sea breeze arrived in early afternoon. Ashore the sun was unbearably strong. In

England we walk on the sunny side of the street, here though even a thin band of shade along one edge of the road was chosen in favour of the sunny part.

Tuesday 10 June 2003. One night I was invited to eat a curry on a large catamaran. Several of the friends I made when careening were there and most interestingly I met the person who had designed the wind vane from which I had drawn ideas to make mine. The specific innovation he devised was to put holes in the wind vane. The holes increased the drag of the vane in light winds by setting up turbulence. The eddies produced as the wind passes through the holes trailed downwind, increasing the drag of the vane. He did not patent the holes and neither did he make any money from them. In fact I omitted the holes because I used plywood for the vane and I considered it effective enough. The designer, Jeff, claimed my plywood vane would be much more effective with some holes in it. I had several spare vanes of various sizes and thought about trying out a smaller sized vane but with holes.

There was an interesting conversation about the spread of some African snails amongst some Pacific Islands. The widespread use of these snails as food, by ships crews and migrant workers, meant they become established on remote islands. There was a serious risk of a form of meningitis infection by eating undercooked snails, or even, by eating the leaves of plants upon which they had lived. To reduce this problem another predatory snail species had been used to kill the African snails. The problem then was the indigenous snail populations were wiped out. One island was the focus of thirty years of a study in which every valley was found to have discrete species of snails and the object of the research was to find out how the various species evolved relative to one another. The catamaran owner had been responsible for the introduction of the predators and he could only claim there had been huge numbers of the indigenous snails collected and moved to other islands to conserve those species.

Sunday 15 June 2003. The Algarve in July had sunshine dripping from the house roofs. One roof had collapsed while builders worked next door and a clothes rack, small bedroom cabinets, a bed and an ironing board stood exposed for several days, like a doll's house, while householders and builders grew heated on the street below. Yachties commented pompously on the state of the Portuguese economy and how this was a typical example of the way the Portuguese carried on. The builders seemed incompetent, digging deep into the foundations of the stricken house without placing props of any kind. I had seen major building works with scaffolding supported on eucalyptus bows held to the road by pats of cement. The same superior yachties happily went out into the vast emptiness and wilderness of seascapes in boats made with cement over a steel basket. Many ferro-cement boats travelled the oceans of the world with wooden masts - not so technically superior to the eucalyptus props and cement blobs of Portuguese construction sites. Yachties tended to hold an inherent superiority to the shore dwelling people they visited abroad. There were often comments like, 'It is SOOO cheap! How can these people make a living like this?', about the price of spirits in a bar, the cost of a train ride from Lagos to Faro, the price of a boat engine rebuild, an Easy-Jet flight back to the UK from Faro, and so on. Actually Portuguese prices were not particularly cheap and comments like the above came from people who had probably spent the past twenty years working in very well paid jobs in the richer, northern Europe. To me the cost of hauling the boat ashore for a few weeks to do maintenance was high at around 400 Euros and SP was a quarter of the size of the majority of cruising yachts.

Really hot weather had never appealed to me, but the Algarve in high summer was actually very pleasant. I must have been acclimatizing well because I loved the heat. I would greet friends with, "Isn't it a lovely day," with transparent irony and they would reply, "But, all the days are lovely". Weather for sailing was almost ideal - each day a sea breeze blew between lunchtime and mid evening. The barometer, such a valuable indicator of change in UK waters, in the Algarve wavered about within the 'Fine' sector for months on end, the only variation a daily rise and fall of a few millibars. Occasionally a weather front passed the region and brought a fresh breeze for a day or two. Once in a while a weak low pressure system danced free of the Straits of Gibraltar or from Morocco and whirled out into the Atlantic to give a couple of days of cloud and perhaps a hint of rain but what rain there was had hardly finished falling before being eaten up by the zigzag heat haze just above the ground. Rain was a fading memory and the sea spray on SP remained as a coating of corrosive salt crystals. The other coating on SP was a reddish brown dust from inland, carried on the prevailing north westerly breeze. The same wind continued all the way to the Canary Islands, to the south-west, tearing around the nine islands to become the north-east trade winds reaching across 3000 miles of open Atlantic ocean to the Caribbean.

Each week or two, batches of fresh tourists slouched along on gleaming white legs, treading the dusty, sun hard roads between the beach and the town. The men in baseball caps and overhanging bellies; boys in baseball caps and football shorts. Women with legs full of stress carried heavy packs of beach accessories; girls had Barbie complexes and temporary tattoos. Fish restaurants did well with large charcoal grills searing the cobbled road beside the terraces and the smell of charcoal fires began mid-morning and ended at midnight. Thursdays and weekends bands or buskers played on the quayside - the ubiquitous on-pan-pipes tune of Simon and Garfunkel captured the diners tastes, 'I'd rather be a hammer than a nail, yes I would, if I only could, I surely would, mmmm,' chew, chew, gobble, slurp, as they collectively picked through the evening shoal of char-grilled fish. At the end of each song clapping hands sent unseen fish bones flying from table to table. Delicately disguised by social conventions and etiquette, the feeding frenzy began with hunger and ended with piles of bones as the gorging was policed by waiters in white shirts and black trousers.

Peruvians in traditional dress (not for the benefit of tourists because they wore it constantly) sold hair wraps and weave bracelets cleverly incorporating any forename, such as Barry, Michelle or Damion. Tourism was a set of packaged experiences - a bit of hot sunshine for a tan; some music played by 'indigenous' looking peoples, regardless off where they were from so long as they appeared exotic, and a bite to eat of something peculiarly local such as the huge gaping mouthed bass in the refrigerated display case outside the Restaurant De Rio Da Mar on Alvor quay. The fish restaurants were not cheap with a fresh fish charged at around 40 Euros per kilo. One fish could easily weigh that if it had a good meal before it was caught - the edible portion was no more than thirty per cent and they were sold by pre-cooked, pre-filleted weight and was served with a few boiled potatoes and a slice each of lemon and lime; salad was extra. While the diner awaits the fish, a plate of pate and slices of goat's cheese was placed on the table along with a basket of bread. These were all charged individually if they were touched. The bill, after some house wine, a beer or two, a plastic flavoured ice cream and a couple of coffees, would easily come to 35 Euros per person. A curry with pulses, such as black eye beans was so much more nourishing, cooked up aboard SP on the two ring gas cooker cost a couple of Euros and provided two or three subsequent meals.

In the café Alianca on a Domingo (Sunday) there were plenty of customers and a young Senegalese man engaged two people on the terrace. He was draped with leather goods, a stringed instrument, a drum, wooden carvings, bracelets and necklaces made from silver, set with semi-precious stones. He spoke excellent English. I wondered what book would he write, given the luxury of the opportunity? The Senegalese seller was under exploitative employers because he had a dead beat, resigned look about him and no matter how hard he worked in his job, he would hardly ever do well enough to transcend it.

Thursday 19 June 2003. As usual I had established a regular place to sit for an hour to write. Shaded after three pm and before this time the air-conditioning made it cooler inside than out, even under the shade of an umbrella. Twice I had been offered a coffee by strange men, but the gestures were obviously driven by an unholy interest in me, so I pointed to my coffee cup and said I'd had one and did not want any more. One coffee profferer was a sprightly fellow, aged mid-fifties with a face like a goat. He wore a black trilby and his shirt, trousers and tie were black. Over a long grey beard, rich-brown and sun-creased, his skin framed twinkling eyes. At first I thought he was a priest of the nearby church and for over a week we greeted each other as regulars in the café. On sweaty days we exchanged comments on the hot weather. One day he offered me a coffee and when I refused his familiarity became frustrated and he sat down at a distance to look at me and plan another approach. Another day I'd seen this man. Three doors down the hill from the café was a rotten wooden doorway. Hanging from nails was a collection of musty men's suits and jogging trousers wrapped in cellophane, thoroughly unattractive and unappealing and a piece torn from a cardboard box was pegged above, with in English, *'Only 10 Euros'*, and another, *'Only 15 Euros'*. Curiosity made me peer through the open doorway where a small cooker coated in cooking stains, a sink and a work-top were arranged near the entrance. Bare concrete slabs and girders formed the roof and the walls were also unpainted. Possessions stood against and hung from the walls including more stock - some Adidas golf T-shirts in plastic bags. At the back of the room a steel framed bed was draped with grey blankets and a grey beard slanted upwards from one end of the blankets - the beard of the black-trilbied man - fast asleep in the hot afternoon. Inappropriate offers of coffee could lead to rooms like this, I told myself; and there I sensed there would exist no adventuresome tales by audacious voyagers, or even someone who could make something scary feel possible, or a difficult journey seem wonderfully worthwhile.

Another day, as I walked by the hovel, the grey beard called out, "Eh! Come here!" (in Portuguese) and I slipped away from the hanging grey suits and the doorway as if it were now a lair.

Locals watched the flow of tourists with indifference, In the evenings Alvor became really busy, but also the people who lived there sat in amused groups outside their houses on chairs placed in the street, leaning over windowsills talking and standing in doorways, watching the strange tourists. Tourists wandered past in incongruous beach fashions with sheepish stances which I put down to having watched too many television programs about poorer countries, the result of which was awkwardness amongst the locals. The Alvorenses had witnessed an explosion in tourist numbers during the past 20 years. The average tourist was hardly in 'a country', instead they were taking part in 'a holiday' - a different sort of destination. Anyway, even if the remnants and threads of Portugal of twenty years ago were sought it would take the skill of a detective to find them. I began to feel quite depressed by the sheer weight of tourists and tourism in Alvor and Lagos. I could not remember the last time I had seen a gecko or even a wall lizard and I had to content myself with observing people instead.

Local men sat throughout the day on benches in the town centre. An elderly man leant forward and remarked to his companion about the gnarled tread of the tyre on a mountain bike resting next to him, saying something like, 'What on earth do they need such a tread for on a bicycle?' Next to him a man with a shiny bald head wore brown corduroy trousers and a bright yellow shirt with white and blue checks on it and the waitress of the nearest café handed him a raspberry coloured ice-cream which he began licking happily, as if he enjoyed life. He and his friends appeared more comfortably off than the retired fishermen who sat under the shade of the disused fish auction building down at the quayside where one of the regulars was usually drunk. Each day I collected water in a ten litre can there was a bottle of white wine cooling in a bucket next to the tap. He would wobble up to me and say things like, 'No probleme, eh?' I would reply, 'Bom dia.' He would return the bottle to the cool bucket and his crackling, partly incoherent, voice would turn towards his friends. He never seemed to cause an affray and I noticed his friends did not exclude him in the ways they sat contemplating the harbour, the tourists and the sunshine. Later in the day he moved up into the town and folded himself up against a wall, on the floor, while the tourists drifted to and fro in bathing costumes. By that time he just blabbered rubbish, talking at the cobbles for hours from under a green and white baseball cap. I heard he had fought in the Portuguese ex-colonies in Africa.

I watched the way two tourists ambled casually by. A man wearing light blue floral print shorts, a pastel yellow shirt and beach sandals. A woman wearing a red swimming costume, a brightly printed wrap, around her waist, to dress up the swimming costume and beach sandals which draw attention to her toes and ankles. They peered at the goods hanging outside a gift shop as if they were really interesting - as if they were seeing for the first time the handicrafts of unknown cultures, although it was just plastic and raffia beach bags, lurid bikinis, bush hats and sunglasses, plastic footballs and buckets and spades, beach mats, plastic windmills and so on, the same stuff which hung outside every seaside shop from here to Stavanger. The older men on the benches glanced up at her bare, tanned back and she ignored any attention by looking at a line of baskets filled with colourful ceramic gifts, such as ornamental versions of the Algarvian chimney pots with hooks so they could be fixed to a wall with a light bulb inside them.

Midsummer

Saturday 21 June 2003. I discovered Alvor by night was another dimension. Cruising folk mostly stayed aboard their boats in the evenings and there was nowhere much better to savour the cooler air, while languishing under a blazing sunset, but by the time night had fallen the shore life had hardly begun. People arrived in droves to fill the fish restaurants and further up the street into town the bars resounded with karaoke and 'Will on the Guitar' entertainments. Out at the anchorage, just 200m away, all I could hear was the occasional swirl of accordion or Peruvian pan pipes. A wander ashore in Alvor at night was a strange experience because so much was different to the tranquil, heat exhausted tourism of the daytime. A glance inside a bar run by a horribly affable Irish Dave revealed a narrow room leading back to the bar, a channel containing a smiling throng of holidaymakers there enjoying themselves despite Will on the guitar, who emitted a mash of over-amplified hits. Clothes were typical of the region with traditional holidaymakers wearing bright coloured tops over cleavage launching push-up bras. On the hips were small white shorts and waxed, bronzed legs lead down to strappy sandals with red painted toenails. Make-up glistened in the twirling coloured lighting. Men gambolled around wearing faces that said, 'What? - Uh? and Ehh!' They had army derived short hair cuts and beers held in one hand, just above waist level. They were over-brave and talked like comedians, on the defensive, to anyone who entered the bar - curt, witty, chirpy sentences - and constantly scanned for girls. Most of them were probably married, gay or perhaps both and by the end of the night long-standing alliances remained as feelings for steady girlfriends or familiar lovers re-crystallised under the warm Portuguese night and the haze of large beers and saucily named cocktails seductively drained through straws. Will on the guitar climaxed with *'Layla'* and everyone sang along. As I walked by and glanced inside the bar entrance I saw the whole scenario which may have been the truth or perhaps all I looked at were my own stereotypes.

The Museu Etnografia was actually open at night, right up until twelve midnight. I had assumed it was not open to the public because during the day it remained entirely inactive, its door shut with no indication of opening hours. Inside a brightly lit room had white-painted walls and ceiling and colourful tiles up to head height all round. The building was just one door wide at the front and broadened out inside to become as big as a house. It must have originally been connected to the church next door because a round window connected directly with the inside of the church. I peered past the open, circular window, through four feet of white painted tunnel to see the plaster face of some saint looking out of one of the scenes at one side of the altar. I thought how this deep set window could have been opened unobserved from the next door building to the church and used to listen in on the services. The window itself could not be seen from the church side as it was just a round hole high up in the wall. Upstairs was most interesting with figures of fishermen, lace weavers and farmers. These dummies were of two types, re-employed shop mannequins looking a little too long of leg and fine of cheekbone for their rustic roles originally created to personify the elegant long limbs and high cheeks of rich people, and they looked like amateur dramatists playing the roles of poor fishermen, snail harvesters, rug weavers and so on. The other type were made of papier-mache and had grotesquely shaped and gaudily painted faces, unnaturally short thin legs, shoes hanging from them at impossible angles and faces and hands painted in lurid pink. I was alone up there with these macabre figures but they looked a lot more like poor, arable working class people than the recycled fashion mannequins. The unmistakable noise of a marching band came striding through the open doorway which looked out over the little square with the café Alianca.

The way to the balcony was barred by dummies and as I slid past the leering form of a traditional fisherman, that rocked unnervingly. Nearly at the open door I ducked under the raised hands of a female mannequin, who stared unblinkingly through me and held aloft a placard as part of a local procession. An explanation consisted of the words of a song which celebrated Alvor and the bountiful gifts it brought.

Reaching the first floor doorway I saw the procession filing past, made up of the very same costumes and placards as the one swaying sympathetically behind me. An electric guitarist who had been captivating the crowds of tourists on the square with reverb soaked instrumentals of 'The Deer Hunter' and some tragical song by Celine Dion, played with the same grin which a performing magician wears and the melodies were wrought so lengthily it seemed the guitarist had, above all, captivated himself. He would have kept the spell unbroken if he could, but the sound of massed clarinets, saxophones, tuba and snare drums drew closer and overthrew the attention of his audience who turned away to the roadside. He kept smiling while diminishing his sugary guitar picking to a simmer to maintain possession of the prime busking spot in Alvor.

The procession was divided into men on one side, women on the other and a wide range of ages. Costumes were themed around fishermen, fish wives, snail hunters. Others wore top hats, tails or hooped gowns. Between each pair of bearers was an arch supporting a paper lantern, with battery powered bulbs inside, above a placard. Each placard was decorated with pictures of Alvor, fish, fishing boats and letters of the sponsoring organizations.

The Hunting of the Snail

Some had dramatic scenes depicting the hunting of the snail, wise old figures draped in black cloth were bent double after years of stooping amongst the scrub while deftly wielding plastic buckets brimming with caracois (snails). Once I glanced inside a snail eatery, although I never tried them, partly due to the look of the snail eating customers who stared grumpily out at me, as if to say, 'Eat the snail and live miserably ever after'. I did not fancy sitting for hours removing morsels of gristle from tiny shells one by one with a pin. They say that in the mountains they eat the shells an' all.

The drums rolled the column of marchers along at a brisk military step. However, the melodies had minor thirds and minor sevenths, which made them melancholic and Moorish, even Cuban with the brass instruments. A number of separate processions made up of competing groups appeared and trailed away down towards the quayside where they assembled for a grand finale. I left the museum to follow the spectacle. Columns lined the quayside, their heavy placards dismounted and some remained standing in line while others chatted excitedly with friends sitting along the seawall. There they awaited their turn to perform in front of an assembled crowd seated in an arena made of stacked chairs. Most of the people milling around seemed to be locals but a few smiling tourists were swept along with the marchers, although it was a wholly Alvorense event, not a show put on for the benefit of tourists.

The overall signification of lanterns with smiling sun faces, models of fishing boats laden with nets and floats and costumes of bright silks or fishermen's traditional wear suggested a celebration of life, the abundance of fish and the good life Alvorenses had for themselves. The date was the 20th of June, the eve of Midsummer when the sun was highest. The fish had been jumping for several months now too, gambolling in abundance, although the reason they jumped was to escape prey, but even so the silver flashes and plops did make the place feel lazy and dreamy, as if the fish were carelessly frolicking. There were extensive shoals of fish at the surface, around the boat and the shore and thousands of tiny green ones could be seen moving a little deeper down.

Saturday 28 June, 2003. A really touristy café positioned right on the main street in Alvor let me plug in my laptop computer. I bought a galao and later, for I spent five hours in there, double egg 'n chips. First I saved sixty photographs from the digital camera onto the laptop. This took forty-five minutes. Secondly, I brought together several recent images and bits of text, to make up the monthly calendar to email to supporters of the voyage of SP.

I had a shortage of electrical power on board SP since the two ICP Global solar panels had failed. The panels were a mere five watts output each, but even this would fully charge both the heavy duty batteries, two hundred amperes worth, in twenty days. The two solar panels also fitted exactly the space on top of the sliding main hatch. On opening the faulty panels the cause of the failure was obvious - the positive wire had been pinched by the frame during manufacture and caused broken insulation until corrosion had finished off the wire. I had been in communication with ICP Global via their website but after I declared the cause of the problem ICP Global went silent for several days, until I received an email telling me to take the panels back to the place of purchase for replacements. Trouble was the chandlery in Bristol was now 1000 miles away. I needed a local supplier and a little liaison between the manufacturer and them, but the fact was the products of ICP Global were poorly manufactured.

A Sea of Simulation

Satellite navigation uses a mathematical model of the globe. Sailing amongst gps coordinates was like moving around in a Playstation game - there was the appearance of going from one point to another, from one place to another place, but it was all pretend. However, the model coincided minutely with the coordinates on various maps and charts and so it was possible to move a gps position between two points without further reference to the world outside, such as in fog, or at night. But it was not sensible to do so because many maps remained inaccurate, having been drawn by men with long beards while bobbing around in rowing boats and probably chewing dried cod. Furthermore, the danger of banging into one of the ten thousand containers lost from ships every year, or a blue whale defending her calf was not within the simulation. The radio signal picked up by a gps receiver, every second, from satellites in geostationary orbit, was as weak as a candle flame at a distance of 30 miles. Two other competing global positioning systems were GLONAS the Russian one, and a planned European run system, to be called Galileo. The currently ubiquitous gps service amongst sailors was run by the United States Defence Agency, for free. For £100 anyone could buy a hand-held gps with a geographical accuracy of a couple of meters. Commercial ships used two gps units, one in the bow and one in the stern, to pinpoint the ship within harbours, not only where it was but the angle at which it lay. Some small cruising yachts had a gps receiver linked to an autopilot and a laptop navigation program so they could travel from place to place turning around headlands en route, without even being awake, but watch those sleeping whales and that forty foot steel container, just awash and full of forty tons of microwave ovens. If these voyagers of the virtual gps world missed the flotsam and whales they would probably be run over by a ship, run out of electricity, or if those things did not occur, for sure Windows would crash.

30 June, 2003. The person who served me a galao was called Andrezja. She was studying economics in Portugal and worked as a waitress during the summer, resuming academic work during the winter. She was from Lithuania and married to a German man. Alvor had a diversity of residents. On the whole though the Algarve left me feeling dissatisfied. What was missing was authenticity - the feeling of stepping into a foreign land was nowhere to be found. There were traces of everyday lives - the women leaning out of windows looking onto the heat bedazzled streets

by day and the press of karaoke bar goers by night. There were a couple of traditional fishing boats which rumbled past each evening to spend the night offshore, but where the Peniche boats were great lumbering, filthy vessels, full of diesel, nets and fish guts the Alvor boats were half the size and half the crew and they slipped politely out to sea, waiting until they had passed the headland before opening up the diesel engine to full throttle. The Peniche boats would sweep through the harbour at full speed, with dogs hollering and men barking at each other. I would laugh as the wash crashed around amongst the visiting yachts causing shrieks of alarm from yachties accustomed to the petty politeness of authoritarian English harbours, with their speed limits and notices saying, *'KEEP DOWN YOUR WASH'.*

Peniche and the whole west coast of Portugal was wonderful, but I felt a distinct lack of excitement about being in the Algarve. The whole Algarve was deadened by the tourist trade and the rotting olive groves, with moss covered trees, long wafting, blanched grass was left to riot impotently, for soon the land would be swept flat and bare by heavy machinery, for hotels and golf courses. Where there were cervejarias, adegas and pastelarias, there grew up Irish pubs, karaoke bars and pizzerias. The former with photographs stuck to the menu board showing scenes of wild nights of karaoke and competitions to drink the most cocktails. Irish bars and other ex-patriot owned fun bars advertised Happy Hour as beginning mid-afternoon in the hope of triggering a drinking session. Cocktails, beers, wine etc. cost a few Euros each, but English people thought a Euro was little over half a UK pound and therefore a couple of Euros for one drink was still cheap compared to UK pub prices, where a pint of beer was about £2. Actually the prices in the non-tourist bars and shops were far less than this. A coffee was usually 70 Cents in the authentic cafés and always at least 1 Euro in the tourist ones. 30 Cents was not a huge amount of money, but 30 per cent was expensive if added to everything. A beautiful picture postcard of the face of a lion captured my attention as I had just finished reading *The Chronicles of Narnia*. A swarthy man emerged from the rear of the shop looking like a Cornish fisherman with a thick white beard and dreamy blue eyes. I asked the price of the card and he told me, "One Euro". I said, "One Euro?" realizing this was extortionate for one postcard. The man shook his head as if to say, 'Take it or leave it,' and I apologized, putting the card back in the rack.

The man was a retired coastguard officer who had thought to run the shop as an easy business. Now he was thinking of shutting up for good because so many gift shops were competing for a capricious tourist market. It was better to sell cheap to three customers than expensive to one, because if one of the three went elsewhere there were still two left, whereas losing a customer base of one was disastrous. After the naturalness of Peniche, which I came to feel deeply for, the Algarve was just how I had been warned it would be - full of English, German and Dutch holidaymakers. Even so the attitude of the Algarve Portuguese was just as open and friendly as anywhere else. After all, in general people treat you well if you treat them well, whether in the Algarve, Gallicia, or the Maghreb, from what I could gather.

It rained for the first time in my recent memory, for the last rain I remembered was in Sines. The boat was being attacked by salt deposited in sea spray which usually got washed away by dew, drizzle and rain but there had been hardly any of these. The rain began at 10.45am and was finished by 10.55am, when a huge sheet of vibrant blue sky appeared along the entire south-western horizon; by lunch time it was shimmering hot as usual. The women leaned out of their windows again, frowning at small dogs as a way to show their love of them. Three ice-creams? hovered past, the very essence of a seaside holiday, each relaying a Euro coin. A grinning and tightly curled beige coated dog turned right at some crossroads without a moments thought. A temporary tattoo turned off the main street and headed down hill towards the harbour, writhing on a young, brown shoulder blade. I was reminded of the last gecko I'd spotted - a week ago - either I was not looking, or the gecko population had migrated away from the tourist rush. I had not been as interested in exploring the surrounding countryside during the last few weeks due to the weight of development and upheaval, so every inch of land had been turfed around, scoured and trodden by man.

The Algarve marketed itself as a haven for wildlife, from the estuaries and salt marshes of Olhao, Faro and Tavira, to the broad coastal plains at the western end from Portimao to Sagres, but apart from the novelty of storks nesting on chimney stacks and the frequent flapping presence of egrets, there was hardly anything to be seen. Thinking back along the coast I remembered with most excitement the Alentejo region, at Sines. There I'd seen a tiny black snake dead, a live black snake and lots of basking geckos. The Alentejo had the heat of the Algarve with the rainfall of the western Portuguese coasts. I would be keen on sailing the 75 miles back up to the Alentejo coast at Sines for the end of July, if Cabo Sao

Vicente, with its persistent strong northerly winds, was not such a formidable gateway. It would doubtless be very worthwhile to visit the free world music festival held inside Sines castle, but Cabo Sao Vicente was not a headland I would wish to confront more times than absolutely necessary. Damage to a sailing boat was as serious as it was to a sea-bird and as habitually avoided.

Tuesday 1 July 2003. I took a bus to Lagos to pick up the photocopy of a sailing pilot book of the North African coast, and I had two borrowed charts to copy - one covering Lisbon, Portugal to the Gambia, West Africa; the other was a passage chart of the Canary Islands group (passage charts give a wide area view to enable a boat to pass through a region without containing enough detail to go very close to the coast). The copies would each consist of eight sheets of A3 paper and I looked forward to lots of sticking together and matching up of longitude and latitude scales and afterwards the task would be to colour in the charts - blue for sea; green for land; and yellow for drying areas like beaches and rocks. Otherwise they would be difficult to interpret while heaving around at sea. The cost of sixteen A3 sheets was a reasonable two Euros and I made just over two Euros by blowing my saxophone for a couple of hours in Lagos. My Psion hand-held computer was in use daily and was kept in a neat case made of ABS plastic, so it was dropped there was some protection but the case was not at all water-proof. To protect the computer while I rowed to and from the boat I kept it wrapped in two heavy-duty freezer bags with Zip lock seals. The bags were a hassle to unwrap and open and deteriorated with constant use. A chandlers in Lagos had a case very similar to the one I used but with a rubber 'O' ring around the edge making it completely water-tight but at a cost of thirty-five Euros I decided not to get it straight away in case I was trying to lose myself in the acquisition of new things instead of going sailing. There were many identical Psion computers available on the web at Ebay, for as little as £20, but the value was in the work held on the computer rather than the computer itself. Even if I did regularly back up everything, there were brief periods when a large amount of writing existed solely on the Psion while I happened to be rowing ashore in fresh winds. Preferably I would use only the Psion computer which had served for the entire voyage without problems, despite being rowed ashore in a bucking dinghy, carried about on gecko hunts and other rambles in my rucksack, every day for nearly a year. Previously the Psion had taken me through my final two years of lectures, essays and revision as a social sciences undergraduate. Once a block of text was placed into a word processor it became a useful resource and I had with me the complete set of lecture notes and essays, two years after graduating. I found it interesting to be able to look back at things I had studied. When I met the French sailor, Michel, in Sines, who had a great interest in the ideas of Sigmund Freud, and I was able to look back over my notes on psychoanalytic theory on the Psion.

Most of the people I had known at university would think it weird to carry lecture notes around several years after graduating but I used the knowledge base held on my Psion computer as a miniature reference library, uniquely formed around my own experiences and interests. There were also thousands of pages of my own writing, book quotes, poems, song lyrics, interesting emails from friends, technical details, instructions and a database of addresses and contacts. Half a minute of immersion would obliterate the whole lot.

Wednesday 2 July 2003. Feeling energetic I went early to Lagos after avoiding drinking a coffee in Alvor to stay with my sparkling mood. The library where I used free internet PCs was shut until three pm on Wednesdays and an exhibition of photography in the council building was not open until the evening, so I arrived at the bus stop prematurely. Amongst those waiting for a bus were two from Sheffield. Northerners often like talking to strangers with a fundamental trust in human nature. I knew I was in a particularly outgoing mood because I had on my north-African hat, in the shape of a simple dish with embroidered spirals and zigzags in warm orange and black, on a leather base. It set off my saxophone playing with heated solos in melodic minor scales - a different set of notes going up than down - and diminished scales, which move in steps of one whole tone and then one half-tone to produce a rootless, curving progression. Frequently my playing was lost in coils of unresolved melodic fragments, brashly but feebly executed and lacking technique, and that was how I liked it. Ever since I'd stopped trying to learn how to play the saxophone my playing had relaxed and improved no end.

The bus squeezed past living orange groves, derelict olive groves, an airfield with little planes coloured silver or fluorescent green, and donkeys in yards. A wide paddock with no shade whatsoever contained twenty or so thin looking horses, many with foals and a goat with a desperately sweet looking kid. The fields were flat with small rises topped by farmhouses in the delta of the river estuary which flowed past Alvor from the mountain range of Monchique. It had silted to become grazing land or roads and garden centres, swimming pool superstores. A giant hotel kept some people for almost the entire two weeks from leaving its confines, swimming pools, sporting facilities, bars, and restaurants. While waiting at the bus stop several plush coaches dropped off bewildered looking people from these hotels. Emerging from the air-conditioned coach after the air-conditioned hotel into the 30C heat blast, they wondered which way to walk to get to the beach. The shops sold exactly the same as that on sale in the on-site hotel stores - buckets, hats, inflatable toys, sunglasses, sun-block and so on.

From the bus I noticed a field of bulls coloured rich red brown and with strong curved horns. Standing close to the legs of these bulls were ten or so cattle egrets feeding on flies and insects attracted to the animals. Stone troughs supported several feet above the ground and winding in channels across the fields formed water-courses following natural streams, rather than being straight, as such constructions tend to be. A man on the bus exclaimed, "Look there's proper grass, like you see on the garden". He sat wondering how nice green grass could grow in the dry heat of the Algarve and then explored his thinking further, tapping the shoulder of the man in the seat in front, he said, "Could be that genetic stuff?" Both men wore shorts, sunglasses, short-sleeved shirts. One in duck egg blue with a lemon check; the other in plain blue. They sat next to wives. The women tolerated the excitement of the men by looking at everything passing outside the bus windows, but without talking to their partners.

At the bus station in Lagos two scruffy travellers with rucksacks noticed a sleeping dog just as I looked at it too. We talked about, 'letting sleeping dogs lie' which was amusing and when the talk failed to extend into either allegory or positive silence I sensed an addictive quality to the couple. He lit a cigarette and smoked it through his closed hand like a joint. Their speech was damped down within the neck as if the voice was guarded, each word shed from the mouth with a little shake of the head, as if it was difficult to let go of speech. On another day one of them spotted me and after the greeting, hung in front of me expectantly, calculatingly and after several minutes I worked my way to the dregs of a galao with him standing in front of me. Then he showed me a packet of batteries and asked if I would like to buy them. I did not want them really but he seemed to need to sell something in order to get along and so I bought them. He left with his inferiority complex and I thought what an odd feeling it was to be treated as if I was older and wiser, even if I was.

Suddenly it was 5.45pm and I still had to pay for my galao and then walk to the bus station with two full size Admiralty charts, photocopies of them, plus two photocopied North Africa Pilot books, a rucksack full of groceries and my saxophone.

Then I realized I had not got enough money for the bus and it was the last one back to Alvor. I found a cash machine and ever so slightly stressed, got to the bus station just in time. In the bus station ticket office was an attractive woman wearing a white cheese cloth blouse and a pretty, colourful necklace. She stabbed hard at the computer keyboard and I said, "You can make it better by prising the keys off and cleaning them," but she said, "No, throw it in the marina and get my boss to buy a new one". Her bright red hair made me wonder if she was a witch, a way of saying, 'This is what I look like' sort of glamourised. She seemed to be presenting a picture of who she wanted to appear to be. Witches do that because a copy is transcendent. A reproduction is much easier to handle and mould than an original. This technique was not occult, there was widespread mobilisation of images of the self used as tools in the media, by politicians, and entertainers. The 'local' self-image, or self-images a person deployed is largely unconscious. Witches just happen to have specialized in it for hundreds of years, maybe thousands.

The boat from Bristol Marina, Havsula (the name meant 'gannet') was still anchored nearby. In the cabin hung a comically grinning witch on a broomstick, not a simulacrum or persona but Jim and April's hearty sense of humour.

Thursday 3 July 2003. A small fat dog with short legs and a black and white coat trotted past. A ginger-haired woman working in an ice cream and crepe shop called out to the dog with kissing lips and a smiling greeting. The dog glanced up at the woman, briefly recognizing her and continued on its way with a toothy grin and a happy bounce in its four short legs. Portuguese people seemed to treat animals as genuine friends and I had never seen so many happy faced hounds as in Portugal.

Friday 4th of July 2003. A man dropped a hunk of raw meat in front of a little free dog which looked up at him, sniffed the morsel, licked it and began to eat. The man picked up part of the meat and placed it into a more tidy position where children would be less likely to kick it and the stray continued swallowing. The little dog eventually flaked out in the middle of the pedestrianized road, content to lay digesting for an hour or two. A smart woman who looked non-Portuguese arrived and placed another morsel between the dogs paws. It sniffed, looked up into her eyes and began to chomp. Next the woman deftly placed a blue webbing collar around the dog's neck as it ate. As soon as the tug of the collar was perceived the dog cowered, but it was held by the captor. The woman comforted the dog, patting and stroking, trying to relax it out of resistance until finally picking up the dog and carrying it away. The expression on the dog's face said, 'Hey!' but all resistance was quashed by the persuasive tactics and food. Another one for the dog home, possibly to be homed in an ideal place or to be killed after weeks of rejection. The dog had looked perfectly happy on the crossroads in the centre of Alvor, but this was a naïve view. Strays were poor, lost souls, uncared for and unloved, often dying of chronic neglect. Later that night the moon was waxing and the free dogs all over Alvor called out, 'Hey! Hey! Hey! Hey!'

Later in the small hours the dogs fell asleep to the sound of millions of insects - a high pitched, continuous, ringing layer. One of these insects had landed on my elbow when I was walking in daytime through the tall, dry grass beside the town. It was a mixture of grasshopper and beetle, with no long springing legs, but large, dragonfly like eyes. Folded wings extended for 40 mm behind it and shone living gold where the sunlight touched them. I held my elbow still as I gazed at the creature resting there and my mind's eye lifted over my head to take flight over the grassy hill where I stood. The imaginary eye saw a picture of a gecko hunter, standing solitary still, with one elbow held up to the sky. Far away, the town gave way to dunes and beyond was the ocean. In the other direction purple-shaded mountains unfurled clouds from the northern sky. My mind's eye spiralled around, taking in all angles of the scenery, until pulled back inside by a silver thread, I focussed on the creature sitting on my elbow, wings glinting soft gold in the sun. A fingertip touched the creature and it flew into the impedance of tall grasses. Tonight it would sing again. The hills brimmed with life, but a ramble revealed only dry grasses and tired olive trees, as every living thing within 100m hid itself at my approach; apart from the butterflies, usually red admirals, sailing skilfully between branches and flowers, circulating in pairs, flying around and around, and up and down with each other.

A charity shop existed in Alvor in aid of domestic animals. Shelves of English books served a mainly English concern. Someone brought in a pile of books and said to the person at the counter, "I read twelve books a week. Can I give you these twelve and take another twelve away? I'll bring them back next week to get another twelve. Each time I pay one

Euro, the other lady lets me do that," then a pause as the convoluted request was processed by the volunteer until in a Yorkshire accent he said, "Well, it's not really a charitable act is it? I don't think so, no. How can you expect to get twelve books for the price of one? No, it's not a charitable act". The heavyweight reader told the charity shop worker she read mainly Mills & Boon, saying, "Well the shop gets them back to sell. They are only Mills & Boon and I read so many I don't want to spend so much on each one, the lady who is here on Mondays lets me do it". The man behind the counter did not see the logic of the weekly donation of one Euro in exchange for a clump of books.

Thursday 10 July 2003. To-ing and fro-ing amongst the boats anchored at Alvor produced good results. Friendships strengthened, books were exchanged, charts photocopied and stainless steel fabrication done. In Portimao, twenty minutes bus ride away, a copy shop gave a price of 13 Euros to reproduce a sailing pilot book containing 280 pages and bind it with an acrylic cover. This was three Euros less than the offer in Lagos and I collected sailing directions for the north African coast and the Atlantic islands.

To buy these two essential publications new would have cost at least one hundred Euros In the fish dock area of Portimao, on the eastern bank of the river Arade, I had a stainless steel spinnaker pole fitting welded; for just 2 Euros It was done instantly. A productive day, in fact a good week, so much so that I was even saying to people, "Does it feel like Saturday to you?" One reply was, "Well a friend in the UK phoned this morning and he said it was a Friday, today's Wednesday isn't it?" On this UK boat, a 48 foot yacht built by the owner, I was able to use a vice to shape a piece of stainless steel to fit SPs mast. Pete offered to tidy the roughly hacksawed shape with a grinder. He leant over to a switch panel and a generator started somewhere in the fore cabin. He plugged in the mains electricity powered grinder as I stood in awe of the convenient way he had arranged this power system. Pete let me have that months 'Yachting Monthly' magazine to read. It was already falling apart from being passed around the anchorage before I got to it. The following day I passed it on to a UK couple on a new Bavaria 32. These yachts were built in Austria using a production line from which the yearly average was ten boats per day. Phillipe and Paulo were hoping to sail to south America. With them the conversation gravitated towards the horrors of malaria, from which one child died every half an hour.

Malaria affected just one of the islands within the Cabo Verde group due to the type of terrain specific to that particular place which allowed mosquitoes to propagate. One of the Cabo Verdes group was covered in nothing but sand dunes and date palms and as a result it was described as a little piece of the Sahara desert floating in the Atlantic. There would be no mosquitoes without standing fresh water. It was at this point the liberally illustrated pilot book to the Atlantic Islands, with harbour plans to all the various islands, came into my hands for photocopying.

A diminutive boat, intrepidly sailed single-handed from Brittany by Alain, had a half-built wind vane steering device on the stern, in a similar design to SPs. I offered my experience with the difficulty of getting the control lines to slide easily but my valuable knowledge from producing a highly effective wind vane were overruled by Alain's overly self reliant determination to personally confront the problems of long distance sailing. One morning as the sun beat down and I lay in my bunk Alain rowed over with armfuls of ropes someone had given him and that he did not need. This was very welcome because after wintering in Peniche my mooring lines had all been damaged to the point where there was not a single really long line left intact. I had plenty of short lines because each time one parted the result was two short ones. Solar panels had become the subject of serious talk. Of the two which failed, one was repairable, but due to shoddy design it was obvious it would not last much longer, so I decided to put it down to experience and never buy anything made by ICP Global again.

I had been avoiding Alvor beach because of the steady stream of fresh tourists plodding over the dunes towards it. I knew it would be a depressing scene of sweating bodies and rippling muscles being competitively 'cool' and I found sand so difficult to walk across, especially when it was too hot for bare feet. When I did go there I enjoyed it, collecting some delicious shells and paddling up to my denim shorts in the cold water. I felt vaguely sad on tourist beaches. Ten years previous when I sailed to Walton-On-the-Naze, with a Pakistani friend, Riaz, in the middle of August, the sky was grey and an easterly breeze ruffled the gulls feathers. Riaz and I looked over the sea wall at the families in bathing costumes huddled behind wind breaks. All the elements were in place for a sizzling summer holiday apart from the sunshine. The sand looked like damp brick dust and Riaz remarked how he thought it was sad to see such cheerless people, he said, "For a couple of weeks each year they come here to be free, to relax and enjoy life. The rest of the year they live in joyless inner city housing, with over-demanding kids and relations strained by dismal jobs. Those lives are so unhealthy and miserable".

Meanwhile I continued to walk around in sturdy suede shoes with thick walking socks on and I must have looked eccentric to people whose only wish was to lay on the sand sunbathing, wearing something skimpy and fluorescent, but I was not necessarily happier than them, just different. The Algarve stretched away to the east and west. At my feet the cool, blue Atlantic lapped the sand. Hardly anyone was actually swimming but for the occasional splash as a child dived in. The rest of the 2 mile beach was populated by bathing-suited people strolling along the water's edge. The water was still quite cold, around 17C, quite a shock from a noon time air temperature of 30C. The beach was divided into portions where either your own parasol could be used, or a sun bed rented. The white plastic beds looked like emergency stretchers in a field hospital, organized into tight lines and with draw around curtains. People lay motionless, one knee raised here, an arm trailing to the floor there. Some sat watching the sea, a power boat cutting white gashes into the middle distance. It felt odd to have stopped at the crest of the sand dunes to just look at the people on the beach. Everyone, it appeared, was arriving, leaving, or being on the beach. To actually look at it was odd, for what was there to look at? The answer was nothing. You don't go to a beach to look. In a harbour there was endless activity to watch but at the beach nothing happened besides a blinding sun aggressively tanning the sunbathers.

A wooden path lead to a wooden pavilion, reserved for people who could not walk across the sand. Another wooden pathway led into the distance either way. Walking east, in the direction of Portimao, I passed huts where surf boards, wind surfers, and sailing dinghies could be rented for twenty Euros per hour. I soon swung off the beach pathway and headed across seven hundred meters of spiking grasses and dunes criss-crossed with trails. Each trail led towards a distant hotel block, or apartment complex and one or two led into dense bushes where there hung shades made of fishing nets, broken pots and pans, fish boxes and the marginalised figures of fishermen, or alcoholics, or both. Always mending nets, or flaking long lines into containers, these unshaven men probably found refuge from tourism in their little dens.

I was walking through an air-conditioned supermarket when I realized I had been avoiding the beach and I was saddened by the whole idea of the Algarve. It had been several weeks since I ad seen either a gecko, or a wall lizard. Had I stopped looking, or was it too hot during the daytime for them? I certainly had not given up wandering about in search of reptiles, perhaps they were nocturnal. Mosquitoes did their biting in the early hours which brought on such an inflamed wakefulness I just wanted to annihilate them. Blood engorged mosquitoes would make wholesome snacks for lizards, a reptilian equivalent of black sausage. My problem of no-see-ums had been almost entirely solved by nets. A square was attached to the open fore-hatch with pegs and a large veil dropped from the rear of the spray hood which was ideal, allowing passage in and out of the cabin with a mere flick of the wrist and giving privacy, while I went through my morning wash. During the night this mosquito net allowed the sliding hatch to be fully open and both hatch boards left out to cool my sleep. Night noises penetrated the mosquito nets, the earthy singing of insects, a harmonic rising through the silent windless hours.

Occasionally I practised a little contented insomnia, waking around four am and supping a mug of tea while pondering the quiet state of both the world outside and my own world inside. Clear thoughts came in the still night - the glass was empty - serene, clear, just a glass. Accumulated projects, jobs, possessions, gifts, clutter, tools, books, drawings and notes of everyday life looked more objective and instead of pressing tasks and problems wanting solutions, I saw interlocking patterns of projects and creative ideas. In those lucid moments I could perceive the futility of something and make a decision to scrap it and cut the losses. At night I reflected on who and what I was, and I did doodles; spirals drawn in three planes. I did small organizing tasks such as putting four rechargeable batteries into a tight plastic wrap to keep them grouped together; I admired the freshly cleaned stainless steel hob top surrounded by pans, plates and utensils and the matching brass cased clock and barometer, the clock face with a disc of paper inserted behind the hands to make it easier to read the time. Some people spend time maintaining things as they were originally constructed. I spent time altering things to suit me and I could be quite destructive in this, although I did spend much time thinking before I acted. Fantasies and inventions flourished in the quiet hours before dawn. The daytime left little room for loose, untenable ideas, under the scrutiny and judgement of other people. Daylight was for getting the job done. Darkness was for dreaming the impossible.

My sister and family decided to go on holiday in the Swiss Alps and I wondered if my critical observations of package holidaymakers at the seaside had put them off the idea of sun, sea and sand. The Swiss Alps stood in stark contrast to the seaside.

One morning when I'd been sailing towards Spain with 250 miles still to go, the sea was a vast realm of peaks with tumbling white crests and waves advancing to the horizon where they formed a slowly writhing line. Waves heaved upwards out of the ocean and I'd thought, 'This is really a hostile environment to be in, awesome, dangerous'. SP had fluttered and swooped in utter wilderness. No wonder I felt dissatisfied among the relentless package holidaymakers of the Algarve. At least my sister and family's trip to the Alps would give breathtaking views and a sense of wild nature in the towering snowy ridges and peaks. There was very little to be sensed of wilderness in the seaside resorts of the Algarve. To find it one must go into the open ocean with Peace Four, Aeoli, Alcaide, Stravaig, Little Annie, The Dawntreader, Alice, Stenfis, Alpha Carinae, Wanderer, Varuna, Havsula, and Storm Petrel. Most of these voyagers went alone, treading lighter than pens and writng their journeys only in the wind.

Chapter 5

The Light, The Silence

'The light, the silence, the tingling smell of the Silver Sea, even (in some odd way) the loneliness itself, were too exciting.' (C.S. Lewis, The Chronicles of Narnia, The Voyage of the Dawn Treader, P. 538).

Wednesday 23 July 2003. Ferragudo lay between a fishing quay that looked across the river Arade to Portimao and a white church on top of a hill. Looking from the church southwards, two concrete arms formed the river mouth and each ended in a cylindrical steel light tower, red to starboard, green to port. Within a clutch of streets and stepped passageways lived a small, happy poodle. Her friendly nature was transmitted through carrier waves of black curls and she had never travelled the 2 miles to the sea. Ferragudo had its very own busker, a lone figure who mechanically fingered melodies - Greensleeves, English Country Garden and a Simon and Garfunkel song about hammers and nails - while standing at the edge of the café terrace facing the customers. She was as expressive as a ten year old schoolgirl who has been asked to play a grade 2 piece for friends of parents. At another time of the day she sat dangling her legs over the quayside, and looked dreamily out over the water. Wind instruments stimulate the player as the breath vibrates a column of air within the body of the instrument. Woodwind leaves an oxygen debt, a light-headedness in the the player and the quayside at Ferragudo soothed and replenished the wind player, old fishermen and sailors all.

Movement stimulated my social life. When I arrived at the anchorage in the river Arade I made friends with four new sailors and even better, I met people whom I had known years ago in the UK, on a large yacht called Sheben with a family aboard whom I'd known in Cornwall when I was living there. Those days I played the saxophone every day, like the Ferragudo busker and I too would spend hours resting by the (Penryn) river, resting an overworked embouchure. At the time sailing to Spain was an ultimate goal, far from possible, a probably-never-will.

A second large yacht in Portimao was owned by a couple whom I had met while organizing a car hire in Milford Haven, on a previous sailing trip. We marvelled at the way sailors could meet again in far flung ports of the world. The offered for sale a tiny rowing boat, freshly painted bright blue and named the 'Blue Brick' due to its being too small for a couple and so frightening them a little by being so low in the water it had a tendency to sink. For a single person it was ideal and rowed twice as fast as my Avon inflatable. The deciding factor was whether it would stow on the foredeck. To do this it had to be less than 2m in length and fairly narrow at one end. It fitted neatly, so after rowing it around for a few days I decided I could not do without it. I needed a poor looking dinghy to use in places where the Avon inflatable would attract thieves. An Avon inflatable would fetch hundreds of pounds on the second-hand market and it would cost nearly £1000 to replace with a new one. A tender was one thing I could not do without. It got me ashore and to other boats where friends waited with open arms to ply me with wine and food in exchange for the wondrous tales I could by then tell about sailing alone across the Bay of Biscay. Invariably I would be grilled as to how I managed to get enough sleep to remain clear-headed during a week alone at sea. When I explained how to take fifteen minute snatches of sleep using a kitchen timer to wake up the usual comment would be, "Oh, I could never do that, once I'm asleep nothing would wake me". I explained the haunting image of an ultra large bulk carrier ship bearing down on you and it was this fearsome reality which the 'beep, beep, beep' of the kitchen timer evoked in the mind's eye of the just-fallen-asleep sailor. However tired I felt, I obediently swung my legs off the bunk and stood up to scan the horizon, every time I heard the alarm.

Friday 25 July 2003. A large yacht named Celtic Castle was enjoying the rural feel of Ferragudo. There were only one or two other cruising boats there, the rest being local craft on permanent moorings. Closer to the quay a fleet of small open boats sported bright primary colours with contrasting borders and bow motifs.

A fisherman grinned and nodded approvingly at the blue brick as I rowed by. I think it struck him as different to the ubiquitous grey inflatable dinghy used by most other yachties. In this grinning appreciation of a painted boat I understood why the Portuguese boats are kept so prettily decorated. It was simply an expression of personal pride and kinship with the home port. Ferragudo bows were painted white with a slanted border from the foremost water-line, backwards to the topmost plank. The white curved triangle thus produced stood out strongly, like an open mouth. Painted motifs were universal; a ship's wheel, a compass-rose, an eye, a squid, a dolphin and, of course, a fish.

I cleaned the bottom of the Avon inflatable which was encrusted with barnacles and green slippery weed. I had never worked so hard at removing growth and usually it took ten minutes with a scouring pad and water, but barnacles had established themselves inside the seams and needed hooking out with a hard plastic scraper. Even so they left white, calciferous, footmarks of glue. The inflatable had worked hard and showed it, so I was glad to have secured a second tender. Then I rolled away the inflatable for use as a spare and as a cheap life-raft. To that end I collected all manner of equipment and supplies to aid survival if I had to abandon ship. I bought a wide-necked, orange polypropylene bottle to keep the items in a single place and free of moisture. A garden light designed to enhance the winding, pseudo poetic paths of villas captured my imagination and I bought it to use as an automatic anchor light. It did not fulfil the legal requirements of brightness but it was wholly automatic and autonomous, switching on at dusk and off at dawn and recharging via a small solar panel in the top of the unit. It solved the problem of how to show an anchor light each night when I went away from the boat to visit the UK In August.

Ferragudo had several useful shops. They were old, stocked with dusty items and inhabited by elderly shop keepers. I was pleased to find two gallons of paraffin and a replacement glass for the paraffin burning cabin light. Ferragudo improved my mood absolutely and I felt the joy of being in Portugal, as I sat listening to the chatter of an african-grey parrot in a cage by the door of the pastelaria.

Saturday 2 August 2003. I chose Alvor as the best place to leave the boat while I visited the UK And so sailed back there one morning to greetings from friends on the anchored boats. The presence of boats with friends aboard had swayed my choice - if you're going to blow into another yacht, better one you know rather than one you don't. In Alvor access to the shore was made easy by pontoons to which a dinghy could be moored and by the proximity of anchored vessels to the town. Living aboard in Alvor was like being part of a flock. There were always at least seven or eight tenders clustered at the pontoon. This gave safety in numbers because the chance of one dinghy being stolen was divided by how many others were available. When I rowed ashore one Saturday morning a man lay sleeping on the pontoon. He was mid-thirties and had thick sun dried hair and a 'gone beach' look. Thinking he may wake and row off in the first boat he clamped eyes on I tied up the dinghy well away from him. Then a second man appeared, who looked equally unseaworthy and asked me if he could borrow my tender for a few minutes, "just to have a go?" he explained. I answered, "No, sorry," and then eroded his will with some tedious information about pedalos for hire in Portimao. He then told me I must speak to his friend, who was still asleep at the other end of the landing pontoon,"Why?" I asked defensively, to which he replied, unconvincingly, "He likes to meet people like you. He is always travelling". "Is that a reason to talk to him?" I asked unkindly, attempting to finish it off for good because I sensed a snare.

The anchorage awoke early one morning as a thunder system loomed, smiling ear to ear over Alvor. Strong gusts came from unexpected directions between periods of brooding calm. A large German yacht had a habit of re-anchoring every time a gust of wind arrived. Two days before, under another perturbance the Germans spent two hours motoring around and around, endlessly re-anchoring, hauling it up again and dropping it to try to settle the boat among the others. Eventually dusk settled them down and they went to their beds. The same thing happened that morning. I was awake with the first of many tiny squalls which lasted no more than two or three minutes each and blew no stronger than 25mph. The luxury German yacht, adorned with fields of solar panels, a wind generator, arrays of whip aerials, satellite phone transmitters and a sun awning, caught the breeze and dragged its anchor out of position time and time again. They even had an automatic water-pump to wash the anchor and chain as they came up, pulled by a cockpit controlled windlass. Despite all that the b****y anchor would not hold.

One evening I cleaned thick green weed from SPs water-line. I bought two good quality scouring pads, the ones for non-stick pans were good on fibreglass because they were just aggressive enough to remove stains and weed but without scratching the hull. In the past I had used stainless steel scouring pads which removed more or less everything but added thousands of scratches which held slime, where weed grew in the little furrows like rows of beans.

Sunday 3 August 2003. One night I watched *Terminator 2*, on a laptop with dvd drive aboard a friend's boat, named 'Whale Song'. The effects of the film were entertaining. The scene outside was one of peaceful eventide and the large yacht rested quietly at anchor, looking fine against the last light in the west. Inside three figures relished the violent images of *Terminator 2* grinning in the flickering light of a tft screen.

In almost every harbour a gaggle of boats flew the frayed flag of the 'Entropy' yacht club. Neglected boats descended through layers of decay and the long thwarted aspirations of the owners. It may be bad luck, such as illness, which had separated owner and boat and produced creeping dereliction. With whisky at £3 a bottle in Portugal many fine captains succumbed. When asked how long they had been anchored there, the reply was often hesitant, not because weeks were being summed up, but years. The reply went, "I got eer in, um, now let's see, it was around the time of the Gulf War," I thought how he had not moved since 2003 as the sailor continued, "Yeah, that's it, er nineteen, er, ninety, um, I think. What's that, it's gotta be twelve or thirteen years". Suddenly I saw the intractable layers of crud covering the poor wrecked, but not wrecked boat. All manner of broken, rusted, obsolete, sun-damaged, salvaged, nicked and donated items would be loaded on deck. The clutter outside reflected the chaos inside. The boat would be un-sailable as well as un-sellable and it would take a year to clean it up and repair it. It was simply easier to get drunk.

The inner mind of these lost sailors was cynicism, rendered as humour; hopelessness, blurted out as wisdom. These alcoholic ex-voyagers surfaced daily out of the mess, like hatching caterpillars, around mid-morning when the sun has made the bunk too uncomfortable to lay in. They looked across the water at each other under yet another quadraphonic blue sky and cursed the day with their fatalism, calling to each other, 'Another f****ng day in paradise' and laughed cruelly. Port authorities occasionally cruised around spot fining anchored boats which did not comply with basic rules, but maybe the authorities were also concerned to break these downward spiralling lives out of their spin. A part of the Portuguese economic development program centred on attracting international sailors with big new marina developments financed partly by European Union development funds. These luxury marina projects divided sailors into two distinct groups, the haves and the have-nots, the first group making up about 15% of the second, so for every cruising boat keen to spend a night, and spending it in a marina, there would be twenty anchored nearby for free.

In Portimao I thought it would be sensible to go into the big new marina, once a week to collect water, recharge ship's batteries, have a proper shower and use the laundry, but I could not justify, let alone afford, the 'high season' price of 20 Euros for a single nights berth. I ended up surreptitiously collecting water in cans from the marina taps. I used the solar-powered garden light as an anchor light to avoid the fussy fines by the maritime police. I carried on doing my laundry in buckets of cold water, which worked perfectly, even in sea-water as long as fresh was used to rinse. I ran the engine for an hour each day to maintain the batteries and I cut down on electricity use to an absolute minimum of brief cabin lights usage and transistor radio. This made me feel more complete, rather than poor, as I became adept and resourceful, just like a 'real' cruiser. More importantly, I managed to evade the heavy drinking which had been a feature of life aboard back up the coast at Cascais with my Swedish friends and Pedro the saxophone player. Pedro would say, 'Life, lasts only 2 days, but don't worry, because carnival lasts 3 days.' His other favourite expression was, 'Come on! Clarissa, don't break my balls!' and he used this forcefully and annoyingly, to win most arguments. Finally I did 'break his balls' by sailing away to look for my autonomy again. And so, the ship sailed on, skirting the treacherous 'Sea of Entropy', rounding the formidable 'Cabo Pedro' and slipping safely past the discordant shallows of 'Karaoke Bar', to anchor safely in 'Whale Song Bay', a safe haven where SP could lay unattended for a couple of weeks.

Wednesday 6 August 2003. My flight to the UK was later in the day. In Portimao I had to wait several hours for a train to Faro after I got the train times from 'Algarve Life', a small magazine in English but completely in error. Luckily I left several hours early, just as well what with the heat and Portuguese buses and trains. The next train did not leave until 3.30pm, so I had several hours in hand. It was a hot day so I hid in the shade of a restaurant. Fried chicken and chips with bread, butter and salad, and a glass jug of red wine kept me busy for an hour. An Irish couple came in and tried to ask for fish and chips, saying, "Er, fish, and chips," The waiter said, "Yes, boiled, grilled, fried?" Irish couple, "Er, in batter," Waiter, "No," Seeking to emulate some kind of fish and chips the Irish couple threw in a concession, "Fish, cod? Grilled? With chips?" Grilled should not be a problem, we all thought. Finally the waiter called through to the kitchen, "Bachalau assada con battatas frites," and they got rancid dried cod, with chips.

The Irish couple, young and good looking, serious in the heat, should have had the frango assada con battatas frites (fried chicken with chips) for the fish was always a bit of a mess in my opinion, but I did not intervene. Bachalau was a national institution of Portugal which was imported from Norway. Stinking mounds of the stuff made grocery stores no go areas. Apparently, once salted and dried, fish remained edible for years. Soon the Irish couple picked their way, bone by bone, through a pair of grimacing fish - a far cry from the fish 'n' chips they'd wanted.

I found my way along the coast to Faro airport and in the evening I caught my plane. A view from the tiny port of the Airbus A321 reminded me of the tumbling heights of Aslan's country, way, way, above Narnia. More the tourist, but still feeling the wonder of adventure I was carried through the cloud vaults into a high, rare land, although there were no soft growling words, nor the touch of Aslan's velvet paw. Instead, I was distracted and subdued by a hot mash of consumerism: British Airways fare came in little bottles of red wine and within a tray full of plastic lids and packets I discovered a three-course meal. Despite returning to England, I was not going home because by now the idea of 'home' was situated at SP. The voyage was where I lived, rather than Bristol Marina, which was merely a pontoon I happened to be moored at twelve months previously. The Airbus A321 windows were too small to gaze through and allowed only fleeting glimpses downwards onto high cloud, and far below this a dense carpet of cloud obliterated the Iberian peninsular. Overhead LCD screens showed an image of the plane travelling across a map.

The plane shot over Portugal, Spain, the Bay of Biscay, France, the Channel Islands and the English Channel. At 32000 feet the outside air temperature was minus 52 F. At 15 minutes to touch down I saw the United Kingdom swirling closer below us, like a glinting orange tea tray floating upwards through the black pool of night. I'm sure I heard a voice singing, 'Hello friend, welcome home'.

Three weeks later, on the first day of September, I returned to Portugal. It was late summer and I had sailing plans to work on. While I was away a gale had dragged the anchors of SP, but she was tended by friends on other boats and suffered only a broken navigation light. This would have cost around 70 Euros to replace, but Tony, a musician friend aboard Tarnimara, a Rival 32, close by, wanted to try out his new hot glue gun and did a great repair job on the light fitting. A nasty cold got into me, but with the illness came a feeling of healing - since the high season of August had passed Alvor was quieter, softer, with a much more tranquil atmosphere. Daytime in Alvor felt relaxing and dreamy, just how I had come to know the west coast during last winter time.

Instead of the clamour of kids and parents fighting each other over limited holiday resources in a mass of noise, now the individual voices of more relaxed holiday makers could be heard saying things like, "I could spend the whole time here, I think Alvor is really nice," and, "Now this is what I'd imagined it (Portugal) would be like, really laid back and tranquil". These were the out of season tourists who had come for rest and quiet. Now the 'Prevailing Super Guns' and 'Whale with Handles' (two beach toys for sale in tourist gift shops) would remain unsold until next year's high season. I felt an incredible relief in the tangible tranquillity of Alvor in September, despite my cold which made me feel quite ill with headaches, running nose, a feeling of mild dizziness and bouts of sneezing.

In the shaded terrace of the café Allianca, I sat regulating my body temperature, like a lizard, by leaving one arm and one leg unshaded. From a gift shop across the road I heard a cd consisting of recent chart songs played on saxophone. My anti-Algarve feelings dissolved as the gentle music reached me soothingly in the sunshine at the heart of Alvor. When I was away the weather had been extremely hot with temperatures described by Jim and April aboard 'Havsula', out of Bristol UK, as, 'Almost survival conditions - you just couldn't do anything from ten in the morning until evening. The only way to handle it was to damp yourself down with wet sponges'. Jim and April told me how the huge wild fires throughout Portugal had blotted out the sun one day, like an eclipse. They said the smoke was choking and ash rained down onto the boats, even though no fire reached within 4 miles of Alvor because a dual carriageway running the length of the Algarve had stopped it. They had, they told me, been ready to up anchor and move out to sea if conditions worsened. I cheerfully said, "And I was not at all worried about SP because I thought the fires were all in the Lisbon and central areas". Oh well 'out of sight out of mind' and I had got away with grubby, soot ridden decks which I did not mind because it gave me motivation to wash and scrub the boat, which resulted in me feeling much happier all round.

A new phase had begun, in which I was busy preparing the boat for an audacious voyage. Each time I bought food I tripled the quantity of things which would keep without refrigeration and made careful note of sources of the best quality perishables. On my little hand-held Psion computer I had a detailed supplies database, with costs, quantities, sources and alternative brands etc. However, this was mostly useless, because it was based on supermarkets in the UK Such as Asda, Sainsbury's, Scoop-n-Save, Tesco's and so on, all of which had been within 10 minutes bike ride of Bristol Marina. Alvor had only one main supermarket, a very poor and expensive 'AliSuper'. It was solely there to supply self-catering tourists with 'a bit of shopping' and the prices were extortionate. There was a Lidl supermarket in Portimao, but without a car it took half a day to get there. I needed to take SP into Lagos, or Portimao marina for a few days in order to stock up properly with three months worth of food and water. For safety, it was sensible to carry stores for three times the amount needed for a particular passage, to allow for unforeseen circumstances. If I went to the Canary Islands I may, I repeat may, then be inclined to set out on an Atlantic crossing. Such a voyage might take one month if all went well and therefore three months worth of stores was appropriate.

For now though, I could hardly imagine leaving the coast of Portugal. I had only just begun to gain an affinity with the complex sounds of the language. I realized this as I copied a page in Portuguese from a textbook. It was information about geckos words used to describe the biological characteristics of the Osga (Portuguese name for gecko) came surprisingly easy to reproduce - the structure of the language had become familiar to me - such as the sentence,

'Os deidos sao curtos, separados, quase iguais, alargados na extremidade, onde formam discosadesivos.'

Which seemed a perfectly understandable explanation of the adhesive feet of the gecko.

During the long days spent wading through the long grasses, olive groves and tinder sticks of the soon to be blazing Portuguese countryside, I had assimilated a language - the words of fishermen overheard as I untied my dinghy from the quay - bitter exclamations sent flying out of shadowy bars at midday by an unemployed typewriter repair man - what the washing machine service engineer said in reply - greetings from old men, cheerful to be wished a 'good day' by this tall, blond, English sailor - complicated discussions during diesel engine complications - All these and other words had bobbed about in my mind like flotsam, as I sailed solo, literally and metaphorically, in Portugal for the past year. Part of me wished to spend longer in Portugal, to learn to actually talk Portuguese, more than the sound of the language and a small collection of words. Another year would see me using sentences and phrases with alacrity. But part of me understood it was a mistake to think happiness was a treasure buried in a faraway land. The voyage of SP was more an expression of pleasure in living than the search for it.

The storm petrel (Hydrobates pelagicus) is a tiny bird, not much bigger than a swift. In a poem by Maxim Gorky, the Storm Petrel is a hero. 'Now he flouts the black sea-water, Now he stabs into the cloud-ranks, Hurling on them cries defiant'. Storm Petrels were named thus because they were seen after being driven ashore during storms, being too small to resist heavy weather, as was my SP. She was tough but her strength was in the ability to offer as little resistance to the environment as possible.

The poem gets worse, going too high, 'And the petrel in the cloud-heights,' And with too much electricity, 'The one rival of the lightning,' Imagine sitting on the one object higher than the seas surface for miles around with lightning striking the surrounding sea and waving overhead, stirring the crackling air was the mast, like a maestro's baton in some Wagnerian concert. Steel wires ran to the tip of this long metal tube, while electricity cables, a cluster of lights, wind sensor and radio antenna enhanced the attraction for lightning. To increase the chance of pulling a lightning strike this tempting pathway was wrapped in ropes and sails, all damp with salt-spray and night air. Lightning loves a wet, metallic direct route. The correct procedure was to drape a chain into the sea from the metal rigging wires to give the lightning bolt easy passage to the water, otherwise as it reaches the bottom of the mast it just blows a hole right through the bottom of the boat in its unstoppable charge. 'Rivals the lightning', more like 'cowers under it'.

Hardship in small yachts is somehow rewarding too. There were certainly remarkable obstacles to contend with in sailing and I read the following which said it well,

"Perhaps a person gains by accumulating obstacles. Care must be taken, however, to select large obstacles, for only those of sufficient scope and scale have the capacity to

lift us out of context and force life to appear in an entirely new and unexpected light. Difficulties illuminate existence, but they must be fresh and of high quality."
Tom Robbins (1976), *Even Cowgirls Get The Blues*, Pub. Bantam, P. 181.

Thursday 11 September 2003. The little old square in Alvor was again my favourite place ashore. The first café I found in Alvor, the Dragao was a bit parochial for my needs and I chose other places where there was a mixture of tourists and locals. I did not always plonk myself in the midst of Alvorans daily lives, even if in doing so I may have presented them with a remarkable obstacle. I preferred to observe from the edge of things without causing too much turbulence. The café Allianca attracted an ideal mix of tourist and local. I sat, with a galao and a mixed toastie and became aware of a figure looking out of an upstairs window, open and looking over the café terrace. In defence against the leering gazer, I exercised my peripheral vision, trying to observe as much about him without looking up at him. I noticed how colours on the edge of my vision were blurry and shapes indistinct, more like tastes than objects. My attention shifted about the visual field, like a tongue when the mouth is chewing. Movements stood out clearly as the lower brain monitored the field. My experiment in vision resulted from a program I had recently heard on the BBC World Service, about eyes, perception and seeing. The program told how when the pupils of another creature are directed at another, special nerve cells, in the eye of the watched, pick up the discs and alert defensive or fleeing instincts. As creatures we are acutely sensitive to being looked at or watched. When the man in the second floor window looked directly at me, I thought I could somehow feel the pupils. Next I asked myself what 'people watching' actually was. My eyes scanned the people enjoying sunshine and chatting on the terrace and I saw eyes averting; fingers touching chins; lips drawing back over teeth in smiles; hands casually flopping around, moving from head to table, to legs. People watching, I decided, was participation. I strongly felt the role I was playing in the scene, which was to do what everyone else was doing. If I openly stared at people, the whole terrace would become uneasy and I begin to perceive increased amounts of threats in little stabs of direct eye contact, so I turned off my sociological imagination and just savoured the relaxed mood of the café. A young couple with Irish accents strolled towards what they thought was the café entrance. They realized the open doors led into the church and about-turned, stumbling out and sniggering.

Later I met Danish single-hander, Beil, and another Dane called Lars, down at the quayside for a late afternoon tumbler of wine. We got talking to Edie, an old Alvorian, born in 1918. He told us he had raced yachts between the Algarve and Lisbon. Writing on a paper napkin, Edie listed the boats he had owned, raced and sold, with the price he had paid and the amount he had sold each one. He had made quite a lot of money from his yachts. He was currently responsible for the lovely Museu Etnografico da Alvor. I asked Edie whether the church bells in Alvor were rung exactly the same as the ones in Ferragudo. I had heard them both and been surprised to hear, what sounded like, the same tune. It was a chaotic tune, full of unresolved melodic and rhythmic fragments, but each time I heard it the ragged, angular pattern was consistent. Edie described the bells of Portimao, 'din, din,' and those of Ferragudo, 'din, dom,' those of Alvor, 'din, dom, com cacas de burbigao.' Which meant din, dom, with shellfish.

There were always dozens of figures out on the sand flats of Alvor. As the tide swirled inwards again they lugged bucket loads of shellfish. It was interesting to view the ebbing and flooding tides as a bulge of water gripped by lunar gravity. The earth revolves beneath the inertial sea. Continents and islands plough along through the standing lunar wave. Into every trough go the cocklers and musselers, like ringed plovers dart into the spaces between waves to pick up prey from the seashore. Instead of fleeting moments, in which to collect food, the tidal wave took six hours to cycle. Somewhere, at a distance to this estuary at low-water a wave was flooding in the direction of this tern enchanted estuary. There was time before the tide arrived again, but not much, hardly the skitter of a sandpiper. Summer was nearly ended. Later in the week I made ready for sea and re-anchored in the fairway, at a distance from the boozing, joking, happy-but-stuck cruisers. I was afraid I would grow long ears and start braying like a donkey. It was time to leave Portugal.

I sailed to Lagos to get the boat hauled out, so I could coat the bottom with a good quality anti-fouling paint and this led to the discovery of a broken rudder bearing. It could have resulted in loss of the rudder. I asked the boatyard to do the repair, insisting on much stronger materials than the original. I had substantial work to do on the self-steering rudder and there were many other small jobs to do so I trusted them to do a good job and at a fair price. It cost just over 200 Euros and I was pleased with the work so my judgement was sound on this occasion. Meanwhile I'd glued, with epoxy resin, two cheeks to the self-steering rudder at the point where most strain occurred. These fifteen mm. thick pieces of marine plywood added immense strength. I was most grateful for the epoxy resin given to me in Bristol by Anne and Nev aboard Peace Four. One part of the boatyard housed a small collection of antique engines, big old cast iron, single-cylinder engines, six decades old. I decided to remove the wood stove, to save weight and space and after lowering the cast iron stove from the boat on ropes I placed it among the old engines, where it looked perfectly in keeping with the other objects. When the owners of Sopramar saw the stove they were delighted with my gift. I had increased the goodwill around the boatyard and when it came to paying the final bill I felt certain I was not overcharged. Some people I met in Alvor who had been several years on yachts in the Algarve told me negative rumours about Sopramar, but I was completely happy with the work done, and the cost of it, plus the haul out charges were reasonable. It had been correct to ignore gossip and choose my own path as some people gossip just to have something to say.

Saturday 4 October 2003. I finished anti-fouling, refitted the self-steering rudder and after a Saturday morning re-launch, filled up all water-tanks. With drying laundry strung around the rigging I moved to the fuelling pontoon to buy extra diesel, then I went to a supermarket to buy a white cabbage, a bag of potatoes, wholemeal rolls and fresh butter. A couple of hours later the only reason to wait until tomorrow was the lateness in the day, it was 4pm, usually a good time for a cup of tea, to relax and laugh with the BBC World Service program, 'Just a Minute', a homely clutter in the cabin and spicy aromas of boaty cooking, a view out of the cabin of drifting gulls, strolling people and the encroaching evening. And safe. Usually.

I decided there was no time like the present and put to sea in the direction of the Canary Islands, 600 miles to the south-south-west. The course set was a rhumb-line which cleared the bulge of north-west Africa by 60 miles. But before the sea was nearly a mile of straight river and the wind and current were with me so when the engine failed and would not restart I made a split second decision to raise sail and carry on towards the sea. The alternative would have been to anchor in the busy, narrow fairway, then get a tow back to the moorings to face the possibility of being stuck for weeks in Portugal while mechanics poked around and cost me money and it would only take a spell of unsettled weather to trap me into spending a second winter in Portugal.

I was hanging on to things like a frightened octopus; a hand on the engine starting key; an arm to unfurl the foresail, a hand hauling in the jib sheet, a leg controlling the tiller, an arm steadying me as the sail drew, a hand to rescue the gps, as it rattled across the cockpit with the slight heel and surge forward of SP; a leg to free a foot from newly writhing coils of rope, and a hand to clear a riding turn on the winch.

I wondered if it would have been better to have stayed in with the radio and cooking smells, but I was alert with harbour walls, jetties and other vessels flowing past and my quickening heart beat fell in love with the going. I sang a merry song of letting go, 'Sail away, sail away, sail away', SP slipped rashly along with her brand new anti-fouling and I sang, 'Carry me, on the waves, to a land I've never been', *Orinoco Flow*, by Enya. Soon I was free of the harbour mouth and Lagos rapidly diminished like gravity as I escaped outwards. A few twists of the self-steering gear and it locked with a course just west of south, away from the Algarve and the continent of Europe. When it was dark I began to feel ill and spent much of the first night and the following day being sick and feeling sweaty with a headache. I lay in my bunk with the wondrous self-steering wind vane guiding the boat.

The second night saw SP 155 miles from land and by the third day I felt stronger, after eating muesli for breakfast. The sea grew calmer and I gave myself a crash course in diesel engine maintenance. I read the Volvo Penta MD1 manual and identified various air bleeding points in the fuel system. This was not easy because I had to poke my head upside down through the cockpit floor while holding a mirror, a torch and a spanner, while the boat jostled through the waves. The wind vane self-steering gave me great confidence by working perfectly and I had plenty of time to think about why the engine had failed. Finally I remembered I'd switched off the fuel tap before the boat was hauled out two weeks previously: I was extremely pleased to find the tap was off. I'd found the reason why the engine had stopped.

After I reopened the fuel tap the engine still would not start. So I reasoned it must be air in the fuel, drawn in after the pump had pulled everything from the pipes up to the closed tap. This was correct because after bleeding the fuel pump, injector and fuel lines the engine did start. I was delighted to have overcome this difficulty.

On the fourth night I could sense Morocco as a strong presence in the mental map I held of the voyage. A photocopied navigation chart showed the bulge of Africa nearing the 640 mile rhumb-line linking Lagos with Lanzarote. A rhumb-line is a straight course which takes no account of the curvature of the earth's surface. It is accurate enough for distances under 1000 miles, although longer distances involve drawing a curved route, known as a 'Great Circle'.

The sun set into the west and uneasy instincts came with nightfall at sea. I felt I should be on land, protected, Moroccan music on the radio made me feel even more uneasy. A dramatic and fearsome noise like a film soundtrack to a battle, or a tragedy - sweeping strings, crying vocals, the knocking and popping of struck drums and rapped percussion left my nerves frazzled in the oceanic gloaming. The following morning, just before sunrise, I had to change sails and after settling the wind vane steering back on course, a blood orange sun appeared where Morocco lay, the closest land, 60 miles to the east. I switched the radio back on and heard music from Casablanca. I was struck by the optimism in a singer at one with the dawning day. The sound of his voice was as joyful as a father manhandling a chuckling baby. The dawn singer was life affirming, warm, open and beautiful. Clouds illuminated in rose gold piled up beneath the morning sun. An hour later the eastern sky turned to silver and the radio was giving the serious talk of the day. There followed a couple of days of calm which was challenging in new ways. The strong heat, endless wobbling blue sea and strong sun had me contemplating the danger of this vast salt-water space. I imagined how unpleasant it would be if I became stranded in the open ocean in a dinghy, sitting wracked by cramps and sores, the scorching days would pass inexorably while whatever water and food supplies dwindled. There would be little chance of rescue. The need for an emergency radio beacon became paramount. At least other people would be aware of a cry for help and I would hold some hope of rescue. After two more days of largely calm weather during which the boat wallowed and the sails slatted uselessly to and fro, the sky became wholly overcast and at night a nearly full moon shone through this dense filter of cloud with an eerie silver light, colouring the sea fish-skin grey.

A breeze arrived, firm enough to operate the wind vane steering and give SP 80 miles in 24 hours. On the fifth night out the wind increased until I reduced the main sail down by two reef points, to half its full size. During the night SP sailed well and comfortably and I knew the boat was prepared for stronger wind if it came before dawn. The following morning a squall came from the east, picking up steep, two metre high waves. Being contrary to the regular swell from the north, the young waves were rude and boisterous and their troughs beckoned the boat in, even as the hollows convexed into sneering grey movement. With the boat pressed over to starboard by the wind and water curling over the bows to splatter across the spray hood I gave up trying to sail and heaved-to, which is a way of stopping and holding a sailing boat in a fairly comfortable aspect to the weather and waves. Then I sat watching the waves from the protection of the companionway seat under the spray hood with occasionally seas breaking over the boat, but I was safe and dry and eventually I decided to go below and get some rest. Preparing the boat for a blow and the thought of approaching strong wind had been tiring and drawn nervous energy, so I fell fast asleep with the canvas lee cloth holding me securely in the leeward berth.

As usual, I kept 15 minute watches using the kitchen timer. After the squall died away to a force 4, I was able to get under way again into lumpy waves which reminded me of the Bristol Channel, although it was warm, at around 25C and the squall had been hot and dry. When I had gone below to sleep I'd had to drag off water-proof trousers, life jacket and rain coat, after which I felt much more comfortable. I had not worn shoes since departing from Lagos and I felt happiest moving about the boat, day and night, bare footed. When there was less than 60 miles before Lanzarote I made the same mistake as when approaching La Coruna the previous year. This was to lose sleep in the hope of covering the distance quickly to ensure arrival during daylight the following day. I sailed through the night and in the early hours what looked like a huge ship heading toward me through grey gloomy moonlight appeared ahead. The ship lights came relentlessly onwards and I made haphazard course alterations, derived of the navigation manual known as 'Over Tiredness'. After an hour it had not reached me or passed by and I assumed it must be anchored. Any course alteration I made to avoid it was matched exactly, in the same way the moon appears to keep pace with a moving car and the 'ship' had not moved in the way an object within 3 miles would, so eventually I realized it was the 500m cliff top called Mirador del Rio, the northernmost point of Lanzarote.

Black against black, a saw-toothed splodge, I spotted the Roque Del Este, an isolated rock, unmarked and unlit, despite rising 264ft above the waves. I was still over 20 miles north of Lanzarote. Over the next five hours I closed with Lanzarote to within 3 miles. I lectured myself about landfall procedures: *Rule 1 - Never approach land if you are over tired and at night.*

I repeatedly fell asleep.

Even when I arrived at Lanzarote I still had to coast down to Arrecife harbour. This was when I felt most tired and I strained to keep awake with shipping and a rocky shoreline nearby. My head frequently fell forward into involuntary micro naps. I had no choice but to stay awake. After a long voyage the last 20 miles seem insignificant. It still took 5 hours at 4 knots. It was light by the time Arrecife slid into view with its DISA oil containers huddling ashore and docking structures branching out to seaward. I had a strong impression of having stopped at a harbour overnight and having talked with sailing friends about lowering the spray hood to make it easier to see forward when coasting. I knew I had not stopped anywhere but over tiredness made my mind a synthesis of thoughts, dreams and reality. Deep inside, a quiet eye watched the situation; the voyage drawing to a conclusion; the position indicated by the gps; the compass and the boats motion. A part of me knew exactly where I was and where I was going. The morning light revealed an arid rocky Canary island with dozens of rose and sand coloured volcanoes. I took photographs of the morning sunshine radiating from behind a cloud with the tantalizingly delicate figure of a tiny sailing boat arriving at Lanzarote at the same time as SP.

Puerto Naos was deeply nestled between an industrial port and the reef which formed the original harbour. Arrecife meant reef. Dilapidated Puerto Naos harboured large trawlers which had lain unused for years. The African coast was washed by an up-welling cold current and a decade previous the fishing grounds between Lanzarote and Mauritania were some of the richest on earth, until European quotas killed the industry.

I anchored at 8am on Saturday 11th October after six days at sea. SP was near to a bright yellow Wharram catamaran with audio speakers laying on the cabin top with techno music playing. The people aboard hurled boozy invitations to me, "Storm Petrel, come and have a beer!" I acknowledged the calls until repetition forced me to become annoyed at which point I ignored them. I was too tired to feel anything. Volcanoes peeked through buildings everywhere I looked. The sky was a high frequency, island blue. Airliners decelerated with a curving scream, as if they had just spotted the island and applied the air brakes hard to avoid missing this sliver of volcanoes.

My instincts were still at sea and a part of me was trying to say this was all a dream. Arrival was made surreal by the insistent calls to have a beer from the catamaran called 'Dignity'. After settling the boat into harbour mode I set about launching the dinghy. The techno music catamaran did not give up and finally my tired frown broke into a laugh as they shouted over, "Storm Petrel! We're not your enemy! Come over for a beer!" So I rowed over and met carpenter Richard, English teacher Caroline and naked naturist, Dani. They became good friends while I was in Puerto Naos over the next three weeks. I had managed to arrive in time to invite a Bristol friend, Annemarie, to take her holiday and I was very pleased to have come all this way and kept to a schedule. I looked forward to enjoying a week of sight-seeing and holiday-making with a close friend.

Thursday 6 November 03. Lanzarote was a barren island composed of volcanic rock with areas of rough lava fields. I visited Famara beach on the north-west coast which was backed by cliffs rising more than 500m. We had been taken there by Dave, a sailor who was also a hang glider, to look at the spot where he launched from. I cherished the view from the surprising height with dark shapes sliding across the coastal plain. As my perception adjusted I saw those strange moving splodges were cloud shadows and moving cars appeared as big as full stops. Next we drove down to the beach where Dave, Dani and Annemarie recklessly stripped off and got swept along in the rough waves while I walked towards the sloping land at the base of the cliffs to look for geckos Under a large stone two geckos disappeared as I lifted it. A third stayed on the stone and as I cupped my hands around it, the gecko moved onto me. It had gold bronze eyes and pressed its belly against the warmth of my palm. The gecko index clanged and flashed like a Blue Peter appeal fund reaching a target.

Days in Lanzarote were dominated by earnest preparation for cruising further. Huge chandlers near to Puerto Naos remained from the vanished fishing industry and it was bewildering to be confronted with everything I had ever wanted for a boat - stainless steel fittings, fixings, raw materials that did not rust or rot and marine equipment stacked in bulk warehouses. None of the large trawlers moored in the port were operational and a Senegalese man lived aboard one as a watchman. He had worked as crew but had not received wages for three years. He always smiled when we passed along the harbour wall and I wondered what his life story might be, if he could write it. Supermarkets brimmed with storable foods, such as tinned beans, lentils, peas and rows upon rows of different brands of tinned tuna. The amount of navigation charts and sailing pilot books available to make copies of was overwhelming. I spent 100 Euros on photocopying alone, but I was pleased with the information thus gained which covered the whole southern North-

Atlantic in pilot books for Senegal, Gambia and the Cabo Verdes. The collection would have cost a fortune to buy new.

I wanted to see more of the islands in the canary archipelago and so a festival of world music, called WOMAD, was as good a reason as any to go to Las Palmas, the capital of Gran Canaria. I left at the same time as Dave and two German friends aboard his boat, 'Asylum Seeker', to cruise to Gran Canaria in company. The journey from the island of Lanzarote to the island of Gran Canaria was 115 miles. The first half ran fairly close to Fuertaventura with its beautiful sand dunes, but frightening waves. There were steepening rolling waves well out to sea where the depths changed from 1000m to 60m. The shoal lay at the north-west tip of the island and a light tower marked the outer end. SP passed within a mile and I saw the horizon ahead buckling and folding like a mat sliding up against a wall. Asylum Seeker was positioned closer inshore of SP so I called them on the radio to warn them, but they did not respond because their vhf radio was on the wrong channel. Eventually the other boat turned abruptly offshore and I knew they had met the steepening swells and, just inshore, huge breakers.

Overnight the two boats stayed close although Asylum Seeker sailed half a knot faster. When she drew more than about a couple of miles ahead I used the engine to catch up again. In the early hours I closed to within shouting distance. Both boats were under full sail, moving at 4.5 knots through sparkling silver moonlight, swirling around the two little ships whose sails were indistinct in the darkness, appearing as faint curved lines tracing downwards from the masthead navigation lights and upwards from red night-vision lamps in the cockpit. Voices reached across the sluttering gap, losing most of their meaning to the steady breeze. A couple of boat lengths between us, we swayed to the same wave surges and as both were helmed by wind vane steering so we headed along equal wind paths.

A navigational warning came over the ships radio about a swarm of locusts in the area. *Gosh, I thought, this is travelling.* We kept within sight of each other throughout the night. At three am an irregularly blinking light faintly loomed dead ahead. Asylum Seeker called on the radio to ask what I thought it was and after an hour of chart work and gazing ahead from the bows we decided the light was the 660ft tall La Isleta - the first sight of Gran Canaria. The chart showed this light as being visible from 20 miles away, but we were nearly 31 miles distant when we'd first spotted it. The early hours went by slowly and only the wind grew lighter as the sky remained dark until eventually at six am the island was clearly visible and shipping could be seen converging on Las Palmas. Mystical mountains did the usual trick of turning into clouds as Gran Canaria changed from a distant dream to an actual island. The mountains reappeared high in the air, Roque Nublo being 1,803m above the sea and another pinnacle reached even higher at 1,949m.

Some weeks after arrival I went with the two German girls into those mountains and took a photograph of Roque Nublo. We hired a car between three of us and crossed the island from north to south. Part of the route was amongst mountain peaks on unsurfaced roads where hire cars were not allowed, but both Marie's and Linda's driving was impeccable and I managed to enjoy the experience of encounters with other vehicles tentatively passing between skyward rock walls and precipitous drops. Beyond a view of mountains was a blue space which looked like the ocean. Beyond the blue realm was a ruler-straight line of cloud with a volcanic cone above. It was the snow capped Pico del Teide, the 2.5 mile high volcano on the island of Tenerife, 43 miles away.

Las Palmas was super, for at last I was back in a proper city. It surrounded the anchorage like a filthy towel, with cars, lorries and motorcycles rushing constantly along the main road. It was wonderful, I could wander into those streets and just evaporate amongst ships chandlers, electronics bazaars, cafés and shoe shops, all in splendid heat, usually 25C, which was absolutely perfect. The Spaniards and Canariones were rumbustious and it was hard to remain in one place for more than half an hour without feeling like a mop in the corridor. I found it difficult to find a peaceful café in which to sit, reflect and write.

Thursday 13 November 2003. At one time La Isleta was separated, but a narrow neck of land grew to connect it with the main island. On one side of this peninsular was a huge port complex called Puerto de la Luz, where SP sheltered from the trade winds blowing fresh from the North. On the other side was the beach, which faced the prevailing wind and was popular with surfers. Las Palmas was capital to the three eastern-most Canary Islands - Lanzarote - Fuertaventura - Gran Canaria.

In 8 days I'd found little opportunity to wander. There had been the Womad Festival which took place over 4 days and was really enjoyable. After the festival was over I spent several days feeling tired having been involved with the problems and needs of friends, perhaps as a way to take rest from my own far flung position. The time to make huge decisions had arrived, such as where to go in the next few months and how to make the boat as safe as possible out in these vast tracts of ocean and in non-European countries.

The yacht 'Asylum Seeker' had come to Las Palmas for a haul out and I agreed to give them a hand going into the travel-lift dock. When Asylum Seeker swooped by SP to pick me up she caught my rigging in her bowsprit. Ten tons of steel brushed against two and a half tons of fibreglass. My complaint was that the assailant kept moving at three knots in all circumstances under way. A steel bowsprit began to play my rigging wires like a mechanical road digger strumming a Spanish guitar (the strained rigging wire attachment would subsequently fail 850 miles south of Las Palmas). Luckily, I had put out two large fenders and it may have been those which pushed SP far enough to the side to prevent Asylum Seeker's bowsprit engaging with SPs fore-stay. As it swept across the foredeck I leapt aboard the other boat with beating heart thanking those fenders for saving SP from being hooked like a tuna fish. We arrived into the marina holding a thousand yachts, Asylum Seeker put the wind up several other yachties with her formidable kinetic motion being heedlessly wielded - it was all engine thrust, either hard forward or strong reverse. I sat gripping the ten tons of steel under me as it moved with long powerful bursts of engine, while moving ahead, astern and abaft, into an aisle where two hundred and twenty-five posh yachts had gathered for the imminent ARC (Atlantic Rally for Cruisers). Virtually all the ARC yachts had hugely expensive and painfully vulnerable wind vane steering devices at the stern. On this very point of concern I had refused to take part in an entry to the marina under sail alone when the engine of Asylum Seeker was inoperable for a period. The merest touch of another boat against a wind vane gear could sweep it from the stern and here were whole rows of Aries, Windpilot, Haslar, Atoms, Autohelm, Monitor, Cape Horn, Navik, Wind Hunter, as well as the precious self-built ones, as priceless as my own, could disappear in one uncontrolled veer.

Being on other peoples boats was just too painful for me to bear and later I sought solitude in the grimy streets full of roaring vehicles and little bars, banks and travel agents. I walked past grubby blocks of buildings, deeper and deeper into the heart of Las Palmas until a startling view of tumbling white waves and a wide bay appeared at the end of one street. I gasped at the sight of a beach with hills to one side and mountains on the other. Joggers swerved around my palpable wonder as I stood and stared.

Earlier I had been to the U.S. Consulate to enquire about getting a visa but was disappointed to learn I could only apply for one in the UK if the boat was registered there. This situation had made me feel obstinate and I thought, 'Sod it then, I'll go to Cuba instead'. The news riled me and I suddenly felt that sailing across the Atlantic was just too difficult. I pondered my situation and nagged myself, 'Why not stay in the Canaries and forget about ocean voyaging for a while?' Another voice did not nag, but instead was self-confident and nuzzled me onwards, 'It is getting time to sail again, you have done so much work to prepare for the next part of the voyage, you can leave soon'.

Tuesday 9 December 2003. Waves tumbled onto a reef laying 200m from a surfing beach. I found some shade and sat just watching and letting my tensions and concerns dash against the reef with the waves splitting into white. Occasionally a surfer held on to a wave right up to where it dwindled to a line of foam, way up the sand from the water. Topless teenagers sunbathed with no more than fluorescent string covering their bits and a perfectly blond, rich-tanned lad spun two bright coloured sticks around his body like dragonfly wings. Two young girls pouted like catfish into the middle distance, ignoring him. Other teenagers volleyed a ball back and forth with crazy skill and I wondered whether the young had special genes which gave them fantastic abilities. Further along the beach I saw a group of middle aged men who were at least as vigorous with their ball. Walking along the beach was a way to gain space for reflection on my voyage. Sometimes it seemed the voyage was yet to begin, as if the past year and a half had been mere preparation for the next part. At other times I realized this was the voyage, and life in general seemed to have the same problem of perspective.

Since the middle of summer I had been stocking up with extra tins of food and a myriad of small spares, fuses, electrical tape, bulbs, sail slides, sail repair twine, sewing needles, spare sail cloth, charts and sailing pilots. That was five months ago and it intensified with me replacing whatever I ate with three times the quantity. Sometimes I bought ten cans of a certain food at once, when it was particularly suitable as when 'ofertas' - special offers - coincided with a particularly tasty and long lasting food. My arms were stretched from the frequent weight of carrier bags. I came away to sail, not to shop.

The Canary Islands were beautiful for the warm climate - 23C on the ninth of December. I spent many pleasant days with Robert, a Swedish single-hander, met in the Rias of North Spain the previous year and met again in Las Palmas. His cruising philosophy reminded me of Eeyore, in Winnie-the-Pooh, as when he said, "I don't really want to sail across the Atlantic for a fourth time, its just a lot of water for 4 weeks, it's borwing". Robert's unexcited, 'It's borwing', approach to much of what went on was nonetheless cleaved through by his love of secluded anchorages which he repeatedly described as, 'byutiful'. He was a welcome, sobering influence, redolent with practical tips for keeping boat, sailor and voyage on an even keel. The best aspects of spending time with Robert were; he went to bed with the sunset, got up with the dawn, he did not drink excessively. I attached great significance to Robert's advice because he had sailed to Australia and South Africa from Sweden. The yacht he had at the time was just 7m long (SP was a little bigger at 8m). I too developed a habit of waking to watch the sunrise over a cup of tea and later at around nine am Robert would appear and we would go off together in search of the days 'Ofertas'. I spent the extra hours between seven and nine am organizing the boat or doing laundry - a phase of early rising, and hardly drinking any alcohol.

In early descriptions of the Canary Islands they were invariably viewed as idyllic. The Romans called them the Fortunate Isles, although they were not always fortunate for the original inhabitants, the Guanches, as half of Europe, the French, Italians, Spainish, Portuguese, perhaps Nordic mariners too, drifted down on the Canary current to convert, attack and harass them. The Guanches were hunter gatherers, lived in caves and mummified their dead. I saw some in the Museo Canario, along with a room full of Guanche skulls which made for a humbling sort of day. A year later a true Guanche man invited me for a drink after I'd given his son a catapult when we met on a beach, but there was a long way to go before the voyage returned to the Fortunate Isles.

I had certainly found my islands; here beautiful sunny weather continued throughout winter and even the Canarian summers were not as hot as in southern Portugal due to the fresh trade winds. The Canariones were generally very friendly towards me as a visitor, one amongst millions of other holidaymakers, although the bulk of tourists congregated in the south of any particular island, whereas Las Palmas was in the north of Gran Canaria. In general all the islands were wetter and cloudier on the northern half with the opposite - sunny dry conditions to the south.

There was a distinct unwillingness in Canariones to learn English and I sensed this as a form of resistance against mass tourism as well as the

British Isles being far to the north and not particularly relevant to Canary island life. The southern part of Gran Canaria was really horrible, with egg box apartments stacked into the landscape and beaches crammed with row upon row of plastic recliners.

I found myself wandering around the huge southern resort of Maspalomas (just do not go on holiday there, it is truly vile), in the early hours, after I could sleep no longer in a cramped tent with two friends, and I went to find a café to watch the sunrise. I walked up some steps away from the beach where we had illegally camped overnight and soon found the town filled with drunken Englishmen swaying about demanding, "More chips!," from sold-out kiosks, while drug dealers hung around looking like drug dealers. I overheard one saying to someone, "Do you wanna do business, or I go make a deal with somebody else?" A group of young African prostitutes smiled at me and as I passed one approached and took hold of my arm, saying, "Do you want to have sex with me?" I said, "No," adding, "I am a woman," to which all eight of them giggled. On a bench outside a library a couple were having sex. The woman made loud exhibitionist groans as her lolling eyes followed me. She was straddling a man who was silent while another woman came across the road towards them shouting, "Leave this man, he is a bad man". The couple ignored the intervener.

I felt sickened by Maspalomas and went back down to the beach where, in the young light of daybreak, a suspicious looking figure stood just along from where my two German friends were still asleep in the tent. Beyond this figure was a couple who were having sex in the sand - he was obviously a pimp watching over his client. Most tourists spend a week or two in this horrendous place and never venture further than the beach, nightclubs and apartment. The drunken men, the immigrant prostitutes, the tourists in their apartments, living their boxed lives all depressed me terribly. I was also deeply pleased to be so different to 'them'.

The past two months in the Canaries had spiralled into higher and higher degrees of organization and planning around the boat's gear and stores until I found a couple of days during which I took refuge in the mall - a decking balcony in the open air overlooking the docks and the city - I had kept away from El Muelle, a giant shopping mall next to where cruise liners docked, but now it provided just the right breezy, airy, modern atmosphere I needed to reflect. How tightly coiled my desires, intentions and preparations of late had become. It was amusing to have travelled to these lovely islands at the end of the known world (yet another 'Land's End') to chose to sit in a shopping mall. But the view from El Muelle was lovely - two or three layers of successively taller mountains to the west. Southwards the glittering harbour with colossal container ships and fast hydrofoil ferries churning and dashing about. Sixty tiny sailing dinghies fluttering off towards seven anchored ships a mile out to sea, while I wrote my journal.

Christmas passed by with a whirl of shoppers. New Year with ubiquitous and breathtaking fireworks. Robert finally left on Little Annie towards Madeira and I was almost ready to sail, but disinclined to untie the ropes. I purchased fresh fruit and topped up the engine oil level - actions usually signalling imminent departure but still I prevaricated and caught myself wandering around in 'Todo uno Euro' shops (everything 1 Euro), finding trivial items to buy, a tape measure, new kitchen scourers, shoelaces, biros and writing paper; until a really big distraction arrived in the Queen Mary II coming brand new to Las Palmas, and then leaving in the evening with a massive firework display.

Thousands of people lined the harbour and seafront to see Queen Mary II looking hugely elegant, hovering mid-harbour, dark navy hull and white topsides crowned with rose pink lighted funnels, while hellishly expensive fireworks broke the ears of every dog in town. Actually apart from the mighty fashionable rosy pink highlighting she looked like an apartment block, nevertheless I added SPs red, green and white navigation lights and a xenon strobe to take part in the bright goodwill. The liner had an unreal appearance, like a special effect, a computer generated Imax screen image. Earlier in the day I had gone to El Muelle to look at the ship in her berth. There were many people doing the same and many posed for photographs with the liner in the background, keen to be associated with the spectacle, as I'd been with my lights.

In the shade of a glass and metal entrance to an underground bus station a spread of African goods lay on the pavement. I took to the shade and was curious to see if there were any carvings of geckos, among the hippos, crocodiles, giraffes and storks. The seller approached two men who stood arms linked, at the stall, smiled and asked, "You like?" and as the couple nodded she asked them if they were from 'The ship'. They were. I said I liked the hippo carvings which looked like shiny mahogany eggs with hippo faces. She asked me where I came from and I told her, "England," She said, "Ahh, England, good country," I asked her where she came from and she told me, "Senegal, my mother is from

Gambia". I said, "Ahh, Senegal and Gambia".

The names of those countries were sound pictures and the seaward approaches to Dakar, capital of Senegal and south of there, Banjul, the capital of Gambia had recently become ingrained as images on charts and sailing pilots, but dare I go there?

To save space and weight I sold some power tools, an outboard motor and the dinghy, the 'blue brick'. I had cleared three lockers of clutter to stow extra food and water containers and in the fore cabin I hung five nets in which to stow extra food. The level of preparedness was becoming intimidating. I wondered whether, really, I would be happier to just relax and remain in the Canary Islands. Meanwhile, I continued to prepare SP, enjoying the DIY work and shopping, along with Robert.

In December substantial support had come from my family which enabled me to obtain three essential things to continue sailing long distances. As the Canary Islands offered no choice in this and I was 700 miles south of Portugal I ordered online and had them delivered. The three items were firstly a new unsinkable dinghy (a Sportyak made by French firm BIC) which I adapted as a budget life raft. Secondly, an emergency position indicating radio beacon and two spare, user replaceable, batteries. The unit (Mini B300tm ils EPIRB) had a duration of twenty-four hours per battery. Satellites, ships and airliners receiving the 121.5 mhz distress signal would ignore it for twenty-four hours in case it was a false alarm and so I considered it essential to be able to transmit for 72 hours minimum in order to attract attention. The batteries were expensive at 12 Euros each. Thirdly, the radar alarm called, Mer Veille (a French pun between the two meanings of 'marvellous' and 'sea guard'). Mer Veille would indicate, by flashing lights around a plan view diagram of a boat, the direction from which a ship's radar came and emit an audible alarm. The range was up to 10 miles. Additionally I managed to arrange the following resources aboard SP:

6 months stores of food.

44 weeks supply of water aboard (225 litres - 5 litres per day).

A new xenon strobe light, visible at far greater distances than the ten watt navigation lights. Nav lights used 2 amps while the strobe consumed 0.15 amps. In the International Rules for Avoidance of Collision at Sea a strobe light would identify SP as a hovercraft, however the most important thing in my mind was to be visible and for that visibility to be sustainable. There would certainly not be any hovercraft out there and so the strobe would surely grab attention from other vessels.

Malaria prophylactics and a course of treatment should they fail.

A course of antibiotics (available over the counter in pharmacies in the Canaries).

21 gallons of diesel fuel, enough for over 4 days of continuous motoring - around 300 miles at 3 knots.

Charts and sailing directions for Senegal and The Gambia.

Detailed planning and chart work for the 850 miles from Gran Canaria to Senegal.

Finally there were two ropes holding my boat in the marina and within them lay strand upon feeble strand of hesitation and prevarication. Somehow despite my amazing success in getting to the Canaries and preparing for the next part of the journey, I was not quite able to cast off those lines, at least today.

Seven or eight tenders clustered at the pontoon. This gave safety in numbers because the chance of one dinghy being stolen was divided by how many others were available.

My instincts were still at sea and a part of me was trying to say this was all a dream. Arrival was made surreal by the insistent calls to have a beer from the catamaran called 'Dignity'.

From the island of Lanzarote to the island of Gran Canaria was 115 miles. The first half ran fairly close to Fuertaventura with its beautiful sand dunes.

Good Day Madam, Have You Bread?

Tuesday 27 January 2004. I left Las Palmas marina at 4pm with 856 miles to sail. I saw my first ever flying fish within an hour. The wind was light from the north-east or east and the sky was cloudy. I slept half hour periods all night with the new radar detector working which was a good reason to increase sleep periods to half an hour. When the alarm sounded a vessel was identified and it continued to beep sporadically as the vessel passed over the horizon. Often I reduced the sensitivity, so the alarm began again only if the vessel got closer, otherwise the continuous beeping was distracting. Some rest could be taken even with ships about, until the alarm became persistent and the number of flashing lights increased, meaning a close watch had to be maintained or avoidance taken. Mer Veille was a simple device and I very quickly learnt to interpret variations in the alarm characteristics. A single pass of a ship's radar beam, say when a far off ship lifted over the horizon on a large wave, produced a single 'pip' sound and a single flash of one LED, whereas occasionally a radar lit up all four LEDs as a strong signal swamped all four sectors of the aerial. At times there were several pips in succession when a ship's radar was being used to ascertain more accurate information about its object and radar operator increased the power. I often listened to this scanning behaviour as ships slid past.

Half hour sleeps were much more comfortable than 15 minute sleeps. I had eleven days ahead and while 15 minute sleeps had previously worked well for up to week, my well-being would suffer over 11 days. As I wrote inside the cabin, for the sun was hot, an alarm sounded - LEDs indicated a 'paint' from the port bow and I looked out to spot a ship just below the horizon, with bridge only, so it must have been about 5 miles distant. I marvelled at the increased safety brought by the Mer Veille.

Wednesday 28 January 2004. Position at 11.19am: 40 miles south of Gran Canaria. I sailed down the eastern side of Gran Canaria overnight and fell away from the bottom of the island during the morning until even the mountains had gone below the horizon. The masthead tricolour navigation light failed during the night and I switched to the fore and aft navigation lights attached to the pulpit and the push-pit. Battery voltage remained above 11.5 volts and the solar panel lifted the voltage back up to 13 volts during the sunlight hours. I saw several whales, or it may have been one huge one, half a mile astern.

Three Portuguese man-o-war jellyfish sailed by flipping up, or inflating, transparent domes or crescents, edged with purple, about seven inches long. Another passed by and I could see they were not domes but crescents, or more like Cornish pasties. The wind was light from the north-east, blowing force 1, the sea was very calm, with a low swell from north-east. The sun was very warm and the cloud cover three octas.

Thursday 29 January 04. 11.00am position: 100 miles south of Gran Canaria. Heading south. Speed 2.7 knots. I ran the engine on one third throttle in a variable wind of force 1 with a calm sea and a swell from west-north-west. The swell came in the dawn with the hope of firmer winds. The previous afternoon I'd seen two large turtles about the size of lawnmowers. A pod of pilot whales with ten or fifteen individuals appeared around 5pm. Heavy shipping appeared overnight, with three or four vessels in view most of the duration, so I slept only in 15 minute periods as a result of keeping watch. During the dawn not a ship was to be seen and up until 11.30am there had been no ships. It was peculiar how a cluster of ships arrived over several hours and not any at other times. A school of feeding tuna, around 50 fish, moved along together, feeding from the surface with fins slicing through the surface in long straight slashes, either to catch prey or scooping mouthfuls of fish offal. I saw strings of oily bubbles wending along over a wide area which probably would have come from a trawler, or might possibly have been signs of an upwelling ocean current. A feature of this sea, known flippantly as the African Channel, was a deep, cold upwelling.

During the night dolphins played around the boat. They were large, at over two meters length. I first saw them after being surprised by a sound like a rubber dinghy being punctured - a quick expulsion with a sharp attack and a wheezy follow through - then another sound as air was taken in. Goblets of watery silver light trailed behind the dolphins and they themselves were cloaked in jewel-like phosphorescence as they darted about with abrupt changes in direction, followed by limpid silver whirling tubes.

At 1.30pm a ship called 'Asahi' passed close in a lazy, slow, deep blue sea. Through binoculars I saw someone on the bridge, standing outside looking back at me through binoculars. We waved and I felt a surprise in my stomach, a human connection and love for the person waving and regarding me. After the encounter I adjusted the wind vane by loosening the control lines so they ran more easily. It was a hot blue day and at 6pm I dipped the diesel tank to find it three-quarters full with 37 litres. I motored all day in a feeble south-west or variable wind. The electronic autopilot steered, as the wind was too light to make the wind vane work. The solar panel seemed to sustain the substantial current drain of the auto-helm, helped by the engine generator. Previously the auto-helm had switched itself off after a couple of hours use due to lack of power and there were several reasons for the change. The batteries were topped up after two months in Las Palmas marina with mains power. The solar panel had been repositioned and the voltmeter showed high power levels during the day. The wind vane assisted with steering and so the auto-helm needed to do less work.

I saw a lovely big turtle in the afternoon. He looked up as I passed. Later I threw a coin into the ocean and calculated if it sank at one metre per second, it would take an hour to reach the seabed. The depth was 3,600m. At sixty seconds in a minute and sixty minutes in an hour that made three thousand six hundred seconds in an hour. I pondered the peculiar geometry traced by the progress of SP, also moving at 3.6km per hour, at 90 deg, tangentially away from the coin in its descent: an isolated isosceles triangle, or was that a right angle triangle? Both? I mused away a long hot calm afternoon with the engine singing the journey along. I'd felt anxious about the calms since leaving and was motoring in the hope of there being more wind further away from the Canaries.

I read *The Famished Road* by Ben Okri, an apt metaphor for my dissatisfaction with progress. Mile after mile gradually passed behind, but there was barely any feeling of passing through the flat empty realm and 750 unfulfilled miles lay ahead. In the late afternoon I was overwhelmed by a breathtaking sunset, two giant feathers of golden orange reflecting in the intense calm and swimming cloud reflections engulfing the distance between boat and horizon. I photographed liquid orange red, lapping toward SP, but such a flamboyant sky also made me anxious as I could not help thinking there must be some seething, incipient force coiled up in such phenomena.

With the engine stopped, the ocean was soundless and I had never been so drenched in silence. A tangerine saturated sundown promised a green flash, but I watched until the sun sank out of sight and there was none. I made a cup of tea, put on a fleece and arranged the two blue cushions under the spray hood I often sat there in the evenings, between dusk and midnight, not quite happy about the long dark hours ahead, my anxiety a reaction to nightfall, but by midnight I usually settled into the reassuring routine of watch keeping and sleeps.

Wrapped snugly in a quilt, laid on the bunk along one side of the cabin, a long series of half hour snacks of rest and forgetting dispelled the tensions and tiredness. Interrupted sleep was full of dreams, with freedom from shore based obligations to sleep well all night long, I could easily become quickly alert and active at any point in response to a new breeze, or to monitor shipping more closely. Also I could resume sleeping whenever the opportunity existed, be that 9am, or whenever. Nights at sea were some of the most beautiful hours, dolphins arrived, penetrating, perceptive, responsive, the moon was usually waxing because I mostly tried to set out with this in mind as it was far more pleasant to sail while the moon was bright, although a full moon flared so white at sea it was hard to see stars and planets because the heavens were brimfull of light and the surface of the sea splattered silver. A breeze often filled in with the colder air of night and the main sail and jib were parallel curves, indigo up against the sky. That sky I'd come all this way to see.

Friday 30 January 04. Heading south-west. Speed 2.5 knots. Cap Blanc was 270 miles ahead. I motored from midnight until dawn with the autopilot steering. I set full main sail and a half rolled foresail for balance with the wind coming from the North and at last I felt SP was free of the wind shadow of the Canary Isles, now 120 miles South of Gran Canaria. I had been warned of the turbulent wind effects from the mountainous Canary Islands when Robert had shown me a satellite photograph with whirls and eddies extending 120 miles downwind of the Canaries. The previous day the wind had come from the west in the evening, quite firm, giving 4 knots at times and this wind had come the previous night too, also dying away at midnight. Now the sky was populated by cumulus clouds with a light northerly breeze, almost the trade winds. During the night light coloured dolphins stayed with the boat for hours, playing and swooping underneath the hull, rushing forward over the surface of the water while standing on their tails, overtaking, all wrapped in light like submerged comets. Torpedoes. Meteorites. Two storm petrels (hydrobates oceanodrome) appeared. Heavy shipping arrived all night with three ships at a time in view, so sleep periods were reduced to 15-20 minutes.

The gps showed 660 miles to Dakar, 180 miles from Las Palmas and 1703 miles from Bristol Marina. The Southern Cross constellation rose almost dead ahead during the night and I felt jubilant although I wondered if it was the False Cross, but I decided it was the Southern Cross with the False Cross being to one side and slightly lower in January.

French radio forecast 11.38am gave wind north-west, force 4-6 for Cap Blanc. My noon position: 70 miles off the coast of Mauritania. Speed 2 knots. Heading south-west.

At 2.15pm I saw a cory's shear-water (calonectris deomedea), a delicate, smart, pretty bird I could not recall seeing before. I shifted a waypoint ahead that was 40 miles off Mauritania to 60 miles offing, because with fresh winds and larger swell forecast some extra distance from the land would avoid sailing onto the African continental shelf. The preferred course line stayed in depths of at least 1200m, avoiding 'shoal' patches of 50m depth, where a heavy swell would increase dramatically in size and break. I topped up the engine oil as 2/3 had leaked out. I checked the tension of the fan belts.

Saturday 31 January 04. I sailed well all night with the autopilot and navigation lights on as the batteries seemed able to keep powering the auto-helm and I thought this was due to repositioning of the solar panel. In the morning a breeze from the east was beautiful and had SP pouring through the waves at 3.5 knots. I wrapped the autopilot in a plastic bag to protect it from spray. I got plenty of sleep during the night with several half-hour dreams, but in the early hours slept for over an hour after forgetting to reset the kitchen timer. At least with Mer Veille on guard this was less risky.

French radio forecast: Cap Blanc, wind north-west, force 1. Noon position: 70 miles off Mauritania. Speed 4.1 knots and heading south-south-west. The distance to Dakar was now 590 miles and distance covered was 260 miles. Over four days at sea the average speed had been 2.8 knots and the average daily run was 68 miles

I ate sprouted beans and chick peas splashed with olive oil for breakfast and still had a portion of sprouting chick peas left for a snack in the afternoon. Next I put soya beans to soak in an ex-coffee whitener jar with holes in the lid. These beans had come from a Korean shop in Las Palmas (2.75 Euros per kilo). To be able to create fresh, living food under way was exciting and I felt far more competent on this trip with improvements and investments made, the most significant of which were:

Solar panel
Mer Veille radar guard
Sportyak unsinkable emergency tender
Grab bag for emergency abandon ship. Food and water stores
Reefing lines removed from luff of main sail.

Main halyard removed from cockpit and led straight to base of mast.
Spinnaker pole eye riveted to mast.
Use of preventer on main sail.
New electric auto-helm.
Foresail repair and ultraviolet light protection completed.
Cockpit tidier, I now automatically tidied lines.
12 volt powered, nimh AA battery charger.
Wind vane self-steering.
More experience with course work, gps, waypoints, noon positions.
New anti-fouling paint below water-line.
Rudder heel repair.
Better range of navigation charts and sailing pilot books.
Tiller bolts replacing screws after they repeatedly worked loose.
Buckets on port cockpit deck, 1 for cut vegetable stowage, 1 for salt-water dish wash, 1 to contain washed plates.
Recently added really deep third reef to the mainsail to reduce the sail area in very strong winds.

Sunday 1 February 04. 11.38am French radio forecast: Cap Blanc, wind north-west force 4-5 Noon position: 300 miles north-north-west of Nouakchott, Mauritania. Heading south-west. Speed 4.1 knots. I'd lost my fleece hat while removing the spinnaker pole as the wind increased in the dark the thrashing fore-sail swiped it into the sea. I immediately accepted this as the dark closed over it in the wake behind. Last night the wind blew force 6, north-east and I'd kept a course with a tiny portion of the foresail unrolled as waves swooshed around and the wind whistled. A Storm Petrel fluttered around the boat, in the navigation lights, squeaking, I think trying to mate with SP as she passed into the Tropic of Cancer. I was tired by the chaotic movement of agitated waves and soon the weather became lighter, but the sea remained disturbed and my sleeping quilt was smelly with sweaty, salt damp patches.

Distance to Dakar 490 miles. Distance from Las Palmas 360 miles. Distance to the waypoint off Cap Blanc, Mauritania 96 miles, bearing south-south-west.

I changed the gas bottle, one was empty, one full and in use, one was full and spare. I greased the stern gland to reduce water ingress.

Monday 2 February 04. With 6 miles to the waypoint (50 miles west of Mauritania) I altered course for Dakar having reached Cap Blanc, a headland upon which the city Nouadhibou was built. My track now led between the original course and the altered, safer course, as the weather promised a low risk of large swells. The gps was now locked on to the course and distance for the next waypoint, 3 miles clear of a reef at Presqu'lle de Cap Vert, a finger of land called the Green Cape where Dakar was situated. Dakar was 384 miles due south and I estimated arrival in 5 more days; by Saturday.

I plugged the unused gas drain with a rag as a possible source of excessive bilge-water after I found the gas locker had filled with water that had spurted up the drain hose. 11.38am Radio France International marine weather: Cap Vert - wind north-west 4-5. I saw gannets for the first time since north-west Spain. My noon position: 210 miles north-west of Nouakchott, Mauritania. Heading due south. Speed 5 knots Wind easterly force 4. Sunny. Waves rough.

Steering just with the wind vane. The electric autopilot had proved excellent over two days and nights non-stop, Friday and Saturday. I'd expected the autopilot to drain the batteries as I was using navigation lights at the same time, but the autopilot went 48 hours, 24 of which were with navigation lights on too, with no problem. Previously I'd only managed to use the auto-helm for a few hours before it squeaked to a halt with insufficient power, but the sun was now really strong on the solar panel.

All the previous night and the following morning a radar had been 'painting' SP from varying directions, although I spotted no ships. When ships came and went there was an evolution in the alarm and the vessel could be mapped as it approached, passed to one side, and receded, even when not visible, but the signals overnight gave me the impression I was being shadowed, perhaps by the Mauritanian navy. A ship passed mid morning and the radar then left me alone. Of course it may have been a trawler. Later I heard several tales of Mauritanian military vessels harassing fishing boats and a fighter aircraft repeatedly flying extremely close to the mast of a Spanish sailing boat. I think it was only a trawler and that I was a little exhausted; my shoulders and neck were aching and tired; 24 hour watch keeping was demanding.

My bird book, by Alan Richards, *Seabirds of the Northern Hemisphere*, gave the size of a storm petrel (hydrobates pelagicus) as 14-17cm. I thought they must be slightly larger, although not as big as Leach's petrel (oceanodroma leucorhoa), at 45-48cm, surely the storm petrel must have a wingspan of at least 20-30cm.

Tuesday 3 February 04. The batteries became completely flat after the solar panel wire became disconnected. I tried hand starting the engine but failed. Now I used the strobe light overnight which worked perfectly even with a battery voltage down from 14v to 8.5v. Batteries are widely considered terminally damaged even at 10.5v. The strobe light was highly visible but it felt illegal because I knew it did not comply with sea laws, however my sole intention was to be visible. One ship paused for half an hour and the Mer Veille showed it to be scanning me, so I indicated movement aboard by switching on a battery powered camping lamp and shining it on the sails. Eventually the ship seemed content to slide away into the night time.

One week before arrival I began malaria prophylactics as the doctor had ordered, 2 Avloclor to be taken on the same day each week.

11.38am French radio forecast: Cap Blanc - wind west or north-west, force 3-4. Noon position: 160 miles north-west of Nouakchott, Mauritania. Speed 2.7 knots. Distance to Dakar 304 miles, due south. Distance from Las Palmas 523 miles, north-north-east.

Wednesday 4 February 04. Stomping along at 5 knots under foresail alone. Wind force 4-5 east by south. Visibility very hazy. Dirty red dust coating the back stays and solar panel. Seeing storm petrels hourly. Last night there were many ships, two or three every hour mostly on the same course as me, or on a reciprocal bearing. Not so chilly last night, even though 'chilly' had probably been no less than 16C. I failed to hand-start the engine again and the batteries were not up enough to turn the engine over. I used the strobe light all through the dark hours and ships all kept well clear by a mile. I felt much safer knowing I could be seen as with the dust haze it would have been nerve wracking to use the paraffin lamp which was completely inadequate. Heavy shipping continued and visibility was constantly less than a mile. The strobe lamp and the Mer Veille were extremely energy efficient as each morning the batteries had not been drained in the slightest.

The danger increased dramatically as two or more ships coincided, with my little yacht in the middle. One night I was nervously peering at the evolution in the positions of two ships through binoculars as I could not determine the direction one of them was travelling, even though it continued to draw closer, it showed a confusing array of lights, some to show it was restricted in its ability to manoeuvre, others to show it could only be passed on one side due to equipment extending, or being towed, out from the other side. Still more lights were to declare it was over fifty metres in length and other sets showed its heading and port and starboard sides. In the half hour I spent interpreting this confusion the ship had closed from 4 miles to less than a mile until I saw the wave of foaming water pushed up under its bluff bows dimly gleaming under all the lights. Suddenly a searchlight shone at me from the second ship and I thought at least someone can see me. A storm petrel fluttered into the beam, circled three times round the boat and landed on the prow. It spoke, 'Courage, dear heart,' spread its wings and flew off ahead, bearing a little to starboard. I steered after it, not doubting that it offered good guidance. Meanwhile the two vessels must have been discussing the situation on their radios, the safest way for them to pass SP and I imagined their exchange would go something like, 'Can you see the little yacht in your path, there right between us? Look, there in our searchlight?' The vessel showing all the lights seemed to slide away across my stern although it did not alter its heading. The searchlight ship, having paused in a dark grey band of steel, rumbled at a very slightly higher pitch and moved away too. Nights alone on a yacht at sea are a mixture of heavy shipping and heady imaginings.

The weather forecast for Cap Blanc was wind, east force 3-4 and at Cap Timiri, wind, east force 3-5. My noon position was 118 miles northwest of Nouakchott, Mauritania. Heading south. Speed was fast at 5.7 knots. WHOOSH! CRASH! SPLASH! HISS! I reduced the foresail to slow down as SP began careering along at 7.1 knots. Many drips from the ceiling and windows came from waves on deck and the bilge took 1 gallon per hour. By late afternoon the wind was light again leaving a big sloppy swell. In this primordial realm three large sharks swam close to each other 100m astern, dorsal fins looked to be about 2ft tall. One of the creatures jumped half clear of the water and the body looked about 12ft long with a tail fin neither distinctly horizontal or vertical. They may have been thresher sharks (alopus superciliosus) with the French name of 'reynard a gros yeux', which I translated as 'big eyed fox'. Threshers have large eyes and a long curved tail fin which stuns or kills prey and one identifying trait was their ability and liking for jumping clear of the water. Thresher sharks have small pits covering the skin near the mouth and nose, called 'ampullae of lorenzini', which are electrical sensors able to detect the weak electrical fields given off by all animals. I was not afraid at the sight of those three large predators swimming back in the direction of Cap Blanc, the sharp, curved fins, like three grey scythes appeared and disappeared as the waves alternately tilted them into view and concealed them. I was moved by a scene of primeval nature unchanged for millions of years. But I was also relieved they didn't start following me.

I tried starting the engine as the solar panel had powered the batteries up to 10 volts even after using gps, strobe light and radar detector the duration of each night, it fired a couple of times before the batteries plunged back to 8 volts and the dynastart was unable to turn over the engine again. The battery voltmeter had shown 9 volts, rising to 11.5 volts the day before and today it was 10 volts, rising to 12.5 volts. Engine starting would still need three clear days to build up enough oomph. When I'd been sweating and huffing at the hand starting-handle I'd noticed both port side engine mountings had broken off.

Thursday 5 February 04. Strong wind from the east, force 4-6. Red dust over everything. 11.38am French radio forecast: Cap Blanc - wind east, force 3-5. Noon position 120 miles south-west of Nouakchott, Mauritania. Speed 3 knots. Heading due south.

The foresail vibrated in tension and bilge-water slopped up onto the floorboards as we went up and over waves. The boat was constantly pressed over at an angle of 15 degrees and sometimes a wave broke over the cabin. I had to sponge a bucket of water from the bilge every half hour as the two bilge pumps would not suck until at least an inch of water lay at the suction pipe end, but the water slopped side to side and end to end with the boisterous movement. Using a sponge and a bucket so frequently was tiring and made my hands salt-dry and cracked, but I knew now there was only 140 miles to Dakar. I reached a stage of just wanting to be ashore, to wear clean clothes, hang with friends. England, oh to be in England. I imagined looking back one day at this trip as the most fantastic experience of my life and made a note in the log-book

Be easy on yourself - you have found you can meet challenges, don't get stuck only in meeting challenges. Am I that hungry for experience?

Friday 6 February 04. Noon position, 81 miles north-east of Dakar. Heading due south. Speed 4.8 knots. Radio France International marine meteo: Cap Blanc - wind east force 3-4. From 9am the wind blew force 5-6 from the east and much bilge-water was coming in through the anchor chain hawse pipe. I noticed a stream like a gulping tap entering every time a wave washed over the foredeck. I pulled the bilge pump suction pipe/filter head out from under the cabin sole and removed the strainer to allow the tube to suck closer to the floor. It was much better and I found I could use the bilge pump to keep down the bilge-water level. 75 miles to Dakar, plus 20 miles around Presqu'ile and Il-de-Goree, to the anchorage off an arc of protected beach named Hann Plage.

Saturday 7 February 04. SP sailed the entire north-south axis of the

Sahara Desert. Despite being no closer than 60 miles from land, smells reached the boat. There were just two main cities along a coastline of 500 miles and leathery scents came as I reached a point directly downwind of them, with other smells of a more indeterminable air; ancient, fugitive. Nouhdibhou and Nouakchott came on the wind; a passing gallery of aromas. Whole cities teased out in the offshore breeze into scents like whispers on the wind. During the second half of the voyage the Sahara was plainly visible in the sky as a heavy brown haze. Each evening the sun set as a yellowish white globe dulled to a pearl ball by the dust, and then an hour later the full moon rose in the east, an identical yellowish white disc and the moon travelled overhead to set at the same point the sun had disappeared. After several dark dust-dimmed hours the sun rose again in the east, identical to the moon in size, rising position and colour. This uniformity of size, colour and arc would cause profound confusion in ancient navigators.

It was only the reducing latitude reading, day by day, which gave me any sense of progress in this oceanic dust bowl. 40 miles from Dakar, Senegalese music came over fm radio, always an early sign of nearing land. I spent the evening listening to a phone-in, immediately picking up a reassuring humour and open warmth in the radio host and his callers who spoke Wolof. Music was crammed with blattering drums and the taut, flexing voice of the talking drum added to the tension of rising tempo toward the ends of songs. To imagine the sound of Senegalese music, picture a lorry load of dishwashers, each full of plates and cutlery, being dumped down a long, steep cliff, even though the music was completely coordinated. The vocals surf this thick bed of percussion knowing every twist and turn of the dense structure. Senegalese music seems a synthesis of the muezzin's shrill, early morning call to desist, and the bubbling, cyclical folk songs of the rural tribes. In this ambrosial hour a moment of serene tenderness came with dolphins while SP travelled smoothly forward with the radio playing soprano saxophone music. A strong resolution formed in my thoughts:

All I want to do 'next' is concentrate on learning to play my soprano saxophone, much much better.

At 8.23am came the first sight of land. Cap Vert formed out of the dirty air, fine on the port bow. The sky was crammed full of red dust in the easterly Harmattan wind. I had not worn shoes for 11 days.

The waves became moody with agitated patches in which even the smallest crests sucked and belched, the energy of oceanic swells turned in on themselves as they ran higher onto the continental shelf. Over a couple of days the depth of water had changed from 1200m to just 60m. I was glad to have reached the headland with its disturbed diverting currents and waves tumbling into one another as they bounced out to sea off the cliffs, as for the last 3 days, by 9am the wind had risen to force 6 until early afternoon, when it eased again. Headlands and wind force 6 always make rough sailing and I wanted to clear Cap Vert soon. The land evolved as it drew closer, at 3 miles I saw a pair of conical hills and a cube shaped fort structure on a slither of flat low land. A tall thin post marked a reef off the Pointe-de-Madeleine and then a while later the whole lot disappeared behind a cloak of sand dust.

I was squeamish at the thought of mosquito bites giving me malaria and I had started taking malaria prophylactics, as directed, a week before exposure to risk, but during the previous night the east wind had carried a biter out to sea and the little b***er survived a flight of 30 miles over open water. It must have homed in on my flashing strobe light and managed not just one, but several itchy bites. It felt absurd to be feverishly (hopefully not actually feverishly) spraying the cabin with mosquito spray out at sea, but there it was, I had seen the little blighter flickering past the beam of my torch. The east wind had carried insects to the boat for several days, small yellow and white butterflies became obsessed with the sail, flying up and down in the wind shadow as if it was the wing of some great butterfly god and after meeting the great wing they often died there, dropping onto the sea like quivering petals. Hoverflies were my favourite insects. They seemed to choose the same landing spot, the left strap of my sailing harness, right over my heart beat. I amused myself by feeding them minute pieces of dried dates and sprinkling drops of fresh-water and then peering at them in close-up through a magnifying glass. They had yellowish and brown striped bodies, spindly legs and two elliptical eyes, with an expression like a turbaned fairytale prince.

A flying insect came aboard like an incoming rocket, it was as big as a fig. It's sudden arrival made me exclaim to myself, 'What the heck!?' It could've been anything. My perception was both heightened and wearied by the journey. I was not terribly overtired as sleep periods had been 20-35 minutes; compared to 15 minutes a sleep of 35 minutes was sheer bliss, with time for dreams to work their magic on mind, body and spirit. I had a weird 5 minutes after hearing a 'splosh', followed by a 'clonk' on deck, giving me the unshakeable impression something had leapt out of the sea onto the boat, and in the light of a torch thought I could see an object clinging to the deck about halfway along beside the cabin. I thought maybe an octopus had been washed aboard and was clinging to the rigging attachment points, but it turned out to be nothing more than my excited imagination.

In stronger winds a couple of small squids had been stranded on deck, the first died as the morning sun came up and dried it out, but the second was rescued with a bucket of sea-water to sluice it back overboard. They were small transparent tubes about four inches long, with two large, black eyes and tendrils at one end. I was amazed at how tidy and organized I kept the boat, with eight separate ropes leading into the cockpit remaining coiled and hung over a cleat or winch every time they were worked. The inside of the cabin was also neatly kept. In the past sailing had mostly been a chaotic activity with everything slipping into a sodden heap on the floor as the boat bounced and swooped through those North Sea waves. The process of tidying up used to be carried out when it was all over, a way to recover sanity once we had scraped into port against all odds, but nowadays I constantly kept everything in its place, so I could move about the boat without treading on things and breaking them, or myself.

In morning sunshine I passed a small local fishing boat, sweetly sheered and flared at the bows, like a Portuguese vessel and smartly painted blue and white, with a barking dog, always a barking dog, and then figures waving, suddenly filling me with human presence, black men grinning and laughing across the distance between us on this sunny Saturday of arrival.

I still had to sail the 20 miles down around Cap Vert to approach Dakar from the south, but the city was by now sprawled along the cliffs and beaches just 2 miles to the east. Thankfully the regular morning squall did not arrive with the light east wind and I had all sail set. The wind gradually slowed to nothing leaving SP bobbing around at zero knots. My instinct was to edge away from the cliffs using each small puff of wind to make progress. I still could not start the engine so 2 miles was plenty close enough to the sight of Atlantic rollers transforming into surf on a rock ledge. The surface of the water changed into small, lively wavelets, like navy blue icing and I whistled nonchalantly for some wind, frustrated at being becalmed and really wanting to get there by late morning, or at least in daylight. Next, like a blaze erupting amidst a summer picnic, a squall hit, dropping from the cape with violent suddenness, and immediately I was fighting in spray and gusts, so hot they felt like the whoosh of a flaring bonfire.

Ten minutes of struggle and amazement at the wind and I had the boat reefed and trimmed so she ran free in the waves and wind, with white water drenching the foredeck. I had whistled up a wind and it had responded so instantly. So this is what the sailing pilot book had meant when it told of the 'bewitching' effect of Africa.

The rest of Saturday morning was hot and almost windless, so I drifted, becalmed again on a south going current past Ile-de-Madeleine until in late afternoon I made minute progress by paddling towards Ile-de-Goree, hoping to stay out of the way of ships moving to and from the oil refineries overnight.

The local fishing craft were called pirogues, and there were many of these inshore as I gradually rounded the peninsular and gained the security of the large bay under its southern side. A pirogue with three fishermen aboard came alongside and the first human words spoken at me since Gran Canaria were, "Bonjour Madam, avez vous du pain?"

THE END of Book One.

Continued in Voyage of Storm Petrel. Book Two. Up the River Gambia and Back to Britain.

Mile after mile gradually passed behind, but there was barely any feeling of passing through the flat empty realm and 750 unfulfilled miles lay ahead.

Next, like a blaze erupting amidst a summer picnic, a squall hit, dropping from the cape

The author.

Clarissa Vincent was born in Huntingdon, Herts 1961. As a toddler she sailed with her parents in a GP14, general purpose 14ft dinghy, but never liked it because she was too young to take control. This early experience gave her a deep sense of security as she headed offshore for different lands in later life. In 1990 she sold a house in Peterborough and bought a boat with a big dream to sail to Spain. A big voyage remained a dream throughout twelve years of cruising with progressively audacious trips setting out from the harbours and rivers of the East Coast of England, to arrive in France, Belgium; then the South Coast of Britain to Cornwall and eventually around Land's End into the Bristol Channel. She settled in Bristol for five years and graduated with a BA at the University of the West of England. Sociology taught her to organize large written texts and sailing alone provided rich experiences. Bristol was the turning point which led to this book: *The Voyage of Storm Petrel.*

CPSIA information can be obtained at www.ICGtesting.com
Printed in the USA
BVOW031019200212

283338BV00010B/156/P